Political Theorists in Context

Focusing on the historical context in which political theorists have developed their thinking, this textbook is an invaluable introduction to students of political thought. The authors address a series of canonical major thinkers in the context of three world-changing epochs – the English, French and Industrial revolutions. The theorists' ideas are assessed with reference to the politics of their time and show how they responded to or interacted with the political events and issues of their day.

Key political thinkers include:

- Milton
- Hobbes
- The Levellers and the Diggers
- Locke
- Montesquieu

- Jean Jacques Rousseau
- Edmund Burke
- John Stuart Mill
- Karl Marx
- Mikhail Bakunin

With key concepts, further reading and revision notes in each chapter this student-friendly text is ideal for students who come to political theory having little existing knowledge of cultural and historical developments.

Chris Sparks, whose previous titles include *Montesquieu's Vision: Uncertainty and Modernity*, and *Uncertainty and Identity: The Enlightenment and its Shadows*, currently lectures in sociology and politics at the Institute of Technology, Sligo and is Visiting Research Associate at the Centre for the Study of Democracy, University of Westminster.

Stuart Isaacs, whose research interests include classic and contemporary political thought, is Senior Lecturer in Social Policy and Sociology at London Metropolitan University.

Political Theorists
in Context

Chris Sparks and Stuart Isaacs

Routledge
Taylor & Francis Group

LONDON AND NEW YORK

First published 2004
by Routledge
11 New Fetter Lane, London EC4P 4EE

Simultaneously published in the USA and Canada
by Routledge
29 West 35th Street, New York, NY 10001

Routledge is an imprint of the Taylor & Francis Group

© 2004 Chris Sparks and Stuart Isaacs

Typeset in Century Old Style and Futura by Keystroke, Jacaranda Lodge, Wolverhampton
Printed and bound in Great Britain by TJ International Ltd, Padstow, Cornwall

British Library Cataloguing in Publication Data
A catalogue record for this book is available from the British Library

Library of Congress Cataloging in Publication Data
A catalog record for this book has been requested

ISBN 0–415–20125–X (hbk)
ISBN 0–415–20126–8 (pbk)

To Oliver, Claudine and Helen; Brigid, Kate, Sheila and Arthur

Contents

Acknowledgements

The authors would like to thank the following colleagues, friends and institutions for their help in preparation of this book: Kate Duke, Claudine Rausch, Gerald Taylor, Sabri Carmikli, Craig Fowlie, Jo Foord, Jeremy Moon, The Centre for the Study of Democracy, London Metropolitan University.

Introduction

Politics

Any society's capacity to endure and develop over time is dependent on its possession of power; that is, its ability to make its constituent elements – human and non-human resources – behave in such a way as to establish an ordered design. However, in every society, power is disseminated disproportionately among different social subgroups, and these groups – each with its own interpretation of the best ethical, economic and cultural mode of living for their society – use their share to try to shape the direction of social development in any number of diverse and often contrary directions. As a consequence, the order of every society is shaped by the push and pull of its contesting elements, each developing its own ideas as to how things should be ordered and engaging in strategic action towards their desired outcome. This is the 'stuff' of political life.

While the need for survival and the common desire for peaceful and sociable existence often calms the struggle and aims it towards consensus, social co-existence is inherently combative and conflict-prone. The factors that play a significant part in whether a society falls into destructive internal conflict or endures peaceably with its internal differences are often circumstantial, unforeseen environmental changes, and novel technological advances can unhinge social arrangements and set groups against each other. These historically contingent factors ensure that the particulars facing any given society at any given time are always unique. Different historical periods throw up different types of problems for people to deal with. For example, the major issues faced by the Aztecs upon meeting with Don Cortez are not issues which the Mexicans of today have to deal with, while the major issues of current times, such as the problems attending the production and potential use of nuclear weaponry, would not be meaningful to people of earlier times. Yet, despite the historical relativity of much politics, sets of issues revolving around the possession and use of power arise again and again, shaped into various guises by the particulars

1

of the current events of each historical epoch. The concepts and language of political theory enable people from different historical situations to engage in an ongoing analysis of perennial issues which are involved in and are definitive of the political condition in much the same way as the concepts and language of medicine have enabled physicians to analyse, discuss and further their understanding of the biology of the human condition across generations.

Political theory

Political life is therefore a rich mix of action and ideas, played out dramatically over time. The role of political theorists in the political world is to provide an understanding of this mix. Theorists critically examine the coherence of commonly held ideas about politics; they observe the effect of such ideas on political action and analyse the social constructs which are built by that action and which in turn provide its social context. As critical examination always reveals incoherence at the level of ideas, and confusion at the level of action, theorists invariably suggest modifications and alternatives to the political world they observe.

Seen in this way, the political theorist appears as a kind of objective observer, viewing the life-world of politics as if from above, but theorists are not external observers since they are involved in the world they reflect upon. Theorists live and work within a political world and their theorising is bound to be affected by the cultural norms and values, as by the academic methods and intellectual puzzles which prevail in the world of ideas of their time. In addition, like all members of a political society, theorists are affected by the prevailing concerns and sometimes dramatic events that shape or disrupt their common world.

This involvement is not just a case of theorists being influenced by their environment; in many cases, the critical reflections and the prescriptions for change produced by theorists have had such an impact on the prevailing understanding of their contemporaries or on later generations that they have been deployed as directives for common political activity. In this way, theory often integrates with action. The arguments and analyses of the most influential political theorists have significantly affected the course of political action and, with it, the shaping of the political world. In order to understand the ideas of particular political thinkers (and to provide a substantive critique of their work), we must take them in context, not only the context of their times, their particular historical setting, but also their philosophical and theoretical context. If we abstract authors from their intellectual and temporal environment we are in danger of distorting their work and of committing the crime of turning their ideas into the worst kind of dogma.

Thus, there is a central tension involved in the activity of political theorists. Their goal is to be critical observers, viewing the political world as if they stand outside it, and yet, in order to achieve the truthfulness required for accurate observation, they must recognise that they are also actors involved in the world they attempt to observe.

Anyone who hopes to understand the social effects and political functions of political theory must address this tension in the activity of theorising, the specific questions it raises about the relationship of the theorist to the world of action on which they are commenting and helping to shape, and the more general questions it raises about the relationship of theory to action. These questions are the underpinning themes of this book.

Dealing with the first question brings with it an engagement with the exciting dramas of political lives. The theorists we discuss are all individuals with a deep commitment to the goal of establishing the best order of life for humankind. Each in their way shows profound insight into the political condition of human life. In many cases, their arguments attracted such angry responses from powerful and at times dangerous opponents that their activities as theorists required great personal bravery. Examination of such scenarios focuses our attention on the theorist as political actor, reminding us of the traditional role of the political theorist that has now become lost, due to the professionalisation of the theorist and the safe and sanitised academic environment that most political thinkers now inhabit.

Addressing the second question is intellectually exciting, involving, as it does, the consideration of the relationship of ideas to the author's conditions of being. More importantly for our purposes, it is also the starting point in any journey towards understanding the centrifugal force that this relationship holds on the spinning political world. It is only when one has an understanding of the general relationship of moving ideas to moving action that any valuation of the importance of a particular theorist to the world of politics can be made.

Book outline: theorists in context

The two questions we have set ourselves to address are the question of the relationship of particular theorists to the world of action on which they are commenting and which they help to shape, and the overarching question of the relationship of theory as an activity to action in general. For this reason, we shall keep our focus upon the theorising situation – the exciting point of convergence between thinking upon and acting into the political world. This interest not only influences our choice of political theorists for discussion, but also directs our treatment of the philosophical concerns and political issues they address. The political theories selected for consideration have not been chosen because they are outstanding examples of political philosophy (though many of the arguments we cover are generally recognised as being so), but because they are highly influential representatives of a tradition of political theory that is umbilically tied to the political world which the theorists struggle to interpret. To have any sense of the place of political theorists within the political sphere, one must have a sense of them as political actors. Far from writing from 'ivory towers' about political affairs, these theorists were deeply embroiled in their political worlds. John Milton risked execution, John Lilburne was imprisoned, John Locke and Karl Marx both had to write incognito, in exile or 'on the run', since their ideas inflamed revolutionary imaginations, threatening various national political orders and the power of those who dominated them. Rousseau struggled with his exclusion from and his antipathy towards French aristocratic society, a struggle that when expressed in writing fired the imaginations of the French revolutionaries, although only after it had reduced their author to a state of isolated semi-madness. Edmund Burke presented his arguments in the hothouse atmosphere of the House of Commons. These were not members of an aloof elite, tossing out clever theories while waiting to be immortalised in stone. They were actors and thinkers, living dangerously and writing against treacherous opposition in the hope that they were contributing to a better world. For this reason at least, we owe them the debt of treating their work and lives as public statements of a commitment to political life.

In order to help locate these theorists and their ideas in historical context, we have ordered them into three broad historical settings, each of which is defined by a set of central themes. The contextual setting for the first section is the turbulent England of the 1600s, the civil war of the 1640s, and the events leading up to the 'Glorious Revolution' of 1689. These events map out the crises of religious and political identity in the shape of constitutional conflicts. During this period, the newly assertive monarchy found itself challenged by radical Protestant liberalism at the levels of ideology and action. The debates among political theorists during this time set out the struggle to establish ideological grounds for sovereign authority and to assert definitive power over the national terrain. We explore this struggle through a presentation of the arguments of John Milton, whose career as a poet followed his first public life as an advocate of Protestant revolt. We look at John Locke, a revolutionary thinker whose ideas came to be used in later times as an ideological foundation for liberal democratic order. We explore two other profoundly influential political visions that were also cast from the uncertain conditions of seventeenth-century England. The first of these is the work of Thomas Hobbes on the horrors of lawlessness and the ethical basis of absolutist sovereignty. Like Locke, Hobbes' ideas are imbued with a concern for the troubles of his times but have been taken up, reinterpreted and represented by many theorists after him, so that varied mutations of his ideas have endured as influential reference points for political actors and theorists. The second political vision is the democratic and communistic reappraisal of the relationship of human communities to their government and to their environment, presented in the writings and activities of the Levellers and Diggers. Their period of existence was brief, but their ideas percolated the discourse of non-conformist Christian organisations. The eventual involvement of these groups in the nineteenth century in the emergence of the labour movement helped construct a quasi-religious and distinctly non-Marxist brand of socialism.

The second set of theorists is explored in the context of the major intellectual and political events affecting Europe and the colonial world of the eighteenth century. These events included the destruction of the *ancien régime* and the socio-political order of Christendom (a continental power bloc covering the territories of Europe). The period also covers the creation of a range of new liberal nation states in Europe and America. At the level of ideas, this section illustrates the centrifugal forces that built up to the revolutionary changes of the French Enlightenment and the subsequent political landmarks of the French and American revolutions. Two theorists whose works and reputations above all others were posthumously claimed by those involved in the revolutions are Baron de Montesquieu and Jean Jacques Rousseau. Exploration of these theorists' arguments, consideration of their reception during their lives, their posthumous evaluation by revolutionaries and conservatives, and some later evaluations made in the past two centuries, reveal the complex relationship of ideas to world-changing action.

Perhaps the most influential and historically significant piece of theorising was Montesquieu's modification of Lockean theory regarding the argument for a separation of powers. It is also one of the most intriguing, for while Montesquieu's presentation is now widely considered to be a conservative defence of aristocratic power within the *ancien régime*, the intellectuals and activists of the French and American revolutions interpreted it as the core feature of a radical liberal manifesto for constitutional republicanism. Similarly, many of Rousseau's key concepts – most notably the ideas of the 'general will' and the nation state – were adopted by French revolutionaries, taken out of textual context, and adapted to the practical circumstances of building a new republican nation state.

The last of our theorists may also be said to have been interpreted differently by his contemporaries than by subsequent generations. Edmund Burke was a liberal thinking Whig politician who had supported many revolutionary movements including the uprisings in his native Ireland against the British. He numbered many radical Members of Parliament and activists among his friends; yet his thesis condemning the French Revolution has marked him out by commentators as the founder of modern Conservatism. Such a view of his work is only possible if, as with Rousseau, his key concepts are taken out of context. For Burke offers us much more than a mere manifesto for the Conservative Party. He confronts us with a theory of liberty and identity that needs to be taken in its own right, without any regard for the ideological 'box' in which he has been put. Looking at theorists in this way can produce rich and creative results, since we find in Burke not a narrow and sceptical anti-politics, but an engaging theory of rights that makes an interesting contribution to contemporary debates.

The final section of the book sets out the context and concerns of the most influential political thinkers of the nineteenth century. The almost overbearing context with which our chosen theorists engaged was that of the increasingly urbanised, overtly class-ridden socio-economic order of industrial capitalism. This overwhelming new order manifested huge changes in almost every aspect of social and cultural life. Theorists made sense of the new order by conceptualising socio-economic classes, mass society, non-personal social structures and impersonal economic forces. In presenting some central ideas of John Stuart Mill and Karl Marx, we will consider two of the most influential and enduring attempts of the time to understand and evaluate the political implications of the new socio-economic order. Mill's work may be seen as an argument for the modification of classical liberal individualism. He sets out a pluralistic, social democratic vision of society, in which individual liberty can be maintained in the face of progress towards mass society. Marx's work arguably represents the most powerful rejection of liberal society and morality through his analysis of class-based politics. However, these two theorists' work will not only be presented as a case of opposites. Rather, we shall explore how both theorists typified nineteenth-century awareness of history as a moving force, imposing conditions and setting terms for human agency, and how they were concerned to establish the possibilities of human liberty in the face of social and historical determinants.

Finally, we shall explore the subversive theories and activities of anarchism through the political thoughts and deeds of Mikhail Bakunin, as well as the often-discredited work of the anarcho-syndicalist Georges Sorel. Anarchism was a strong and vibrant political movement in the nineteenth century, yet too often political texts have ignored the influence of its leading figures. This is strange, as the anarchist discourse stretches right back through the whole history of modern political ideas. We can trace its lines of thought from the Levellers and the Diggers, through Rousseau and eventually to Marx. It has many overlapping debates with the libertarianism of J.S. Mill and classical liberalism. It also offers a direct challenge to the tradition of state-centred politics that began with Hobbes. Coming at the end of the modern period of political ideas, before we reach the terrain of the 'contemporary', anarchism is a fitting way to end the enquiry into the context of political theory and practice that has been presented here. It brings together many of the themes of the book and points the way to the new type of ideological politics that was destined to be bound up in conflict for most of the twentieth century.

Part I

A WORLD TURNED UPSIDE DOWN: THE ENGLISH REVOLUTION

John Milton

Good and evil we know in the field of this world grow up together almost inseparably; and the knowledge of good is . . . involved and interwoven with the knowledge of evil.

(*Areopagitica*)

Born in London in 1608, John Milton lived and worked at a time in which great social and political changes were sweeping through Europe and overwhelming England. This time was marked by a fearful clash between the political order of Christendom that had held sway across Europe for several hundred years and a loose movement of new Christian-based ideologies (collectively forming Protestantism) and potential new political orders which were struggling to take its place. In retrospect, we can see how this loose movement initiated new ways of thinking which, in the centuries following, were to mature into a secular, scientific rationalist way of life. However, any dip into the politics of the seventeenth century shows that the motivations and understanding of participants in the great clash were far removed from those of secular modern-day society, and it is quite a task to perceive the connecting threads between seventeenth-century English Protestantism and modern Western politics. Milton's political writings are a particular help when trying to address this task; while not noted for their originality, they do present one of the clearest expressions of the political ideas and concerns of English Protestantism during the period of the English civil war – the time in which the earliest forms of liberal parliamentarianism came into being.

In fact, all of Milton's writing – including his poetry (which is not obviously political) – provides a clear juncture between the ideals and arguments of the protesting (Protestant) challengers to Catholic Christendom and the core ideals of modern-day liberalism. We shall see that it also provides information on where and why liberal parliamentarianism moves away from its religious origins to establish secular grounds for political order.

The classical liberal themes which run as a constant thread through Milton's political writing and his poetry include the right to free expression, the right to choose between modes of living and the right to overthrow tyrants. All of these derive from Milton's belief that individual liberty is a requirement for each and everyone if they are to fulfil their God-given potential to act as rational and moral creatures. They derive in a particular way from Milton's perception of the integrated functions of judgement, choice and responsible action in the expression of individual liberty. In *Of Education* (1644) and *Areopagitica* (1644), Milton argued that the need to make choices is central to the activity of learning and is therefore fundamental to the acquisition of true knowledge which, in turn, is fundamental to each and every individual's capability of taking responsibility for his or her actions.

Such ideas stress the freedom of the individual, the role of education and the limits of legitimate rule, in ways which are very familiar as elements of modern liberalism, but in Milton's work they are expressed in the theological terms that were fundamental to the Protestant understanding of his time. All his ideas are conceptually rooted in themes that Milton and most of his contemporaries believed constituted human history. These are the metaphysical scenario of the fall of humankind from grace at the outset of human history (the theme of *Paradise Lost*), and the struggle to return to God and truth (the theme of *Paradise Regained*). In this light, his works may be seen as messages to his contemporaries about the commonly understood sources of the moral and political problems of humankind. Through reading them, we gain an insight into the mindset of the hybrid Protestant-liberalism of his time, and so we are able to recognise the theological origins of many secular liberal ideas of today. By placing them into the context of Milton's life and times in this way, we can also see how Protestant liberalism was originally a vital, revolutionary ideology, forged in the heat of civil war by political actors literally risking their necks – as Milton, and many others later were to do – advancing the principles of representative government and tolerant civil society, in the teeth of great and powerful enemies.

Context

In the seventeenth century, the politics of Europe were dominated by crises. The old order maintained its hegemony through the unchallenged propagation of the intellectual and moral mores of Catholicism. By the seventeenth century, Catholic hegemony in northern Europe was being seriously challenged by various types of Protestantism. The Catholic Church's power stemmed from the secular support of the Carolinian Empire (and, by the seventeenth century, from the monarchies of Spain and France). Over the centuries, the Empire had gradually reduced in size and power, as various monarchies, city states and republics successfully challenged its authority and took over the governance of their territories. The old continental political order was breaking up, and, out of the varying alternatives vying to replace it, one pretender was emerging as the strongest. There was a collection of central-ised, unitary governments that were establishing their power over national territories in a process that would eventually shape them into the form of nation states. The process of development itself, however, was slow, and was characterised by the struggles of varying alternative forms of state to develop.

The politics of England in the seventeenth century are marked by such a struggle between two prospective forms of state, neither of which would ultimately survive. This struggle was between advocates of absolutist monarchy and advocates of a Protestant republic. Locked into combat in the English civil war, neither project found space or time to develop unthreatened by the other (or by the activities of the other's allies among the array of Catholic and Protestant forces struggling for power across Europe). In the end, they produced the rather odd merger of monarchism and parliamentarianism that constitutes the present nation state, known as the United Kingdom.

For those involved in the struggles, the eventual outcome – a secular liberal nation state – was simply not imaginable. For them, the contest was a life-and-death struggle for the souls of the polity and for the people who lived within it. This was because politics and religion were understood as two distinct dimensions of one all-encompassing contest: the contest between God and Satan. So, for all those involved, politics and religion did not come apart. Catholics saw Puritanism as heresy: a fall away from God's law on earth. Protestants saw Catholicism as the corrupted edifice of God's church on earth: what had once been good had become overpowered by lust; the greed for power and sensual and material pleasure – Catholicism, they believed, was now a satanic order. So, for all concerned, politics was the field of play between Satan and God, good versus evil, and the English civil war was understood as a war for the soul of the nation and of each and every one of its people. It was into this hothouse of politico-religious ferocity that Milton was born. His birth fell just three years after Guy Fawkes' failed 'gunpowder plot' to blow up Parliament.

KEY EVENTS

The English civil war

Charles I of England and Scotland wanted to establish the dominance of the Anglican monarchy over the Puritan-dominated English Parliament, but he could not raise the taxes he needed to rule without Parliament's permission. To get around this problem, Charles set up a crown court (the Star Chamber) to impose special taxes and fines, and he dissolved Parliament, ruling without them for eleven years. In this time, the monarchy slowly moved the established Church back towards a Catholic model. This so offended Scottish Presbyterians that in 1640 they invaded England. The King had to recall Parliament to fund the war against them, but Parliament sided with the Presbyterians, and the head of the Anglican Church and other supporters of the King were arrested and executed. The King lacked the ability to control Parliament, as became evident in 1641, when an uprising in Ireland triggered a dispute between the King and Parliament over who ran the army. After a violent argument, the King fled from London to Nottingham whereupon the war with Parliament began.

After a period of inconclusive warfare, the parliamentarians established, in 1644, an army of Puritan volunteers. This 'New Model Army' consistently outfought the Royalist armies. By 1645 the King's forces were beaten and the King held captive by Scottish forces.

The victorious army and Parliament then divided among themselves. The army leadership was inclined to replace the monarchy with a people's republic, but many parliamentarians wanted to re-establish the monarchy on terms more favourable to Parliament. In addition, the Presbyterians in the parliamentarian camp wanted to establish their religion as the official state church – something the independents that dominated the army were opposed to in principle. Taking advantage of his enemies' disarray, Charles turned the Scottish Presbyterians to his side, and, in 1648, launched an attack on England. The Royalist forces were beaten in a series of skirmishes with Oliver Cromwell's parliamentary army who eventually captured the King. At the same time they carried out a military coup on Parliament, reducing it to a rump of army supporters who voted to have the King tried by an army court after which he was executed.

In 1650, Charles' son, Charles II of Scotland, invaded England; once again Cromwell led the parliamentary forces against the Crown, and once again the monarch's forces were soundly beaten. Charles II fled to France and Cromwell was established as Lord Protector of the new English Republic.

The gunpowder plot registered the last gasps of Catholic resistance to the Anglican subordination of the Church to the State, but this end signalled the beginning of the struggle within British Protestantism between the Anglicans (often called Anglo-Catholics, to signal their continuing sympathy with the elements of Catholicism) who dominated the court and church hierarchy, and the Puritans – the Presbyterians who were strong in Scotland, and the numerous independent sects such as Anabaptists, Familists and Quakers who came to dominate the army. This contest climaxed in the 1640s with the English civil war, tailing off slowly over the next forty years before finally ending with the glorious revolution of 1689 (see Chapter 4 on Locke).

FACT BOX 1

Main factions within Protestantism 1

Anglicanism replaced Catholicism as the official state church of England, following Henry VIII's split with Rome. Apart from its independence from Rome, the Anglican church retained many features of the Catholic Church, notably the promotion of its own place in a hierarchy of authority (now one place below the monarch, but unchanged in relation to the general populace, who had to pay tithes – the tax to support the Anglican clergy).

FACT BOX 2

Main factions within Protestantism 2

Presbyterians: Presbyterianism was the largest grouping of Puritanism in England and Scotland. Austere in lifestyle and conservative in modes of living, Presbyterians believed that God had chosen an elect few to join him in the afterlife and that the day of judgement, when the elect would be made known, was approaching (1660 was a popular choice). Presbyterians worked to have their church replace Anglicanism as the official state church of England and Scotland.

Anabaptists: a loose association of groups who commonly believed that individuals had to choose to join the church and thus could not be baptised until adulthood. This challenged the idea of natural membership of a national religion, and so placed them at odds with the Anglicans at the start of the civil war and with the Presbyterians at the end of the war. The Anabaptists' challenge was strengthened by their refusal to pay tithes.

Familists: a sect which overlapped with Anabaptists, but which believed that heaven and hell could be made in this world. Members sought to recapture the innocence

continued

of Adam and Eve by living at one with nature, sharing all their possessions in communal living. They were as much a threat to the emerging commercial ethos of mainstream Protestantism as they were to the Anglican monarchic state.

Quakers: developed away from the centres of politics and commerce in the north and west of England. They believed (as Quakers still do) that the spirit of God dwelt in each individual and moved them – in a non-rational, intuitive way – to understand right from wrong and good from bad, usually by means of interpreting the scriptures. Like Anabaptists and Presbyterians, they placed the emphasis of ethical action on the individual, but replaced the rationality of choice favoured by the Anabaptists with the emotionality of feeling what is right, and, like the Anabaptists, they challenged the Presbyterians' ideal of an established church imposing authoritative interpretations of scripture.

Life and times

Milton's austere Protestantism blended with the ornate romanticism of his poetry to create an unusual mixture of form (classical romantic) and content (Puritan fundamentalism) in his writings. Encompassing the tensions between the baroque flamboyance of the Catholicised old world and the minimalist austerity of the Puritan new world, Milton's writings brilliantly transcended the tension between them by linking the basic ideas of the Protestant parliamentarian cause to the fundamentals of the ancient cultures of Greece and Rome. In doing this, he was able to exploit the creative techniques of classicist forms in the style of his writing, to present classical ideals in the content of his arguments, as the cultural and philosophical roots of some apparently novel (and, to Royalist traditionalists, culturally unfounded) Protestant ideals. These ideals specifically fall into the group which today we would define as liberal, but which we recognise as originating in the political culture of ancient Athens. They comprise the exchange of ideas and argument in unfettered debate, public assembly as the locale for each and every individual citizen's expression and judgement on ideas and opinions, individual endeavour expressed in the thoughtful and pro-active engagement with ideas and opinions expressed in the public sphere.

The sources of Milton's unusual mixture of classicism and Puritanism are his family upbringing, his education and his experiences while travelling in Italy. He was raised in a stable and prosperous family in an area of London occupied largely by the merchant classes. His father – a scrivener (a type of lawyer specialising in loans) by trade – was also a lover of the classically informed high culture of the old Catholicised order, and so Milton's upbringing immersed him in the typical business-headed Puritanism of his community, and also in a world full of classical music and arts. His privileged upbringing enabled him to indulge in a long career of learning that began in the best seats of academia. After studying at St Paul's Grammar School in London, he moved to Cambridge University, where he stayed from 1625 to 1632. It was during his time at Cambridge that he fell in love with poetry and made the decision to devote his life to it. For a short time after making this decision he was able to pursue its logic, and he spent some years after leaving Cambridge in the town of Horton, privately studying and writing poetry. He also began to study and consider some of the novel ideas propagated by various Protestant sects and by political radicals. At this point, the political dimensions of his religious beliefs began to take shape in his mind and to influence his activities. Although the various sects within the Protestant milieu constantly argued about theological and political matters, they were united in their challenge to the hierarchy of church authority. They also commonly held the equalitarian and individualistic notion that every individual's spirit gave them direct access to God (and direct access to each individual for the devil). In the years that followed, Milton's writings reveal that these ideas influenced him greatly. Indeed, they appear to have opened the door to the 'big idea' which runs like a thread throughout his writings – the idea that every individual must choose between possible courses of action and between conflicting propositions, if they are to learn right from wrong and good from evil: no one can have the answer given to (or forced upon) them. Another idea popular among the sects was that the 'second coming' was due. The struggles between parliamentarians and the Catholicised monarchy for the constitution of England was seen as the struggle to prepare God's heaven on earth in time for Jesus' coming and 'the day of judgement' which would come with it. Milton found this notion compelling; the second coming would soon destroy the monarchy and the corrupt Catholic Church. He believed that the radical Protestant revolt against Catholicism in general and the Anglican monarchy in England represented the beginnings of the establishment of God's order on earth. This belief (of which events eventually disavailed him) fired his radicalism and inspired his leap into the public sphere as a fierce anti-monarchist.

In 1638 he travelled to Italy in order to gain knowledge and experience at the high seat of the Renaissance – the home of classical art forms. While on his travels, he witnessed the full dimensions of the Catholic order's attempt to impose belief from above. He saw everywhere the extensive hand of the Church's censorship of new ideas and the policing of public debate. He encountered Galileo, who was under house arrest imposed by the Catholic authorities for his 'blasphemous' challenge to the Church's authority in all matters of knowledge. This experience, combined with his intake of radical Protestants' challenge to Church authority, filled his mind with the encroaching dimensions of the political struggle between Protestantism and the Catholic Church. To him it appeared as a struggle for the soul and, as such, it was unavoidably the subject of the poet's muse.

On returning to England, the strength of these sentiments pulled Milton into the political fray, and his intended life as a poet became delayed for decades by his ever-increasing involvement in the struggle between monarchists and Parliament which dominated the politics of his time. It was during the climatic period of this great struggle that Milton entered the public arena as a strong supporter of the parliamentarian cause. In February 1649 he came out as a strong supporter of the new republic, publishing *The Tenure of Kings and Magistrates*. This article presented a strong defence of the execution of Charles I, which had taken place just two weeks before, and effectively earned him the post of Secretary for Foreign Tongues to the new Parliament. Between 1649 and 1651 he published a series of commissioned papers, explaining and defending the government's activities and attacking Royalist and Catholic objections. In today's terms, he had become a 'spin doctor' for the Cromwellian government – a move which ensured that when the republican cause fell he would fall with it.

KEY PEOPLE

Oliver Cromwell, 1599–1658

Cromwell was a staunch Puritan who rose to military prominence during the civil war, when he led Parliament's forces at many significant battles including the crucial victory at Naseby. After the purging of Parliament, Cromwell was left as the head of a military dictatorship, with the title Lord Protector of England. For the remaining five years of his life, Cromwell used the New Model Army and his political supporters to purge England, Scotland and Ireland of any religious dissidents and of all political opposition. Milton supported Cromwell, at first whole-heartedly, and later, as the dictatorial features of Cromwell's political leadership became evident, through gritted teeth. Cromwell after all shared Milton's vision of a new Puritan order, and Milton thought that perhaps Cromwell could be persuaded to lighten the authoritarian style of his government.

Late years

Milton's faith in his cause and in the rightness of his actions was to be tested by a combination of political and personal misfortunes. On the political front, the collapse of the Protestant cause into bickering camps and the replacement of Parliament by Cromwell's military dictatorship began to shake his belief that he was witnessing the beginning of God's new order. The subsequent disillusionment of many people with the government and the hankering after a return to monarchic government left Milton pleading with his contemporaries to establish an elected ruler; this was the thrust of his *Readie and Easie Way to Establish a Free Commonwealth*, published just before the restoration of the monarchy in 1660. The restoration and the complete routing of the radical Protestant factions that followed reduced his convictions in this respect to the vaguest hope. The terrible unpopularity of the parliamentarian cause which followed Cromwell's dictatorship ensured that Milton – as a notable republican – would be subject to retribution following the restoration of the monarchy. He was imprisoned and faced possible execution, but, possibly due to his connections with one or two Royalists, or to his reputation as a writer, he escaped with banishment from public life. His private life offered little in the way of comfort. A badly judged marriage in 1642 had left him living with debtor Royalist 'in-laws' and an unhappy wife. In 1652 his wife died in childbirth, followed shortly by his only son, and Milton's failing eyesight finally reduced him to total blindness. In 1658, just months into his second marriage, his new wife died in childbirth along with the child. He did not give up on life however; he remarried in 1663, and his writings show that he remained committed to serve the radical Protestant cause: 'I sing with mortal voice, unchanged to hoarse or mute, though fallen on evil days' (Bush 1977: 396). His resolute faith was never fully extinguished.

In the remaining fourteen years of his life, Milton returned to his first love – poetry. He completed *Paradise Lost* (begun during his politically active life) and wrote *Paradise Regained* and *Samson Agonistes*. These three epic poems established his reputation as possibly the greatest poet in the English canon. With his epic tales of the struggles of God and Satan and the fall of humankind from grace, he poetically shaped the dramatic landscapes of his culture and his time, and into this landscape he traced his own experiences of the struggles for the soul of the people, and the failure and fall of the radical Protestant cause. In this sense, his poetry was his continued service to the cause.

KEY TEXT

Milton on divorce

In 1643, Milton went public with ideas about marriage that were fermenting among Anabaptists, but which were considered radical and subversive by the Anglican Church and by many of his contemporaries. In *The Doctrine and Discipline of Divorce*, he argued that marriage was a contract between free-thinking, independent individuals. Its vitality sprung from the fact that it was made by choice and continued through mutual consent expressed in the keeping of the marriage vows. If one party broke the marriage vows, the mutual consent to the vows was ended, the vitality of the marriage lost and the marriage likely to die. In such situations, it should be possible for the hurt party to withdraw consent.

Milton argued that a whole range of hurtful activities could be considered as sources of marriage failure and, in this, his argument ran contrary to the common belief that adultery provided the only grounds for divorce.

Milton also flirted with the idea of women divorcing their husbands, which was highly radical in a time when men were considered to have a lordly rule over women. The scandal caused by his works was such that they bought him his initial notoriety, not as a political actor or as a poet, but as 'Milton the Divorcer'.

Writings

Milton's willingness to mix together elements of the diverse religious/political discourse of his time, combined with a fiercely brave willingness to stand up and argue for a parliamentarian republic, and his awesome talents as a writer, led him to produce some of the most outstanding polemics of Protestant liberalism. His initial public reputation stemmed from his political writing and only later extended to his reputation as an outstanding poet.

While obviously valued as significant contributions to literature, Milton's poems also have historical value as expressions of the metaphysical landscape in which the participants in the political struggles of the seventeenth century imagined themselves to dwell. In *Paradise Lost* and *Paradise Regained*, Milton presented his contemporaries with the familiar story of Adam and Eve's fall from grace, and the struggle of human-kind to retrieve the path back to God's paradise. These ideas operated constantly in the minds of most people of the time. The failing of the Catholic Church, for so long the trusted guide to the good life, presented a massive test of faith to people who were not prepared mentally or psychologically to consider non-theological alter-natives. For them, the issues of the conflict between the Church and Protestantism could be broken down to the issue of who were the good people, and who was working for Satan. In this way, the metaphysical notion of the fall from grace framed the political issues of the time with the concerns of a Christian people in a deep crisis of faith. The poems may also be viewed as more personal reflections on the major ethical issues involved in the political struggles of Milton's life and times. They constantly thematise banishment from paradise, the struggle to know good, the issue of when to obey and when to challenge authority. All these themes echo the struggle of Milton and his compatriots to establish God's society on earth, their eventual defeat by the restoration of the monarchy, and Milton's own banishment from political life.

Most cryptically, *Paradise Lost* contains a strong subversive flavour. It is the devil who gives words to Milton's big idea – that every individual must choose between possible courses of action, and between conflicting propositions, if they are to learn right from wrong and good from evil. In the *Areopagitica*, Milton writes: 'what wisdom can there be to choose, what continuance to forbear without the knowledge of good and evil?' (Bush 1977: 167) In *Paradise Lost*, Satan finally persuades Eve to bite the apple of knowledge and so revolt against God with the words: 'if what is evil be real, why not known, since easier shunned?' (Bush 1977: 454). Exposed here is a strong sense of the sanctity of individual judgement, and with it a strong anti-authoritarian streak: no one – not even God – can *enforce* right judgement or goodness from above.

Intriguingly, Milton's use of the devil as the advocate of his own ideas indicates something which his passionate faith in the Protestant religion perhaps blinded him to. This is the fact that Protestantism, being founded in protest against the established church and being also the dynamic ideological source of protests against the monarchic states which enforced the principles of that church, was actually rooted in a suspicion of organised religion itself. Puritans were very suspicious of the mysticism which is integral to Catholic theology, partly because they believed that religious truths were revealed by the holy spirit, and partly because theological mysticism led to secrecy within the Catholic order and therefore to a hierarchy of unexplained and therefore unaccountable power in Catholic polities. This suspicion of mysticism ensured that Protestants would look increasingly to secular sources for the rationale and justification of the new political orders they were establishing. In this way the roots of secular liberalism grew out of seventeenth-century Protestantism. Milton's works, filled as they are with a sense of the tensions and contradictions of Christian theology and of political governance, provide a rich vein for mining the interconnections and the differences between Protestant fundamentalism and modern secular liberalism.

Milton's grand themes

Milton's political writings are relatively short works, addressing specific events and situations and, on reading them, it is not immediately obvious how they might combine into a grand theoretical engagement with the political condition. However, when these works are placed in the light (and shade) of his later poetic writing, strong political themes may be seen to run through each and every text. The political themes are the nature of *tyranny*, the nature of *liberty* and the relationship of mutual opposition which defines them. The perception of an integral relationship between tyranny and liberty derives, in Milton's thinking, from his philosophical concern with the nature of truth, the nature of falsity and the relationship between them. The interest in truth and falsity is itself derived from his theological concern with good and evil which 'in the field of this world grow up together almost inseparably' (*Areopagitica* in Bush 1977: 167).

Milton observed that the monarchy in the UK and the Catholic hierarchy in Europe both built claims to a divine right to rule, on the widespread use of censorship, and the enforcement of favourable doctrines in religion, politics, science and the arts. In this arrangement, he perceived a circular relationship between evil falsity and tyranny: the tyrant, 'regarding neither law nor common good, reigns only for himself and his faction' (Dzelzainis 1991: 16). The evil lies in the tyrant's propagation of the falsehood that he is God-like in relation to the laws of the state and to the people within it. So the evil of tyranny is derived from falsity, while both the falsity and the evil are maintained by the political conditions of tyranny – censorship, the closure of public forums for debate, the imposition of a ruling ideology – which promote falsehoods and deny access to the truth.

In Milton's thinking (and the thinking of his contemporaries), the political, the philosophical and the theological do not come apart. The struggle for goodness is the struggle for truth, which is also a struggle for liberty, for the condition of liberty is necessary as a space for truth to engage with and to outdo falsity, and so for good to outdo evil.

In this view, the struggle for goodness and knowledge is a fundamental site of political struggle. The great political struggles of humankind are the struggle for empowerment and the struggle for truth. In the end (come judgement day), these struggles will be seen to be two sides of the same coin, since power and truth are ultimately unified in the person of God. However, due to the continuing struggle between God and Satan – a struggle which centres on the world of men and sweeps their fate into the balance – power and truth are not joined readily in human experience, and degrees of power may be held, and often are held, in opposition to truth.

Knowing good and evil

For those of us who see politics in the practical terms of the material world, Milton's strident interconnecting of religion to political life may be worrying on two counts. First, it resembles an example of the inflexible and conflict-inducing thinking, from which the modern secular world has in large part freed us. Second, it seems to root the terms of practical political judgement in a debatable fiction. However, while it is right to be cautious towards political theory that takes its lead from religious assertions, it is worth noting that, in his way, Milton is unearthing what has since become a recognised connection between despotic tyrannies and loss of truth, and between the loss of truth and the loss of ethics. If we look through the religious tenor of Milton's writings to the logic of his arguments, we find an insight into the problematic entwining of good and evil and truth and falsity. Underneath the myth-making, Milton's presentation of the fall is a philosophical exploration of how we get to know the truth and how we come to be moral beings.

The beginning point is to acknowledge that Milton shows how the means to access truth is through the process of knowing. Knowing is portrayed in *Paradise Lost* as the activity of becoming intimate with things. It is the activity of getting to know things through continued experience of them and through judgement of that experience, as shown in the story of how Adam obtains self-knowledge. Like all sentient beings, he begins with unfamiliarity and ignorance, 'who himself beginning knew'? but then,

> myself I then perused, and limb by limb
> Surveyed and sometimes went, and sometimes ran
> With supple joints, as lively vigour led.
>
> (Bush 1977: 422)

Milton shows here how knowing involves the activity of thinking (thus concentrating in the mind) which is applied to experience (which also involves the sensory application of physical being). The human mind is the site of intellectual understanding – it is the place where, by combinations of rational thinking and memory (of previous experience), we order experience into categories of things which we know to be real or imagined and whose existence we know to be true or untrue. Our minds provide the means to judge between truth and falsity.

In *Paradise Lost*, Milton develops a classical Puritan formulation of how humans know good and evil, from a classically seventeenth-century formulation of the relationship of reason to experience. Judging between good and bad is more complex than judging between true and false, for it involves a tension between sensual attraction to or repulsion from experienced things and rational analysis of what they are and their likely effect on us. Things look, feel, taste, smell or sound attractive or repellent in varying degrees, and we react to them directly without thought. The intellect has to impose reasoned order on to these basic sensory reactions; a piece of fruit, or – to modernise Milton's argument – a piece of chocolate tastes great, but it is not always a good idea to eat it. You need to impose restraint on your desire if you are not to be damaged by your own thoughtless, lust-driven actions.

The difficulty for a person in this situation is that the reasons why it is not good to succumb to temptation are not absolutely certain. If you eat chocolate you may get fat, lose your teeth and perhaps even die from obesity, but you may see this is a fair trade-off against the pleasure of eating sweets – you may rationalise that living for pleasure in the present is a better way of living than denying pleasure for a long life of dull healthiness.

Milton plays the Puritan hand strongly on this point. In *Paradise Lost*, Eve struggles to judge whether to taste the tempting fruit dangling from the tree of knowledge and die, or to live for ever without ever possessing that knowledge:

> So savory of that fruit, which with desire,
> Inclinable now grown to touch or taste,
> Solicited her longing eye.
>
> (Bush 1977: 455–456)

In her confusion, juggling all the possibilities, she falls prey to Satan's subtle arguments:

> Knowledge of good and evil?
> Of Good how just? Of evil, if what is evil
> Be real, why not known, since easier shunned. . . .
> Why then was this forbid, why but to awe,
> Why but to keep ye low and ignorant.
>
> (Bush 1977: 454)

Milton is showing that, in trying to sort out such conundrums, the intellect grapples for reference points against which to judge whether experience is good or bad. If there is no ultimate criterion for judging experience of things, you end up in a self-serving relativism – a world in which you decide good and bad purely in terms of how you feel. It is no coincidence that it is Satan who says:

> The mind is its own place and in itself
> Can make a heaven of hell, and a hell of heaven.
>
> (Hill 1988: 404)

It appears to the relativist that they have God-like control over their life and destiny, but, like Satan, they are cut off from the means to judge their desires and feelings and thus to know what is good. There must therefore be an ultimate reference point from which judgements can be rightly made and this reference point is God. For Milton, the ultimate and universal criteria for judgement are those of God. These criteria are not 'good' and 'bad', but are 'Good' and 'Evil'. In this measurement of things, the idea of 'good' shifts from a confusion of technical specification and moral judgement to a fully moral judgement. In the technical language of good and bad, a 'good shot' is on target, as opposed to a 'bad shot' which is sloppy and misses. In a moral specification: 'a good shot' is one taken for a right purpose – for example, to liberate the oppressed or protect the weak – whereas a 'bad shot' is one taken for bad ends – for example, to murder someone. By calling such things as murder 'evil' rather than 'bad', God makes it clear that the bottom line for all judgement is measured out in moral not technical terms.

The relativist is self-absorbed and so only has his or her feelings as a yardstick for judgement, yet the drive of experienced pleasure often pushes against reasoned judgement; we are tempted to do something which feels good, but which reason and experience inform us will lead to a bad end. Surrender to temptation is the fall into evil. Thus, when Eve – prompted by Satan – 'be deterred not from what might lead to a happier life knowledge of good and evil' (Bush 1977: 454) – became confused and wrongly bit into the fruit, it was not simply a technical error of judgement, it was a moral error – a sin – for which she had to be punished. Here again, we see Milton's work exemplifying how Puritanism gives a solid set of theological reference points from which to make frighteningly certain judgements in social and political areas of life. Hence Milton's own judgement that the Anglican flirtation with Catholicism was not simply mistaken, but was 'evil' (Potter 1971: 56). Such certainty leads easily to inflexible doctrinal politics and entrenched political positions that generate and maintain civil unrest and conflict. This tendency may certainly be seen in Milton's unbending support for the Cromwellian purges of King and Catholics.

Milton's political thought is, however, more interesting than simple dogma. Its fundamentalism is offset by a liberal recognition of the uncertainties of human understanding and a sense that there is a place for making errors in the process of learning truths. This liberalism is actually an outgrowth of his Protestantism. In his essay *Of Education*, he writes: 'The end of learning is to repair the ruins of our first parents by regaining to know God aright' (Bush 1977: 137). In the *Areopagitica*, the activity of learning is tied to the idea of being tested by God in order that we improve ourselves – cleanse ourselves by degrees from original sin – and prove to him our worthiness. 'That which purifies us is trial, and trial is by what is contrary' (Bush 1977: 167). This statement is fundamentally Protestant, positing each individual to face good and evil alone under the eyes of God. However, much of Milton's political work is an attempt to set out the necessary conditions of the 'trial', if it is to be a fair recognition of the individual's endeavour. In setting out such terms, Milton moves towards classical liberal ground. His works are full of arguments for the 'free and open encounter' of ideas in public debate, the accessibility of all evidence to those who would be involved in such debate, the equality of each and every person undergoing his or her trial before the law, the necessary transparency of the trial process for the verdict to be understood by the participants, something necessary if they are to learn from their actions and improve (as God wished them to do). In all these elements of Milton's thought, there is a move from its fixed Protestant base towards genuine liberalism. We shall now follow this process in detail through analysis of his three major political works: *The Areopagitica, The Tenure of Kings and Magistrates* and *The Readie and Easie Way to Establish a Free Commonwealth*.

Areopagitica: free debate and the public sphere

The terms of the trial are set by Adam and Eve's fall from grace. 'It was from the knowledge of one rind tasted that the knowledge of good and evil as two twins cleaving together leaped forth into the world', writes Milton and, 'Perhaps that is the doom that Adam fell into of knowing good and evil . . . that is of knowing good by evil' (Bush 1977: 167). Following the fall, we are each compelled to know the world this way: through the trial of attempting to discern good from evil. It is not an easy task; sometimes good things involve bits of evil and sometimes evil appears to be good: 'the knowledge of good is so involved and so interwoven with the knowledge of evil, and in so many cunning resemblances hardly to be discerned' (Bush 1977: 166).

The problem is complex because the opposition of good and evil transfers into the problem of knowing good and bad, and this in turn requires a perception of truth and falsity. It is not a direct transfer. As we have seen, knowing what is true is not equal to knowing what is good, and knowing what is good is not exactly the same as knowing what is true.

For Milton, the difficulties involved in the trial of human judgement set the terms for the best conditions of social life. The social and political order should be arranged to provide the most favourable conditions for the trial which every one of us must continually go through. The best way to get at truth, argues Milton, is to expose the various arguments to the sword of debate. When tested by human reason, coherence, which is a quality of truth, will win over incoherence, which is (ultimately) a definitive quality of falsity. False argument will be exposed, however impassioned its presentation, however cunningly its incoherences are obscured (as Satan eventually discovers in *Paradise Lost*). So the advice Milton gives to those who govern his society is that the foundational principles of any human society must be to provide open spaces for public debate and for scientific and philosophical experimentation.

The argument of the Areopagitica

The *Areopagitica* – named after the people's court of ancient Athens (the Areopagus) – is an open letter written to Parliament, in which Milton puts forward the case for open public debate. Written in 1644, this text is an argument against the imposition of a censure on published materials. Censorship had long been standard practice in Europe. In England, the activity was carried out by the Star Chamber, a high court of the Crown. In 1641, the Star Chamber was abolished as part of the deconstruction of the monarchic state, and with its demise the responsibility for censorship was lost. Thus, for a brief period between 1641 and 1643, when Parliament re-established censorship, there was a 'free-for-all' on the printing presses. The various religious sects and political movements published furiously, and a wide range of radical theology – from some Familists who believed the soul died with the body, to others who believed that Jesus was a mere mortal (Hill 1979: 70–76) – and/or radical political activity – notably that of the Diggers and Levellers who argued for a communist redistribution of property – entered the public arena.

 Fast forward

Go to Chapter 3 where the argument for avoiding schisms is deployed by Thomas Hobbes in his *Leviathan*.

The reintroduction of censorship followed the established reasoning that censorship damped down the spread of wild and opposing ideas, and so ensured like-mindedness within society, avoiding schisms or splits which would weaken society from within and expose it to enemies from without. Milton argued that this practice was based on a wrong understanding of the ways in which humans can get to know truth, and of the ways in which the moral virtues of obedience and communality that constitute good citizenship are produced. The Athenians had shown that good citizenship requires willing participation in the life of the polity. Being inquisitive and wilful (as shown by Adam and Eve's behaviour in Genesis), people will only willingly obey laws that they understand to be right. Understanding of laws can only be had from enquiry into the reasoning of those laws. Enquiry can happen only through open discussion and analysis, which in turn is produced only by open debate. Thus a condition of liberty is required, not a zone of uniformity – 'This is not the liberty which we can hope, that no grievance ever should arise in the commonwealth', but a free space in which to think, talk and act. 'When complaints are freely heard, deeply considered and speedily reformed, then is the utmost bound of civil liberty attained that wise men look for' (Bush 1977: 152).

Fast forward

Go to Chapter 8 where you will find a very similar argument in J.S. Mill's *On Liberty*.

The condition of liberty is a risk-filled arena; both right and wrong and good and evil are allowed to gather to full strength in public discussion, but this is necessary if the struggle between them is to take its rightful place at the heart of society. In this context, it is possible to see how Milton perceived the schismatic state of English society in his time as a good thing and a bad thing. It was good in that, freed from the yoke of Catholic censorship, people were able to imagine new ways of being. It was bad because the multiplicity of often wild ideas which had sprung up indicated that people, unaccustomed to the test of reasoning in open debate, were falling for all sorts of wild imaginings. Milton saw that the wide range of ideas believed by the members of the multiplicity of religious sects was a consequence of a long-term lack of opportunity to get at the truth. Here specifically is the reason for a free press and a public sphere of open debate. 'How can we more safely, and with less danger scout the regions of sin and falsity than by reading all manner of tractates and hearing all manner of reason'(Bush 1977: 167).

The guide of action is belief and the guide of belief is understanding. The power of human imagination to construct compelling fantasies can lead reason into mistaking falsity for truth. Without the constraint of countervailing argument, grand falsities cannot be tempered by the rational appreciation of what can possibly be true. The good behaviour of those untried by argument is simply the product of blind belief.

In making this argument, Milton produces a unique and vital role for books. Books are the material record of argument. Not only do they record all opinion and argument, but they also capture truth in the form of right argument and proven facts in a record which people can see. So he 'who kills a man kills a reasonable creature, God's image; but he who destroys a good book kills reason itself, kills the image of God, as it were in the eye' (Bush 1977: 155–156).

Having made this point, Milton can show how censorship denies the opportunity to develop a capacity to truly understand right from wrong and to see through false argument disguised as truth. Censorship closes down the open space of debate and reduces the plurality of opinion to one single repeated dogma, so that, even supposing that those involved propagated their views with the best intentions, they would act in error and eventually come to an end in confusion and failure. 'What continuance to forbare without the knowledge of evil'? (Bush 1977: 167).

Thus the appearance of virtuous citizenship established by imposed censorship is merely a front, for 'The virtue . . . which is but a youngling in the contemplation of evil . . . is but a blank virtue' (Bush 1977: 167): it is weak and likely to break when tested. As evidence for his argument, Milton pointed to the intellectual poverty of much of the published material during the free press period and the gullibility of many of the people who read it. He argued that, although people now had the opportunity to analyse argument in public debate, they did not know how to do it, because judgement requires practice in the public arena and people had not had such practice for hundreds of years. In the suddenness and completeness of this period of free expression and thought, people were making big errors, 'as children and as childish men who have not the art to qualify and prepare' ideas and arguments (Bush 1977: 170). The answer to the plethora of wild preachings, he argued, was forbearance and discussion. The regular practice of analysing argument would allow the people to develop their rational sensibilities and, in time, false argument would be rejected. Censorship eradicates the propagation of 'false doctrine', but at the expense of allowing people to understand why it is false.

The intensity of Milton's argument stems from its theological origins, but finds its political expression in the argument for a recognisably liberal political order. The theological dimension leads Milton to give a stark warning to Parliament over its renewal of censorship. Censorship blocks access to the truth and is therefore evil. We as individuals 'bring not innocence into this world', but rather we 'bring impurity' that we have inherited from Adam and Eve (Bush 1977: 167). Censorship chains people to their inherited condition of corruption and imperfection, by denying them the trial of judging right from wrong and good from evil. Censorship denies everyone the opportunity to develop their capacity for intellectual and moral judgement – the activity by which they can purify their souls and liberate themselves from Adam's curse. Therefore, censorship is opposite to God's intent and is an abuse of power. Even if it is done with good intent, it is misguided, and dangerously so, for what is against God is fundamentally satanic. For this reason, Milton states, censorship is typically a tool of tyrants, but it is not a fit tool of governance for a new age under a people's parliament. Milton gives his parliamentarians a stark final warning: 'revolutions of ages do not oft recover the loss of a rejected truth, for the want of which whole nations fare the worst' (Bush 1977: 156).

DISCUSSION POINTS

In later works, Milton argued that a limited degree of state control of speech and action was necessary. His shift away from the argument for unfettered access to information and opinion raises two questions that have been constantly discussed

continued

since his time. First, there is the question of power: Who gets to decide what are the limits of expression, and what gives them the authority to do so?

Second, there is the question of judgement: What factors would determine the limits of expression? These two questions remain problematic for advocates of an 'open society' and set fundamental technical problems for legislators in liberal democratic society.

The *Areopagitica* makes it clear that the task facing the new Protestant Parliament is to work at establishing a social order in which the people of England are encouraged to learn, debate and experiment in order to get at the truth and so 'know God aright' (*Of Education* cited in Bush 1977: 137). Of course, to Milton and his contemporaries' way of thinking, such inquisitiveness is what landed humans in trouble in the first place; any society which has free thinking and open debate at its core is open to error, false argument, ideological conflicts and potentially civil war. Milton, living though such a situation, is daringly advocating a politics of risk, when most of his contemporaries are searching for a means to eradicate diversity and difference in the name of security and order. Seen in this way, Milton's *Areopagitica* is a radical liberal argument.

 Fast forward

Go to Chapter 3 where Hobbes' *Leviathan* gives the most notable example of the seventeenth-century English arguments for the overriding need for the security of the nation.

There are three specific elements of his argument that we would now describe as typically liberal:

1. The argument that each and every individual stands equally before God is both equalitarian and individualistic. It is equalitarian in that every person is equal before God (and God's law) by virtue of their common possession of human faculties and their common encounter with the problems of truth and falsity and good and evil. It is individualistic in that each person must think for themselves and act out their own path towards God. In summary: all are equally engaged in the moral choices and judgement, but each makes his or her choice alone. This formulation (which retains a degree of coherence without reference to God) is fundamental to modern liberalism and is the basis of the modern liberal ideal of 'meritocracy'.
2. The idea that a public sphere – namely a social space for open debate – is essential for each and every citizen to know truth and to choose to act upon it has become a fundamental tenet of liberal democracies. It underpins the notion

that citizenship is dependent on participation in the debate and decision-making concerning common affairs. This idea is, in turn, dependent on citizens being educated and informed, to a level that enables them to understand the issues of the day and to give rational responses to arguments and make sound judgements on ideas for action.

3   In arguing that the state withdraw from censorship, Milton is indicating that the sphere of legitimate state policing of society is prescribed in scope and type. It is limited, in that it cannot legitimately enforce ideology or suppress artistic, scientific and associational activities in the name of either truth or order. It is prescribed in type, in that its legitimate role centres on maintaining and protecting the social activities, which involve free thinking and open debate, from corruption and violence. In short, Milton is advocating the liberal prescription of a limited state protecting a civil (non-violent, tolerant) society.

DISCUSSION POINTS

Is it possible to coherently present an argument for the natural equality of every individual, without recourse to a religious notion of 'equal before God'?

Is the idea that people are fundamentally equal a viable notion, in a world where physical, intellectual, economic and socio-political inequalities appear to constantly reassert themselves?

Governance in tension with creativity: from *Areopagitica* to *The Tenure of Kings and Magistrates*

When the tension between truth and falsity occupies the realm of material things, it shapes into a tension between order and chaos. However, the link between the two layers is not simple. Truth provides the principles which give order to the world, while chaos is lack of order and therefore also lack of access to truth. Falsity, on the other hand, is an active agent that can create chaos or live off it, but is not co-equal to it. *Paradise Lost* begins with Satan establishing his own satanic order in Hell. Chaos is the condition which prevails when people are cut off from truth and are not yet beguiled by falsehoods into living under satanic orders. For Milton, the time of the English civil war was exactly such a time. The task for the victors was to establish God's order, before the temptations of power and self-serving false principles could corrupt the new order. It is this concern which sounds through *The Tenure of Kings and Magistrates* (1649), at the outset of the new parliamentary era and through *The Readie and Easie Way to Establish a Free Commonwealth* (1660), as the Puritan era, corrupted by Cromwellian dictatorship, comes to its end.

The argument for the overthrow of tyrants and establishment of a republic

> That it is lawfull and hath been held so through all Ages, for any, who have the Power to call to account a Tyrant, or wicked King, and after due conviction, to depose, and put him to death; if the ordinary Magistrate hath neglected, or deny'd to doe it.
>
> (Dzelzainis 1991: 1)

This assertion occupies the title page of *The Tenure of Kings and Magistrates* (1649) and sets the agenda of the text which was to follow, in terms that clearly establish Milton's belief in the legitimacy of the new post-monarchic order. Believing in the power of reasoned argument and the justice of the rump Parliament's activities, but also sensitive to the difficulty facing people in judging between what he saw as the clever deceptions of the monarchist argument and the claims of the parliamentarians, Milton set himself the task of making clear exactly how the King had been bad, and exactly why it was necessary to replace monarchy with a representative republican leadership.

Fast forward

Go to Chapter 5 for Montesquieu's discussion of tyrants.

Milton argued that the trial of the King was necessary to expose the falsity of the overthrown monarchic tyranny. The trial showed the falsity of the King's claim to a right derived directly from God to rule as protector of the people, by exposing how, in going to war against the people's Parliament, the King had used his powers for his own well-being and in direct opposition to the well-being of the people whom he was supposed to protect. 'We could not serve two masters', he wrote, 'God and the King, or the King and the supreme law, sworn in the first place (*by the King*), to maintain our safety and our liberty' (Dzelzainis 1991: 221). Here, Milton sets out Parliament and the monarch as two duelling representatives of truth (and right and good) and falsity (and wrong and evil), arguing from the outset that the relative legitimacy of Parliament and the illegitimacy of the King both stem from their respective actions in regard to their rightful place as representatives of the people's true needs: 'The power of kings and magistrates is nothing else but what is only derivative, transferred and committed to them in trust from the people to the common good of them all and cannot be taken from them, without violation of their natural birthright' (Dzelzainis 1991: 10). Parliament represented the people's needs by going to war with the King, while the King attempted to bamboozle the people with stories of his divine appointment by God and their duty to obedience to him. Turning the arguments for divine right to rule against the monarch, Milton argues that such a claim, and the actions that follow from it, marked out King Charles I as a tyrant – a ruler 'who regarding neither Law nor the common good, reigns only for himself and his faction' (Dzelzainis 1991: 16). He had placed himself outside the law and thus 'voutsaf'd the benefit of the law' (Dzelzainis 1991: 17). Lawless, lacking society, and dangerous to those who live within lawful society, the tyrant (Charles) – is no more than a 'savage beast' (Dzelzainis 1991: 13) despite all his finery. The danger to society lies in his use of false argument to obtain power over the people (like Satan fooling Adam and Eve), which he then uses to destroy the lawful polity (as Satan destroyed Adam and Eve's lives in paradise). Charles' appeal to a God-given right to rule and his assault on a representative Parliament typified the way in which tyrant kings establish a social order by 'overturning of all law and government' (Dzelzainis 1991: 11) to produce a state of lawlessness disguised as holy order. It is the darkest satanic trickery. Charles, by acting in this way, showed himself to be a tyrant – a 'common enemy against which the people lawfully may do, as against a common pest, and destroyer of mankind' (Dzelzainis 1991: 17). Thus, although many found it hard to imagine the overthrow of an apparently God-ordained ruler, Parliament was acting to cast the illusions from the people's minds and set them free.

This final defensive element of Milton's argument signals a challenge to the substantive reasoning that supported the monarchy's claim to power. The extent of this power, and the depth of the ideological support for it, was such that, even though the King had only just been executed, many parliamentarians and Protestants were against it. The political theories of many of the participants in the war were commonly rooted in a religious perception of the universe as a fixed hierarchical order known as the great chain of being. The political order of the nation was understood to fit into this hierarchy in its own hierarchy of office, with each office obtaining its legitimacy from its fit in a chain of appointments originating from God. There was a fixed hierarchy, with the monarch at the top as chief magistrate and a series of lower magistrates. Non-appointed (private) individuals had no place in this hierarchy and so had no status as political actors.

Political debate and struggles for power were understood as the organic life of the chain. When elements of the chain misbehaved, the other elements were obligated to correct them and put them back into their proper place in the order of things. Thus it was possible for officers of lower orders to correct higher ones.

The struggle between Crown and Parliament was seen by the various religious and political groups aligned in the parliamentary camp as a legitimate struggle of a lower magistrate to call to order a misbehaving higher one. But here the agreement ended. The Cromwellians wanted Parliament to bring the King to account for his actions, at the outset of the conflict and during the war itself. The Presbyterians, however, believed that Parliament's victory in the civil war had achieved the aim of war by re-establishing Parliament's authority and ending monarchic flirtation with absolutism. The Presbyterians had no desire to overthrow the monarchy. They were happy to force the Crown to accept terms which gave Parliament more power in general and greater power over religious matters in particular. To this end they argued that, while Parliament could punish the Crown further, it would be better to let the new dominance of Parliament be enough, and they used their numbers in Parliament to block any act of retribution against the King. This left the Cromwellians with only one course of action if they were to defeat the King completely – they would have to overthrow the lower magistrate in order to overthrow the higher magistrate, which is what they did. Cromwell's army purged Parliament of all those who favoured dealing with the monarch, leaving only 'the rump Parliament' of their supporters.

This rump called for the King to be tried for illegal use of force, and the trial led to the King's execution.

Milton's essay was a challenge to the constitutional theory that only lower magistrates could act against the Crown. Milton was arguing that the authority of a ruler stemmed not directly from God but rested in the function of a ruler within the functional processes of God's order. This meant that, to have moral authority, a ruler's actions had to be recognisably in concert with the principles of the political and social order as a whole. They had to fit within the laws governing the order of things – natural law or God's law. 'A prince is bound to the laws, the authority of a prince depends upon the laws and to the laws ought to submit . . . how then can any King maintain and write himself accountable to none but God' (Dzelzainis 1991: 13). Here, Milton subtly shifts the focus on where the responsibility for judgement comes from. The locus of legitimacy is no longer directly in God's will, but is now derived from the principles which initiate and drive law. Social and political laws are maintained through their observance and enactment by the people. So the observers of the laws of the land are the ones best fitted to make judgement on whether or not a ruler acts legitimately. The lower magistrates fulfil this task, not because of their place as next in the hierarchy of the chain of being, but because they represent the people whom God designed the laws to serve: the children of Adam and Eve. If and when the lower magistrates fail to call a tyrant to order, then the people they represent have the moral authority to do so.

By challenging the authority of the established governmental structure of the time, Milton stands at odds with the mainstream Puritanism of his day and certainly with Catholicism. His argument was not unique, however, but gave expression to a radical new way of thinking, spreading like fire in the debates of Protestant independents. Milton and the radicals both recognised 'the people' as a community of free individuals, each and every one directly in touch with God through their own conscience, and each and every one empowered by God to take authoritative action over their affairs through the use of their intellect in rational analysis and public debate.

Following the fall, God does not expect individuals to simply follow his commands. The fall has set us free, to know through rational judgement what is right and wrong, and Milton presents a picture of citizens considering the parliamentary debate on the King: 'The best principled of the people stood not numbering . . . on which side were most voices in Parliament, but on which side appeared the most reason' (Dzelzainis 1991: 221). Reason displayed to those observers the factual falsity of tyranny. They were able to analytically determine what a tyrant is and what the people may do against him. 'A Tyrant . . . is he who regarding neither Law nor common good, reigns only for himself and his faction' (Dzelzainis 1991: 16). The factual falsity stems from the tyrant's belief that he is God-like in relation to the laws of the state, and that he may use the state as his own private possession and the people in it as his private slaves. In holding this belief and acting upon it, he becomes a violator of God's order. Once the people see a king act in this way – and the trial of Charles, Milton believed, revealed the occasions in which Charles did so (he lists the King's crimes in *A Defence of the People of England* (Dzelzainis 1991: 12,220)) – they do not need to wait for commands from God to act for the good. God wants people to act upon knowledge gained by reasoned analysis. Thus 'There can be slain no sacrifice to God more acceptable than an unjust or wicked King' (Dzelzainis 1991: 17).

In fact, having access to the arguments and possessing the rational capability to observe the facts of the King's tyranny, each and every one of the people is compelled to act with their fellow citizens to overthrow the tyrant. If the magistrate fails to do so, the citizens must take up arms and do it themselves. Hence the Army was right to fight, to try and execute the tyrant Charles I.

There can be no doubting the democratic tone of this argument. The legitimacy of government is determined by the authority of law, which in turn stems from service to the community which establishes the kingdom. Here, Milton introduces the classical liberal argument (later produced in more detail and depth by Hobbes and in another variation by Locke) that the laws of the polity derive from an originating covenant made from naturally self-governing, typically self-serving and therefore mutually dangerous individuals. He writes that, following the fall of Adam and Eve, individuals roamed the earth 'falling among themselves to do wrong, and foreseeing that such courses must needs tends to the destruction of them all, they agreed by common league to bind each other from mutual injury, and jointly to defend themselves against any that gave disturbance. . . . Hence came Citties, Townes and Common-wealths' (Dzelzainis 1991: 8). The laws and the power to police these communities derived directly from the individual members of the community: 'the autoritie and power of self-defence and preservation being originally and naturally in every one of them, and unitedly in them all' (Dzelzainis 1991: 9).

Yet it was impossible for each and every one to police their own affairs independently without the dissolution of the community into anarchic chaos and so, 'for ease for order, and least each man should be his own partial judge, they communicated and derived either to one, whom the eminence of his wisdom and integrity they chose above the rest . . . not to be their Lord and masters but, to be their deputies' (Dzelzainis 1991: 9). The ruler's legitimacy springs directly from his position as representative of the people.

The democratic tendency evident in Milton's arguments was radically novel at the time, though he was not alone in exploring it. In fact, unlike the Levellers, Diggers and Ranters in the Army, Milton's faith in the people was tempered by a degree of elitism typical of the educated middle classes of the time, and, perhaps more significantly, derived from witnessing the emotion-driven factional disputes of his contemporaries in the twelve years of republican government. What finally killed his belief in open debate and elected government as the means to a rational and just society was the general movement towards reinstalling the monarchy. Rather than think clearly and act rationally, the people had bickered over minor points of theology and fought each other for their little bits of power, until the authority and power of the Parliament had fallen away. This seemed to show that each and every individual cannot after all be trusted to think for themselves. The engagement with truth and falsity and good and evil was too difficult, the complex interweaving of the opposites too befuddling for the average mind, the temptations falsely offered by deceivers too strong for the average will to resist. Indeed, by the time of writing *The Readie and Easie Way*, Milton was aghast at the 'multitude (who) would . . . creep back so poorly . . . to their once abjured and detested thraldom' (Dent 1958: 223).

Fast forward

Go to Chapter 2 for analysis of Levellers, Diggers and Ranters.

Like his contemporary, Thomas Hobbes, Milton feared that democratic politics too easily descended into factionalism, endless disputes and struggles for power. Unlike Hobbes, Milton's major concern in witnessing such struggles – even in the relatively undemocratic circumstances of Cromwell's dictatorship – was that while these factional struggles took up all the time and energy of the republicans, the policy-making necessary to build a new order was left undone. Rightly, he sensed that, with the supporters of the monarchy regrouping to overpower the fractious republicans, the opportunity to establish a republican order through decisive and coherent governance was slipping away.

In response, he argued, in *The Readie and Easie Way*, that a new republic could not be fully democratic, but should be ruled by a general council of suitably educated and experienced citizens. This council would be 'well chosen' (elected) by the people initially, but afterwards would remain in power as a 'perpetual' (Dent 1958: 229) oligarchy. In using the phrase 'well chosen', Milton is not only flattering the people who will choose; he also means that the act of the community's choosing meets the requirement that the people entrust their powers of self-governance to the new ruling body and thereby authorises its use of power over them. This, he believed, would ensure that the new oligarchic government would be acting legitimately and lawfully, even when it acted against the wills of the citizens who authorised it.

DISCUSSION POINT

Here, Milton opens the door to the possibility of a new type of dictatorship in which an elite of self-proclaimed 'know-it-alls' overrides and ignores the wishes of those they claim to represent. They may do this with the best intentions, but isn't this the top of a slippery slope to corruption, as unchecked power, combined with hubris, leads 'leaders' to become self-absorbed rulers?

Commentaries

On his death, Milton's political prose writing had long ceased to be acceptable reading, while the political implications of his epic poems were registered by *Paradise Lost*'s appearance in the early 1700s in the lists of banned works produced by the Catholic Church, the Spanish state and several smaller Catholic provinces. By the 1730s however, Milton's epic poems were gaining such a reputation and readership that they could not be ignored. Instead, their reputation as poetry was separated from the reputation of Milton's political prose, which was buried and left for obscurity. Despite this, Milton's political reputation did not completely disappear, and those criticisms of his poems that there were often come barbed with references to 'Milton the Roundhead', 'Milton the Divorcer' and 'Milton the Blasphemer', the most notable critique of this kind being found in *The History of Sin and Heresy* by Charles Leslie (1698).

Since these times, there have been two attempts to return Milton to the fold of political writers, each of which adds some insight into the proto-liberalism of Milton's mindset, but both of which do so partially as they have other points to make.

The first attempt to politically rehabilitate Milton came in a late eighteenth-century flurry of interest by the Romantic poets. On reading *Paradise Lost*, William Blake was moved to declare that Milton was 'of the devil's party without knowing it'. This idea was taken up enthusiastically by the revolutionary Romantic poets Shelley and Byron. The Romantics' big idea was that passion and subjectivity provide the locus of judgement. They took the moral relativism and sensual provocation that Satan presented in *Paradise Lost* to represent Milton's own point of view. Milton, they argued, was the seventeenth century's great purveyor of anti-rationalism and anti-moralism. As has been pointed out by many subsequent commentators, the Romantics' reading of Milton is very non-contextual. Moral relativism was not accommodated by the religious understandings of the time, and Milton's religious and political prose shows a consistent and fierce belief in the rightness of rational study of 'God's' order of the world. Given Milton's steady beliefs, it must be the case that Satan's relativism is a sign of a loss of the grounding that true understanding gives, and the sensual voluptuousness in which the arch-relativist Satan is presented must be designed to show that temptation can blind one to truth. Despite the weakness of their claims overall, however, the Romantics bring to the fore Milton's perception of the complete individual – heart, mind and sensual body – as the locus of all ethical and practical matters. In short, Milton was an individualist, and as such promoted the idea that every order of power – even the relationship between God and humans – was subject to the necessary right of individuals to choose their destiny for themselves and to act accordingly. Furthermore, the Romantics highlighted how Milton's poetic flirtation with the devil's challenge to God's authoritarianism points to the revolutionary roots of fundamentalist Protestantism. These roots are the challenge posed to all collective orders by the radical individualism propagated by Protestantism, and a suspicion of the state which was later to characterise the work of many great liberal theorists, from Milton's contemporary John Locke, through to George Orwell and Frederick von Hayek in the late twentieth century.

In part, the Romantics' claim that Milton supported the devil against the authority of God gains its persuasive strength from the fact that Milton used the devil in *Paradise Lost* as the mouthpiece of his own ideas. This intriguing act indicates that Milton's exploration of the Protestant theology in which he passionately believed gave him an insight that, as a protest against the Church and against the state as a political order which enforced the principles of the Church, Protestantism was actually rooted in a suspicion of religion itself. Here we see the seeds of the secularism that has eventually expelled theology from the centre ground of liberal political thought.

A much more recent attempt to reinstate Milton to the ranks of political writers is Christopher Hill's *Milton and the English Revolution* (1988). Hill's work attempts to place Milton in the context of the radical movement of independent Protestants within the New Model Army. Hill's argument is that Milton's political position fell half-way between radical Anabaptist theology, the egalitarianism of the Levellers and Diggers and Puritan orthodoxy. This thesis does make sense of Milton's initial enthusiasm for, and eventual discomfort with, the widespread participation of common citizens in public affairs (other commentators usually provide no reason, or simply claim that the radical implications of the *Areopagitica* are due to the overly dramatic effects of Milton's writing style).

In raising this point, Hill helps us to see how Milton's uncertainty about whether every individual is to be seen as the holy site of choice and decision-making foreshadows a problem in liberal understanding which has lasted until today. The problem may be put as follows: the ethical ideal of Protestant liberalism is for a political order to be founded in the free choice and willing participation of each and every citizen. However, experience shows that the arguments of the citizens frequently lack the depth of understanding necessary to make good judgements about the condition and needs of the polity, and the activities of the citizens frequently undermine its constitution. Milton, recognising this problem, opted for a ruling elect to act in the citizens' best interests – even if it meant overriding their wills. In making this choice, he raised one of the fundamental problems of liberalism, namely the problem of the possible range and the necessary limits to be placed on the democratisation of power. Once a claim is made for individual choice as the ultimate source of all legitimate action, the questions come tumbling out: On what grounds can such an elite claim better knowledge of the people's needs than the people themselves? Is such an elite prone to corruption in the continuous and unchallenged exercise of power? Conversely: Can the people be trusted to find the best solutions to the many and often complex problems they face? Are the people not prone to converge into emotionally driven mobs at times of crisis? These problems are all aspects of the issue of the democratisation of power. In the following chapters of this book we will see them raised again and again, and always in terms initiated by Milton's struggle with the question of whether the people act for themselves or have their interests represented by an elected elite. In the eighteenth century, Edmund Burke opts for an elite representation of the people's interests, while his political adversary, Tom Paine, opts for a full democratic participation. Jean Jacques Rousseau insists that only a polity in which each and every citizen fully participates has legitimacy. In the nineteenth century, John Stuart Mill wrestles with the issue in recognisably similar terms to those used by Milton in the same city and but a mile or two down the road some two hundred years before.

Revision notes

1   Milton's arguments for an elected republic and an unfettered public sphere, placed in the context of the Puritan revolt against the Anglican monarchy, show the historical link between Protestant theology and liberalism.

2   A conceptual link between liberal notions of civil society and Protestant notions of God's society may be seen in the link between the presentation in *Paradise Lost* of the case for each individual's need to explore their experiences and to test out their ideas

in practice, and the argument in the *Areopagitica* for a free press and open public debate.

3　Milton's assessment of the Protestant revolt highlights how the liberal definition of tyranny (sometimes called despotism) as a situation in which a ruler places himself above the rule of law stems from a theological belief that the law itself represents a higher authority than humankind. Today, a modified version of this idea is expressed in the term 'natural law'.

4　Milton's attempts to show the illegitimacy of Charles I's rule set up an early conception of legitimate rule as stemming from the authority of the people who are ruled over, and so turned the idea of the ruler towards the more democratic idea of the leader.

5　Milton's doubts about the people's readiness to carry out their public role as rational-thinking, public-debating citizens capable of choosing the best leaders to serve their needs, highlights how the democratic implications of arguments for free speech and government in service of the people stand in tension with the traditional liberal concern with individual freedom and the rational construction of lawful policy. Milton signals a classic liberal awareness that in a fully participatory democracy an unthinking mob may trample the individual and the rule of law underfoot in the thoughtless and emotionally driven exercise of its new power.

Bibliography

Bush, D. (ed.) (1977) *The Portable Milton*, London: Penguin.

Dent, J.M. & Son (eds) (1958) *Milton's Prose Writings* (1st edn), London: J. M. Dent.

Dzelzainis, M. (ed.) (1991) *John Milton: Political Writings*, Cambridge: Cambridge University Press.

Hill, C. (1979) *Milton and the English Revolution*, London: Faber and Faber.

—— (1988) *The World Turned Upside Down*, London: Peregrine Books.

Potter, L. (1986) *A Preface to Milton*, New York: Longman.

Further reading

There is a multitude of books available to undergraduates for the study of Milton. Many books concentrate solely on Milton's poetry and, though some have useful contextualising introductions, you would do best to concentrate on Milton's prose writings, which contain his overtly political ideas. These can be easily found in various popular collections (none of which contain all his political work). J.M. Dent & Son's *Milton's Prose Writings* (1958) offers a good selection of works, including all the major political tracts as well as works on divorce and education. It also has a short and functional introduction by K.M. Burton.

D. Bush's *The Portable Milton* (1977) contains a mix of prose and poetry, including *Areopagitica* and *Paradise Lost*, plus a useful contextualising introduction. Lois Potter's *A Preface to Milton* (1986) is concerned with Milton the poet, but contains a finely detailed contextual introduction to Milton, including discussions of the political scene, common modes of understanding, the geopolitical climate and copious biographical material.

The two Christopher Hill books cited in the bibliography are classics. There is a useful appendix on Milton in *The World Turned Upside Down* (1988), and *Milton and The English Revolution* (1979) is a mine of information. J.T. Shawcross (1972) *Milton 1732–1801: The Critical Heritage*, London: Routledge & Kegan Paul is a good source of information on critical responses to Milton over the ages.

The Levellers
and the Diggers

The poorest he hath a life to live as the greatest he; and therefore . . . every man that is to live under a government ought by his own consent to put himself under that government.

(*Putney Debates*)

Following the decisive break with the Catholic Church government in the sixteenth century, the politics of England in the seventeenth century became a struggle between two prospective forms of state, neither of which would ultimately survive. This struggle was between advocates of absolutist monarchy and advocates of a Protestant Republic. Locked into combat in the English civil war, neither project found space or time to develop without threat from the other and, in the end, they produced the rather odd merger of monarchism and parliamentarianism that constitutes the current nation state known as the United Kingdom.

In the brief space in time between the collapse of the old order and the establishment of the Cromwellian dictatorship, the first seed of a new political culture took root; a social movement called 'the Levellers' grew up among the Puritan 'commoners' – men of the yeoman and trading classes – through which they developed conceptions of a radical democratic and, in some cases socialist, republicanism. In their arguments with the monarchists and the Puritans' own Cromwellian leadership, the Levellers initiated the terms of modern arguments for democratisation and redistribution of property. The strengths and weaknesses of their arguments remain relevant to discussions of mass democracy and socialism today.

The exact origin, ends and membership of the Levellers have never been established facts. The original Leveller declaration is usually attributed to a pamphlet entitled *Remonstrance of the Many Thousands of the Free People of England* setting out a manifesto for radical levelling action, written at the end of the first civil war in 1646, though this pre-dates the common use of the term 'Leveller'. The authors of the document claimed that the term was invented by less radical parliamentarians, to define their radical opponents within the parliamentary army. The oldest reference to Levellers found by historians is from that year, but it is used by Royalists as a negative description for radical agitators for a democratic Parliament, 'to cast down and level the enclosure of nobility, gentry and propriety, to make us all even, so that every Jack shall vie with a gentleman and every gentleman shall be made a Jack' (Brailsford 1961: 309). Whatever its origin, it is clear that it was originally a term of disparagement used to highlight the radicals' aim of levelling – that is, pulling down – the political, social and economic structures of English society. It was then taken up, as a positive self-description, by the reforming movement, who used it to stress its socialist connotation of levelling out – that is, equalising – levels of power and wealth within society. In both of the term's connotations, it is clear that the levelling intent constituted the most fundamental of the many challenges since the reformation to the crumbling remains of the Catholic feudal society.

As the ambiguity of the origins of the term indicates, the Levellers were a loose movement rather than a well-defined organisation, and levelling arguments of varying degrees of intellectual coherence and political radicalism were propagated in highly polemical pamphlets, often by anonymous authors, and always in the fierce heat of the ideological and military conflicts which made up the English civil wars. It is therefore impossible to locate a specific doctrine set out in an authorised document.

However, there is a common set of themes running through the many pamphlets from which a clear set of Leveller principles may be derived. Broadly speaking, the demand was for a political community founded on full democratic principles and redistribution of land, and with the opening up of trade to competitive market principles. All in all, the Levellers' demands set out the clear lines of a radical programme for systematic political democratisation and socio-economic reform. Of further interest to anyone considering the history of political ideologies are the arguments put forward by Gerrard Winstanley, the leader of a small group calling themselves the 'True Levellers' but better known as the Diggers. In one imaginative leap, Winstanley moved from Puritan theology, through Levellers' demands for greater democracy and economic equity, to an argument for an agrarian communist utopia.

It is necessary at this point to warn against over-modernising the Levellers and the Diggers. They were very much people of their times, Puritans of the 'middling sort' and not the pragmatic materialists of nineteenth- and twentieth-century political movements. Like all participants in the struggles of the 1600s, their political imagination was framed and directed by theological principles. The construction of a secular nation state was not readily conceivable and yet, in an unlikely mix of religious imagination and practical recognition of the emerging socio-economic changes, they spun out a line of reasoning which took them beyond their cultural and intellectual inheritance towards a sense of a secular tolerant civil society.

To make clear the distinctions and coincidences between Leveller thinking and modern democratic thought, we shall concentrate on the three major elements of Leveller discussions:

1   *The myth of the fall*: Puritan theology drives the ethics of the Leveller position and at its core is the myth of 'the fall' which fascinated so many people during the mid-sixteenth century. For the Levellers, the English civil war was a life-and-death struggle for the soul of the polity and for the people who lived within it. Politics was the field of play between Satan and God, good versus evil, and the civil war was understood as a war for the soul of the nation and of each and every one of its people. The pragmatism and worldly cynicism prevalent in our modern liberal-democratic world would have been anathema to them.

2   *The myth of Saxons and Normans*: By the seventeenth century, the notion of the English as a fundamentally Saxon people had already been long established. The Levellers tapped into this part of collective folklore to build an argument against the aristocracy's control of the land, which, at that time, meant control of the means of production and of maintaining life itself. Exploration of the Levellers' myth-making shows them unfurling the nationalist flag in a way which has become very familiar in the England of modern times.

3   *Notions of democratic and communitarian principles*: From their conception of life before the fall, Puritans developed an ideal notion of humans' proper relationship to nature, which combined individual responsibility to God with a collective inheritance of natural resources. The Levellers built their political programme upon this ideal. Individual responsibility was converted into the principle of the rights and duties of participating citizens centred on the right and duty of each and every citizen to vote for their governmental representatives. While the communitarianism was expressed partially in mainstream

Levellers' demands for redistribution of the land, and fully in the argument of the Diggers, that all land should be used communally. In this way the Levellers formulated an early democratic version of parliamentary representation as an expression of national sovereignty, while the Diggers formulated an early version of communism.

The Levellers in context

In feudal times, all aspects of commercial life – centres of trade, trade routes, legal procedure, valuations of goods – were relatively undeveloped. For the vast majority of people, making a living meant working the land, and while merchants and bankers were wealthy, direct access to wealth lay in possession of land. Throughout the long period of unproblematised Catholic domination, the aristocracy had legitimised and maintained their control of the land through the propagation of their arcane ideology of the great chain of being, the deployment of a Christianised version of the Roman legal system and, following the Reformation, the less successful amendment to the notion of a divine right to rule. The paternalism of the Church and the power of the aristocracy were reinforced on a daily basis by custom and practice of master/servant relationships, a strictly enforced patriarchal family structure and the weekly lectures given from church pulpits. By the 1640s, however, the whole system had long been unwinding. The 1640s was a period of economic and political crisis, as the much modified feudal order finally fell to pieces. The decade was cursed with bleak weather and poor harvests at exactly the same time as the aristocracy and gentry moved to privatise common lands by 'enclosure' – that is, fencing them off from public access.

The enclosures squeezed the rural peasantry, who depended on access to common land, and the yeoman farmers – the lower middle class in the rural economy – who were already forced to pay tithes (taxes) to work farms were losing their means to an independent livelihood and were forced increasingly to became wage labourers disposable and disposed of in the bad harvests which blighted the decade.

As the last remnants of the feudal order fell, the initial development of an emerging capitalist world was also impacting on the national socio-economic order. In the cities and towns, the emerging power of the growing mercantile corporations impacted on the traditional practice of craft and trade. The production and trade of goods was subject increasingly to licensing imposed by 'official' agencies represent-ing cartels of large corporations run from the City of London. These changes imposed restrictions on the urban middle class of small traders and craftsmen, causing widespread unemployment and poverty.

Thus, economic developments in the countryside and urban centres led to the loss of economic independence for many lower- and middle-class people. They promoted widespread poverty across the nation and sharply intensified lower- and middle-class resentment and resistance across the nation. It could be argued that these events contributed to the development of a national middle class; the otherwise distinct urban and rural lower and middle classes shared but one other feature, namely that they contributed the bulk of the diverse and differing sect making up the independent Puritan population of England. The impetus of their common experience of increasing impoverishment, loss of status and frequent clashes with the powerful landowners and big business ensured that, despite their many doctrinal differences, the independent Puritan population was drawn together as a relatively unified protesting body. Out of this body grew the clearly defined form of the political movement known as the Levellers. It was the common grievances of the common people that the Levellers voiced, in public writings directed to the citizenry and to Parliament, and in speeches to Parliament and in the Army's many debates on the future constitution of the nation.

The common feeling of desperation may be felt in the defensive tones of the Levellers' writings typified by this passage: 'When we consider what rackings and tortures the People in general have suffered through decay of Trade, and dearness of food, and very many families in particular, through Free-quarter, Violence, and other miseries, incident to War, having nothing to support them therein, but hopes of Freedom, and a well-settled Common-wealth in the end' (Brailsford 1961: 97). The frustration of these people and the threat they posed to the ruling powers may also be heard in the frequent challenges to Parliament: 'ye must deal better with us', they demanded, as 'ye are only chosen by us the people' (Brailsford 1961: 97).

The New Model Army

The growling tone of the Levellers' demands, although usually written by civilians, expressed a very real connection between the armed forces, the independent (non-Presbyterian, non-Anglican) parliamentarians and the Army's leadership (bodies who merged increasingly into one under Cromwell's leadership); both recognised the reality of the threat. A large part of the Levellers' power derived from their widespread presence within the parliamentary army. The New Model Army's famous discipline and indomitable fighting spirit was driven by the religious faith of its many volunteer soldiers, but the Army was more than a fighting machine. It was also a location for the development of a Puritan counter-culture.

KEY PEOPLE 1

The New Model Army

The New Model Army was formed by Parliament to improve its forces' effectiveness in battle. It went on to defeat all its opponents throughout the civil wars. It fought against the Anglican monarchy and its imposition of Catholicised hierarchical religious practice in all areas of life, and later against the Scottish Presbyterians who also sought to impose their religion upon the nation. In 1651 the Army travelled to Ireland where it put an end to rebellion and the Celtic Catholic culture. By this time the Levellers, who opposed the war in Ireland, had been expunged from its ranks. For more information, see 'Key Event' (Chapter 1) on the English civil war.

The yeomans' Puritanism ensured that the Army's life was run through with religious activity. Military actions and strategy meetings were punctuated with prayer meetings, and the Puritan belief in the natural equality of individuals fed into the common practice of lay preaching. Thus 'it was quite usual for a corporal or private to preach while his less gifted officers listened in silence' (Brailsford 1961: 148). The politico-religious quality of daily life in the New Model Army, combined with the communitarianism of its large Baptist (known as 'Anabaptist') membership, fuelled the common ideological commitment to levelling – the returning of social order to non-hierarchical communality in which all decisions are made by the community through direct participation and expected representation, and in which great inequalities of wealth are readjusted to enable ordinary people, yeoman farmers and tradesmen to make a 'fair' living.Thus, even while the Army fought to overthrow first the monarchy and then the Scottish Presbyterians, it always contained in its ranks many who would challenge even Puritan landowners, such as Cromwell, in their right to governance.

In the years 1647 to 1649, when the English polity paused between its civil wars, the indomitable and battle-hardened New Model Army surveyed Parliament's activities from their encampments across the country. Their large Leveller member-ship found immediate cause for concern in Parliament's dealings with the monarch whom they had defeated. The Army Levellers were worried about the unrepre-sentative nature of the 'Long Parliament', which had been called into being some six years earlier by the overthrown King and seemed likely to strike a deal to return him to power in return for permanent tenure for its members. They gave support to the civilian Levellers' call for a democratically elected Parliament. This support created stress within the Army itself between the Levellers' rank and file and the less democratically inclined Cromwellian leadership. Having fought together against the royal forces and having shared in the strong bonding Puritan communality of army life, the leadership and rank and file sought to overcome their differences. In the autumn of 1647, they gathered for a three-day period of meetings known today as the 'Putney Debates'. The partial record of this event shows the Levellers introducing and arguing for an 'Agreement of the People' – a petition for an elected Parliament, full franchise, and tax and land reforms. The record also provides some evidence that Cromwell and the Army leadership tried successfully to delay and modify the proposed reforms. The debate failed to close the growing rift within the Army and instead set in train a consistent and hardening opposition among the Army leadership to the Levellers' programme of reform. From 1648 to 1650 these internal divisions hardened against a background of civilian agitation, petitions, rallies and parlia-mentary attempts to weaken the Army, until, under pressure to fight a war against the Irish, five Leveller units of the Army rebelled, only to be crushed by Cromwell's forces. Cromwell's move severed the Levellers' links with the Army and ended their threat to the Cromwellian new order.

In subsequent years, the movement dwindled quickly to nothing and, as it disappeared, its leaders, Lilburne, Walwyn and Overton, also disappeared from public life. The political substance of their ideas, however, was strong enough to initiate the movement towards democratisation and through their periodic revivals by later groups (the trade union movement, the British Labour Party and various socialist organisations) to stimulate ongoing movements towards social democratic and socialist politics.

KEY PEOPLE 2

Leveller leaders

The Levellers' leading spokespersons typified the class background of the movement's membership, as well as articulating their common needs and developing political sensibilities. Three of the most notable, **Richard Overton**, **William Walwyn** and **John Lilburne**, typified the spokespersons in general. They were not political philosophers, but pamphleteers and soldiers in the Puritan cause: **Richard Overton** was an Anabaptist and a printer by trade who, on returning from exile in Holland, became a satirical pamphleteer in the Levellers' cause. Along with William Walwyn, he drew up the famous *Remonstrance of the Many Thousands of the Free People of England* (1646) – the initial declaration of Leveller intent.

William Walwyn was an Oxford-educated merchant in the clothing trade, who became an active supporter of the parliamentarians' cause during the civil war and contributed some notable writings on religious and civil toleration. His writings – most famously, *Tyranipocrit Discovered* (1649) – articulated the Levellers' demands for a full franchise for the English people and for a regularly elected Parliament. His writings on toleration, such as *The Compassionate Samaritan* (1644), were the first to move away from religious terms of reference towards the now commonplace secular notions of free choice and the limits of knowable truth.

John Lilburne was a populist and rabble-rouser, who fought in the first civil war as a friend and lieutenant of Cromwell before his consistent challenges to the ruling elite led him to take the Levellers into direct conflict with Cromwell and Parliament. He was imprisoned a number of times for pamphleteering, and his trial and subsequent courtroom victory in 1649 were huge public events, drawing large crowds and much celebration.

The Levellers as Puritans

In the preceding chapter, we saw how the combination of the religious and political dynamised the protesting Protestants to overthrow the Anglican monarchy and to establish a Puritan Republic. The Protestant movement was not a single body driven by a single dogma. The Puritan imagination was rich with different ideas about the 'coming new order', and in the testing conditions of a social struggle these ideas were hewn down into two distinct and, in some ways, opposing political visions. The first of these is what has since become known as the classical liberal vision – a radical individualistic conception of a society of free-thinking and self-interested individuals, constructed and maintained by a contract between themselves to interact on agreed terms of trade, cultural and religious tolerance. The pursuit of material and spiritual well-being is seen as the private enterprise of individuals; society, as far as it follows these agreed principles, is free of politics and its activities are a rightful concern for the state only when individuals violate the principles of free and fair trade and mutual toleration. Chapter 1 set out the arguments for individual free expression, as argued by John Milton. The classic contemporary presentation of the liberal position was set out by the Puritan political philosopher John Locke in 1684. Locke's philosophical argument for private property gave intellectual support to a position held almost by faith alone among Cromwellians (including Milton), as did Locke's arguments against tolerating Roman Catholicism.

Fast forward

Go to Chapter 4 for Locke's theory.

In this chapter, we shall explore Puritanism's alternative political vision – a form of democratic republicanism and economic communitarianism which set the Levellers apart from the Puritan independents and eventually led to conflict between the two parties. In direct opposition to individualism, communitarians view human life as the pursuit of well-being through the integrated activities of mutually interdependent members. While individualism was a core principle of Calvinism, communitarian principles shaped the basic mode of social organisation in Baptist communities. The divergence stemmed from a basic difference in interpretation of the relationship of humankind to the resources which constituted their environment. All Puritans saw the relationship in terms of productive work. It was commonplace to quote the biblical command of God to Adam: 'through the sweat of your brow you shall eat your bread', to express the Puritan view that God set out life as a task; a defined activity with a desired outcome, to prove yourself worthy of his attentions. Thus, to their mind, working through the toils of life was a God-given task through which one proved oneself worthy to God. In Calvinist thought, the relationship of mankind to God is individualised into the relationship of the task-setter and the one who has to undertake that task. This individualism sets the terms for the subsequent considerations of human interaction with their environment and with each other – individuals have to improve themselves through the morally right use of the natural and human resources God has put at their disposal.

Rewind

Go to Fact boxes 1 and 2 in Chapter 1 for more information on Baptists.

In contrast, Baptists believed that God had given the earth and its resources to mankind in common, a notion which framed the ethical ideal of economic and political life in a socialist train of thought. A root idea of all socialist thought is that the identity of each and every individual is shaped by their interactions with others. People do not enter the world or live within it as isolated individuals, but as members of a social group. For Baptists, whose primary concern was with ethical life, the moral identity of individuals was shaped by their membership of an ethical community. The ethical identity was shaped by work – an activity that had to be a collective enterprise if the corruption of Adam and Eve was not to be continuously repeated.

Along with most other Puritans at the time, Baptists believed that the second coming was due in 1666, and believed themselves to be among the elect few chosen to return humankind to its original purity in readiness for this event. However, Baptists challenged the norms of their times by disputing the supposed factuality of the Old Testament. For them, the stories of the Old Testament were to be read as metaphorical ethical guides, and the story of the fall – so significant for those trying to return to the state of grace in readiness for the second coming – was a metaphorical warning about the evil inherent in the act of taking possession. 'The earth with all her fruits of corn, cattle and such like, was made to be a common storehouse of livelihood to all mankind . . . without exception' (Sabine 1941: 270).

Eve, in plucking the apple out of its natural context, abstracted it from the common world of resources for her sole use. The story shows that each time anyone takes from the common store, they corrupt the environment which maintains their happy condition of life. This cumulatively creates a world of division with inequality of access to resources, envy, theft and war. This understanding fired the most communistic expressions of the Baptist movement in Munster, where all property was taken into collective ownership. Following the brutal suppression of the Munster Baptists, the movement developed a pragmatically self-protecting moderation of its communist tendencies.

In England, this modified form was modified further in a merger with the Calvinist individualism typical among the middle classes, until it found expression in the Levellers' claim for a fairer allocation of private property and equal opportunities to trade property in a free market. The full communist idealism also resurfaced in England in the activities of a smaller movement, self-defined as 'true Levellers' but generally known as the Diggers. The Levellers challenged the prevailing control of property and the manipulation of markets by the fractious and disintegrating ruling aristocracy, whose acute divisions, as expressed in the conflict of Parliament and Crown, were already centre stage. Thus the emphasis of the Levellers' challenge fell upon the machinery of rule itself.

In the movement from pure Baptist communitarianism to a Baptist-informed political movement, the shift in emphasis moved from the collective ownership of the means of life to collective control of the political governance of the country. While the Diggers concentrated on collectivising land and labour, the main thrust of the Levellers' movement was to establish a 'people's government' which would ensure an equitable distribution of land and economic opportunity. Baptist notions of collectivism were tied into the Puritans' commonly held equalitarian and individualistic notion that every individual's spirit gave them direct access to God (and to the devil). God made all men equal in their capacity for action and reasoning ability. So all men are naturally free-thinking and free-acting agents: 'All men being alike privileged by birth, so all men were to enjoy the creatures alike without property one more than the other, all men by the grant of god are free, and every man individual, that is to say no man was to lord over his own kind' (Sabine 1941: 611). So, 'no man be questioned or molested or put to answer for anything but wherein he materially violates the person, goods or good name of another' (Brailsford 1961: 75).

The Levellers as democrats

The political ideology of the Levellers expressed the wider political awareness of power derived from a class-consciousness. This consciousness was shaped and framed by the religious understanding prevalent among the lower-middle classes but also pressed towards a secular vision of communal identity in formative expressions of an emergent liberal democratic nationalism, shot through with elements of socialism. As we now know, liberalism, being essentially individualistic, does not fit easily with the communitarianism of nationalism and socialism, though modern Western societies have continued to attempt to 'mix and match' them in practice. The Levellers' initiation of what have become continuous struggles to fit these diverse tendencies of thought into a coherent whole throws interesting light on some enduring issues in modern democratic theory and practice. Their aim was to persuade the parliamentarian leadership to accept that democratic representation could be the only legitimate process for authorising power in a republic. The arguments led them into an exploration of the conditions for a community of independent individuals – a liberal republic. In the course of this, they considered the community of individuals as a source of political authority and the necessity of the community's authorisation for legitimate use of power by the state. These arguments, tying the concepts of democracy to political authority and political legitimacy, set the tone for all subsequent liberal-democratic thinking.

The Levellers' challenge focused on the unrepresentative nature of Parliament. The parliamentarians' challenge to monarchic government had exposed Parliament's condition as a seat of aristocratic power while also revealing its potential as a means of self-government for the aspiring middle classes.

In the 1640s, the landed aristocracy dominated the Houses of Parliament. While the House of Lords was explicitly the power base of the great landowners, the Commons – despite its name – comprised the landowners' relatives and those at the lower end of the squirarchy. It was understood that only 'gentlemen' – that is, individuals whose wealth stemmed from landownership rather than trade or commerce – could become Members of Parliament. Furthermore, Parliament was far from the democratically elected body of today. While elections did take place at irregular intervals, only around one-fifth of the nation's commoners had the vote, very few people could afford the costs of running a campaign for election, and many seats – those which eventually became known as 'rotten boroughs' – were simply bought. So at the time of the initial conflict between Parliament and King, Parliament was in the possession of the landed classes. The landed classes were dominated by Presbyterians; Protestants who needed the support of independents – Baptists, Quakers and the like – to shape an army and to ensure the support of the people at large for their campaign to wrest power from the monarch. The political goal of the Presbyterian aristocracy was to replace Charles' autocratic rule with a collective aristocratic rule, in which the monarch's power was checked and his plans moderated by the aristocratic Parliament. It was equally important to them that the Presbyterian Church was established as the state church in place of the Catholicised Anglican Church, making the Presbyterian religion the official state religion. The church in those days was a vital power point. As the site of regular community meetings across the country, and the place where the clergy traditionally directed the people's religious affairs (which covered all aspects of life), the church pulpit provided a means for co-ordinated nation-wide propaganda. Possession of the official church would give the Presbyterian ministry the power to pump out propaganda for aristocratic parliamentary rule (as opposed to kingly rule).

This was a very different agenda to that of the religious 'independents'. The independents sought the disestablishment of church and state and the construction of a religiously pluralist society, based on the ideal of an equality in powers of reason and judgement combined with the core Puritan notion of free conscience – that is, the God-given capacity to make judgements, carrying with it the responsibility to act upon such judgements, a condition which requires freedom from political enforcement of moral and behavioural codes of conduct. This stance may be Puritan at root and Christian in intent, but the political arrangement to separate political and religious modes of living was liberal in its design. Indeed, it set out the basic and necessary element of a community of independent individuals. The principle for the separation of politics and religion which is consistently expressed in Leveller tracts is 'toleration'. The argument for tolerance was rooted in the fundamentally liberal recognition that all of us have some access to truth through reason and revelation, but that no one has a monopoly on it: 'the truth or the broken gleams of truth appear diversely on the minds of all men' (Brailsford 1961: 86). We share parts of a fragmented whole – the truth – and we are diverse parts of a kaleidoscopic whole – the human community engaging with the truth, which is called the Christian people. Therefore, 'so far as Christ is in us, we shall . . . honour . . . the least particle of his image in others' (Brailsford 1961: 86). Many Levellers saw that toleration provides the grounds for learning the truth through experimentation and public debate. In his piece entitled *The Arraignment of Mr Persecution* (1645) Overton wrote:

> He [Mr Persecution] is an utter enemy to all spiritual knowledge, a hinderer of its increase and growth. For no man knoweth but in part, and what we know we receive it by degrees, now a little and then a little. He that knows the most was once as ignorant as he who knows least. Nay, is it not frequent among us, that the thing we judged heresy we now believe is orthodox?
> (Brailsford 1961: 55–56)

Here we see the Levellers frame the first clear statement of what in later centuries was to become standard liberal argument; through mutual tolerance, people can form a community of like-minded but free-thinking and acting individuals and, in doing so, provide the conditions for the pluralistic pursuit of truth through rational argument and experimentation.

 Fast forward

Go to Chapter 8 for J.S. Mill's influential version of this argument.

The liberal recognition of the virtue of toleration was quickly matched by a recognition that the goal of a tolerant pluralist Christian society was at risk, if the powers of the state remained in the hands of a social and religious clique. In his 1646 critique of the overthrow of the Anglican elite by the Presbyterian-dominated Parliament, Richard Overton wrote: 'the Bishops' courts stripped us of our clothes, but the presbyters courts will strip us of our coats skins, lives and all' (Brailsford 1961: 54). This comment shows the key Leveller recognition that the powers of the state had to be controlled by the citizenry as a whole if it was not to be used by one faction to impose their doctrines upon the rest, 'like inquisition after inquisition' (Brailsford 1961: 54). The practical necessity for a collective control of state by the citizenry was given an ethical underpinning by the idea that all Christians were in fact one community; they were 'all the creatures of one God, redeemed by Jesus Christ' (Brailsford 1961: 55) and, in addition, by an emerging nationalism expressed vaguely in the idea that that the English people (along with the Dutch) were at the vanguard of the movement which would reform the world into a place fit for the second coming. Such ideas are not only common in Leveller tracts. Reports from the time, such as the transcripts of the Putney Debates, reveal that they were commonly discussed by the regulars of the New Model Army and by small traders in the public meeting places of large towns and cities (commonly public houses, or pubs). The logic of this way of thinking, along with the democratic mode of its development and dissemination, opened the way to the notion of popular sovereignty: the Christian people of England had to take collective control of the state, if the state was not to be used by one faction against others to the ultimate detriment of all. This revolutionary idea was the core ideal of the Levellers' challenge to the Presbyterian-dominated 'Long Parliament' of 1646 and remained the core notion throughout their challenge to Cromwell's 'Rump Parliament' of 1648 to 1649.

The first signs of a coherent Leveller challenge are found in *The Remonstrance of Many Thousand Citizens to their own House of Commons* (1646). In this pamphlet, the authors (including Walwyn and Overton) demand that the Members of the Long Parliament – who had sat without any form of public accountability for six years – 'account, how they . . . have discharged their duties to the universality of the people, their sovereign lord from who their power and strength is derived and by whom . . . it is continued' (Brailsford 1961: 96–97). It was not unknown for public statements to assert a basic relationship between the House of Commons and the commoners, but such statements did not usually imply the modern democratic understanding of the relationship. This pamphlet, however, does exactly that: 'Ye are only chosen by us the people; and therefore in you only is the power of binding the whole nation by making, altering or abolishing laws.' It is a sudden and, for the parliamentarians, shocking assertion of the notion of popular democracy. Its logical next step was the demand for a widespread franchise, and this duly came in *The Case of the Army Truly Stated* (9 October 1647) which, among a number of arguments about the role and conditions of army life and the need to end feudal tithes, demands the franchise for 'all the freeborn at the age of 21years and upwards' (notice the gender neutrality here).

The argument for democratic government is presented more clearly in the *Agreement of the People* (29 October 1647) which was presented to Cromwell and other army grandees in the Putney Debates. This agreement set out demands for biannual elections and fixed-term parliaments, the claim for the supremacy of Parliament over the King and the supremacy of the sovereign people over Parliament, equality before the law, the right to free religious expression, and freedom from coercion to fight in the state forces. The overt democratic nature of the document appears to have worried the Army's leadership and it set a line in the sand between the Levellers and the Cromwellians, which was crossed with the eventual refutation of the former by the latter.

The Putney Debates between the Cromwellian independents and the Levellers about the Agreement raise some fundamental issues about the nature of political authority, representation and the ethics of constitution building. Cromwellian resistance to a new democratic constitution rooted itself in a set of profound and perennial questions concerning the making of political constitutions.

FACT BOX

Major points from *The Agreement of the People* (1647)

1 Redistribution of constituencies, proportionate to the population.
2 Parliaments to be elected in regular succession on 'fixed dates every two years and shall sit for six months only'.
3 The power of the representative body is inferior only to 'the sovereign people' who choose it and 'extends without the consent of any other person or persons [i.e. of King or Lords] to all fields of legislation and administration, including the making of war and peace and the command of the militia'.
4 'All are equal before the law and none [meaning neither peers nor MPs] is exempted from the ordinary course of legal proceedings.'

At one level, the questions were ethical and revolved around the issues of the right and authority to construct and impose a constitution on the rest of the social membership. The basic question, 'What right do people who possess power have to use that power to shape the common world as they will it?' was framed in the Putney Debates as a question of authorisation to decide 'Who or what gave the New Model Army and or Levellers and generals this right?' At another level, the questions were about the practicalities of making and breaking constitutions. These issues were the Army leadership's sensitivity to the impositions of contingent circumstances. To put it bluntly, they were concerned with what was realistically possible given the circumstance – the civil war, the continuing mass support for the monarchy, the hostility of the Presbyterian landowners and the anarchic desperation of peasants struggling to stay alive in the failing economy. In practical terms, they were worried that, in undoing long-established social structures, a full democracy would wreak havoc with the social structure of a society already rent apart by civil war.

The debate on democracy

The argument between the Cromwellians and the Army Levellers was grounded in the belief of each party that the other's claim to authority was flawed. While all present strongly believed that they had won the civil war because they were God's agents on earth, there was a palpable common sense that God was not giving them clear guidance on the issues of how to use their newly won power. Both sides in the debate believed that the other was not authorised to speak or act on behalf of the nation. The underlying problem was that it was not at all clear what a proper source of authority for state actors might be, now that both the authority of the Church and the authority of the Crown had been vaporised by the victories of the Puritan independent parliamentarians. In truth, the Levellers and the Independents were facing an existential moment of recognition which was to become consistent with the modern secular interpreters of the political condition. Political actors, without an external point of authority (that is, direct authorisation from an unambiguously higher – international, global or metaphysical – authority), have to look to themselves. They have to look within the political constitution of their collective existence for a relationship which provides ethical grounds for the order of power. While the Levellers' response was to argue for the democratic authorisation of power through elected representatives, the Cromwellian response was to locate their earthly source of authority in the traditional authority of Parliament. This was not a claim for democratic authority, as Parliament had never been elected by the people in the fullest sense. It was a claim rooted in Parliament's traditional place as the locus of legislative power, combined with its newly acquired status as the locus of the executive in the absence of a functioning monarch (the previous traditional executive).

Each party made a good job of demolishing the other's claims. The Levellers exposed the weakness of the Cromwellian position. The Cromwellians' argument hung on the common understanding that the authority of Parliament was based in the combination of its enduring functionality and its (very loosely conceived) status as representative of the nation (rather as the monarch is seen to represent the UK today). The Levellers pointed out that if Parliament's authority was located solely in the fact of its traditional role, then so was the authority of the monarch, which the Cromwellians had successfully challenged. If Parliament's traditional authority lay in its relatively representative constitution – the fact that unlike the royal court, its membership represented the spread of rank and opinion among those with property and education in the country – then this also lay in tatters, since it had been captured and neutered by the Cromwellians in their purging of Parliament to a rump of Cromwell's supporters.

 Rewind

Go to Chapter 1 for further information on the purging of Parliament.

The Cromwellians, however, were able to point to equally damaging flaws in the Levellers' claim to represent the English people. They asked the Levellers what gave people the right to break down the trusted arrangements that maintained the socio-economic structures of the nation – to uproot the economic and social conventions long integrated into a complex and commonly recognised system. This question has conservative implications, hinting at the notion, developed in the eighteenth century by Edmund Burke, that a socio-political order is ethically valid if, by enduring over time, it exhibits the economic stability to reproduce and maintain the citizens and if, through custom and practice, it creates a meaningful cultural home to the collectivity. A full conservative argument remained undeveloped, however, as it was made almost irrelevant by the fact that the debaters had recently conducted a war against the establishment of the old socio-political order. What remained vital and relevant to the debaters was its two substantive elements. Its first element is a question of certainty: 'How can you be sure that you're right (that God's on your side) when you act decisively?' The second element is a question of authorisation: 'What authority do you have to carry out the act of imposing your ideas on others (even if your critique of their actions is right)?'

Underpinning this was the Cromwellians' sense that the Levellers' notion of 'the people' was too broad and loose to provide a clearly defined source of political authority for the Levellers' demands. The Leveller argument for a full adult franchise fully implied that 'the people' meant all the adult people within the national territory and that they were the source of governmental authority. The Cromwellians, while unable to articulate arguments for an alternative earthly source of authorisation to that of 'the people', were able to point to past failures of the ancient democracies and to the precarious state of civil war society as reasons for doubting that God could want a people's democracy. More decisively, they also questioned the Army Levellers' claim to represent the people against Parliament. The question was valid, since the Levellers were not a political party (these did not exist in these times), but a loose political movement made up of various interest groups (to use modern terms). Like many pressure groups since, their claim to represent a social group was undermined by their lack of a clear mandate. The Army Levellers had no formal and transparent processes to obtain the consent of 'the people'. There had been no formal transparent process whereby the people contributed to, or at least scrutinised and authorised, the Leveller manifesto (though the civilian Levellers did later construct internal forums and elections for their members). For this reason, despite all their democratic intent, they lacked democratic grounds to claim to represent the people and therefore suffered a difficulty in claiming authority for their actions. Because of this it was possible for the Cromwellians to argue that the Levellers had no right to insist on change. Furthermore, as army members, they were subject to strict military discipline. Their actions as soldiers were authorised by army officers to whom they were subordinate, and there were none at Putney higher in military rank than the Cromwellians. Therefore, attempts by the Levellers to force radical changes in the economic and political system would be doubly unauthorised and thus unethical.

The outcome of these arguments showed that no one in the New Model Army received their authority direct from the people (and shows why armies cannot be genuine representatives of the citizens). Initially this appeared more damaging to the Levellers' case than the Cromwellians, but ultimately it reveals the weakness of all non-democratic claims to political authority. For this reason, the outcome of the debates points to the necessity of a democratic process of authorisation. Parliament could claim authority only if it could show that its authority was derived from within the polity. In a republican polity – which a fully parliamentarian polity must be – the logical source for authority is the *res publica*, literally, 'the public thing', which is commonly translated as 'the people'. The Cromwellian exposure of the Levellers' lack of such a clear authorisation threw doubt on their moral right to force changes in the governmental system. In doing so, it showed that the missing piece in the authorisation/representation jigsaw is the legitimating act – the ethically necessary and clearly discernible process in which authorisation is provided by the people. To be a people's government, a government has to be rooted to some degree in the wishes of the people. It has to have at least an elementary process in which the will of the people shapes and directs to some degree the form and activities of the government. In short, the minimum requirement for a people's government – not a religious, class or factional government (which is precisely what the New Model Army's Parliament was) – is that there be a process in which the constitution and actions of the government are subject to the consent of the people. For this process to accommodate the Protestant/liberal insistence on individual free choice, it would have to involve the public statement of consent by each and every citizen which occurs in elections. It is this fundamental point that underpins and gives persuasive strength to the Levellers' demands for regular elections with a full franchise.

In the end, the lack of democratic credentials of both parties at Putney is highlighted by the failure of either to show their authorisation from the people. The lack of alternative credentials is also highlighted by the parties' failure to make a case for, or to show, a non-democratic authorisation for their power. The conservative element of the Cromwellian argument, however, does point to the functional argument for the authority of Parliament. If validity is to be found in the secure functioning of an enduring society, then some political authority can be traced to the government's efficiency in performing its *political* function. The communality of the Putney debaters was rooted in the fact that they had fought together to free Parliament of its subservience to monarchic power, so all present could settle comfortably with a new and modern definition of Parliament's function, 'the end of government being to promote virtue, restrain vice and to maintain to each particular his own, one sort of government which we call civil, either is sufficient or by the wisdom of parliament may be made sufficient for these ends' (Brailsford 1961: 65). It is significant that, although this argument was made by Puritans, it is secular in its formulation. It presents the state's authority as a product of its practical function and not as a product of divine purpose. It is also intrinsically liberal, in that it limits government to maintaining a sphere of private property (which other discussions show include intellectual property), but it is not intrinsically democratic. This pragmatism (increasingly shorn of its liberalism over time) became the guiding principle of Cromwellian government after his defeat of the Leveller's cause.

The Putney Debates failed to provide guidance to the participants, but this failure reveals the intensely difficult dimensions for trying to theorise in a practical situation. Indeed, the significance of the debate is intensified by the oddity of the situation in which it took place. Both sides involved in the debate were parts of the New Model Army (more or less the Cromwellian generals versus the common troopers). Their very existence and their situation as a de facto senate presiding over which direction to lead the nation indicated that social structures had broken down already and that they, as the most powerful collection of people in the country, had now to consider the ethical basis and the practical ends of their newly gained power.

Within this odd scenario is the further anomaly that *The Agreement of the People* was a proposition put by the rank and file of the Army to its generals who, as members of the State Council (a self-appointed parliamentary executive body), were also de facto representatives of Parliament. Not only are there strong elements of a homogenised state apparatus – a merger of military, legislature, executive and judiciary – but the citizenry petitioning the executive are also absorbed into the state apparatus.

The significance of the concentration of all aspects of state and citizenry into one military body becomes clear in the light of the eventual fall into Cromwellian dictatorship, especially when one notes that all the people at the Putney Debates (even Cromwell, at least at that time) were minded towards a more liberal and tolerant society. The English revolution was the first but not the last time that the participants in a political revolution set out to create a condition of liberty, but, under the pressure of time and the need to act, unwittingly constructed a despotic dictatorship instead.

 Fast forward

Go to Chapter 4 (Locke) **and Chapter 5** (Montesquieu) for more information on the separation of powers.

It is significant that the first considered argument for a separation of the executive, legislative and judicial functions into separate state institutions (a subsequent bedrock of liberal constitutionalism) was presented by John Locke shortly after the failure of the Cromwellian experiment. Building constitutions has often been done by people in the kind of situation the New Model Army found itself in – a revolutionary situation in which the old system has gone or is going and power is falling to the strongest, who have to create an authoritative order. In such scenarios, the constraints of time and place press heavily on the activity of critical thinking. The time needed to make considered ethical judgements may be seen as an impediment to effective action – practicality can appear as the opposite of ethical consideration, but both activities, in the end, can be produced only by careful critical analysis; people cannot do the right thing until they know what the right thing is. Rarely do constitution-builders find the time to fully complete the necessary cycle of debate and consideration, judgement and action. Often, they produce compromised and oddly shaped constitutions.

DISCUSSION POINTS

1 The democratic ideal of a 'sovereign people' places political authority in the collective and in doing so implies that the collective has rights over the affairs of its individual memberships. How does this square with the liberal prioritising of individual liberty?

---

continued

2 It is not a simple process for a secondary body – whether it be Parliament, a political party, a pressure group or an armed people's militia – to represent the citizenry. Mechanisms for selection scrutiny and recall of the representatives by the represented have to be in place. Such mechanisms would vary according to the type of organisation and the constituency to be represented. Can you think of appropriate constituencies and mechanisms for their representation by the different agencies named above?

Levelling as class conflict

In the seventeenth century, the economic order underpinning the long-standing class system of England began to break up and change. The development of new technologies, the growth of urban trade centres and the expansion of a sophisticated and shared understanding of the market value of commodities among the growing merchant class created tensions between the feudal landowning aristocratic class and the emerging mercantile class. The immediate cause of the tensions was obscured by a degree of social interaction between the wealthier gentry and the economically less well-endowed members of the aristocracy. It was also obscured and lessened by the struggles for power between religious groups which, unlike the mysterious developments of economic power, were clearly recognised and understood by the participants. In contrast, the tensions were brought into focus by the fact that the delineation of the various conflicting religious groups of the time tended to overlap with the delineation of socio-economic groups – whereas the vast bulk of Puritans were small farmers, skilled artisans or independent merchants, the landed aristocrats consisted largely of the hierarchy of Episcopalian (Anglican) families, many of whom had converted from Catholicism in order to maintain their lands and power. Thus, class conflict served to exacerbate the religious conflict and to feed off it.

The Levellers and the redistribution of private property

The Levellers recognised the economic fault-lines within their society – they saw the ruthless control of land, the support of this through taxation including taxes to the Church – but they did not possess a full enough conceptualisation of social class to articulate their dimensions. Instead, they split their argument into two parts. The first was an argument for the equal right of every individual to access to and use of property. This argument included the classic liberal demand for the repeal of taxes such as tithes as an end to feudal obligations such as making oaths of fealty (declarations of subservience) to aristocratic landowners. The second element of their argument was a series of often virulent attacks on the economic and political powers of the aristocracy. In this part, their arguments move from liberalism towards a recognition that there were two distinct classes of people operating within the socio-economic order. However, while the aristocracy was seen as a distinct group whose interests stood in direct opposition to the widening of access to land and trade for the middle classes, the Levellers could not conceptualise the conflict in terms of class. Instead, aristocrats were presented as a group of lazy pseudo-English, whose wealth was originally plundered by Norman (French) conquerors.

Without a clear notion of class, the Levellers hung their arguments for (limited) redistribution of wealth and property on the claim that undeserving individuals owned more than their fair share of private property. Like most Puritans, they believed that individual property rights were the basis of economic independence, and thus of independent action and thought; in short, property was the basis of liberty. Furthermore, many Levellers agreed with the common Puritan notion that unequal distribution of property was no bad thing if the amount and quality of individual property was a direct expression of that individual's 'industry and valour' (Brailsford 1961: 525). What they were opposed to was the aristocratic claim to property through inheritance rather than productive work.

The Levellers' stance did not provide grounds for an articulate assault on the property rights of a large part of the wealthy classes. The moral claim at the centre of their case was that those with surplus property, in a society in which others had little or none, should have their property levelled to an equal proportion to the rest. Yet, by proclaiming the necessity of private property for all and the virtue of unequal property, they left little room to compose an argument in support of this claim. Indeed, the Levellers were forced under pressure from their opponents to explicitly declare that they were 'against an equalling of men's estates' (Brailsford 1961: 525). Without contesting the notion of private property in itself, they had no grounds on which to attack those wealthy individuals (such as Cromwell) who used their land industriously to produce profit and those who benefited from the increasingly profitable trading corporations. Most tellingly, the Levellers' reform programme hung on demands that the state take private property from undeserving individuals and redistribute it to those whose industry deserved it. As their Cromwellian opponents argued decisively in the Putney Debates, if property could be taken from individuals by the state and redistributed to others, how could possession of property guarantee the safety and liberty of the citizens?

The Diggers and the establishment of a communist utopia

Unlike the Levellers, the Diggers – who called themselves 'true Levellers' – did not petition Parliament about the redistribution of private property. They simply took over common land and established a communal, agrarian self-support group in the rural heathland of Cobham in Surrey. Although this group's communism was informed by Baptist beliefs, they typified Quakers in their pursuit of non-violent politics. Through taking over and working the common lands, they sought to return directly to the garden of Eden, to re-establish God's order on earth. The Digger movement barely lasted any time. The Diggers were a small group of no more than a few hundred led by the charismatic Gerrard Winstanley, and this small community was forced to stop digging the common land after a few months of legal and physical harassment by local landowners. Nevertheless, their actions caused enough of a stir to become 'a nine days wonder and they were widely reported in the news sheets of the time' (Sabine 1941: 15). Thus, although limited in scope, their highly publicised actions posed enough of a challenge to the established order to catch the attention of Army generals and of Parliament. Adding to the drama of the Diggers' actions was the impact of the arguments of their leader and theoretician, Gerrard Winstanley, who set out some of the basic tenets of the communist republican arguments against acquisitive individualism which have become a core feature of modern Western society.

Winstanley's political argument for communism appealed to common reason. Its political argument actually arises from a theological conception of 'reason' as the presence of God in humankind. Reason, argued Winstanley, is the process of things working; it is therefore a material sign of a purpose and order to things and thus is evidence of God's work. The presence of reason in humans gives them the ability to comprehend God, through an understanding of the process of natural 'motion'. Winstanley argued that reason is more than a sign; it is, in fact, God known to us through our rational comprehension of natural motion. Thus our capacity to reason reveals that God is in us: reason is God-in-human-being. Reason, therefore, is more than understanding, it is goodness. Reason is the process which gives harmonious order to a world of apparently conflicting parts and makes it function. Humans, whose humanising substance is reason, are microcosms of the natural order: 'The world is in mankind and every particular man is a perfection creation of himself, a perfect created world' (Berens 1961: 59).

This understanding provides the basis for an argument for a communist society – reason is a common quality and a globalising one and, as such, it is a communalising force. However, humans had failed to create a reasoned communal society because, like the earth, humans function though a balancing of elemental parts; in opposition to reasoned caring and sharing is unreasoned passion – expressed fully in lust for pleasure and power. Unreasoned passion can be powerful. It drives towards its ends directly and forcefully through violence and so establishes a social order in which the strong rule the weak through pure force. This corrupting force can be attractive in its directness and in its promise of easily won pleasures, but, warns Winstanley, 'the masculine powers of the poisoned flesh stand it out against the King of Glory' (Berens 1961: 59). This is not the thundering of a 'Bible-bashing' preacher, but a pointer to the practical consequences of unreasoned action. In such societies (defined as 'Kingly' by Winstanley), pride and vanity mark out the rituals of government and, at root, force governs the control and distribution of its wealth. Such an unreasoned social order will fall into a consuming violence – exactly as the kingly rule of his own times had done.

 Fast forward

Go to Chapter 6 to see how Rousseau develops this argument.

Hidden beneath the theology, Winstanley is framing the first sociological argument against individualism (which was being propagated so articulately at the time by his contemporary Thomas Hobbes). The argument – made many times since – is that people will be corrupted if they do not live in a world where their reason can flourish, but rather live in a world where their vices are promoted. 'The inward bondages of the mind are all occasioned by the outward bondages that one sort of people lay upon another' (Sabine 1941: 59). On the other hand, a reasoned society will provide a nurturing of the good traits of every individual – sharing, thoughtfulness, the tendency to discuss difference rather than leap into combat. By pointing to the apparently incontrovertible evidence of selfishness and greed at the time, Winstanley argued that people were selfish, and dangerous, only because they were living in an unreasoned, chaotic and violently imposed order – 'Kingly Rule' – where 'poisoned flesh proceeds the lust of the eye, the lust of the flesh, and the pride of life' (Sabine 1941: 59). The answer was to replace kingly rule (established on the principle that the wealth was gathered into the hand of one) with its opposite: a society where wealth was in the hands of all. Winstanley was able to point out that this is the precise and literal meaning of the term 'common-wealth', used by all to describe the national polity.

Winstanley dug down cleverly into the ethical implications of the commonly held idea of a commonwealth: 'common-wealth' refers to the collective wealth of the community and collective wealth is distinct from private wealth, in that it is shared wealth. To be shared by the people it must be accessed, controlled, and, of course produced, by the people. In this largely agrarian society, wealth, indeed the very means of life, was ultimately rooted in ownership and control of land. So the idea of the common wealth could be translated as collective access to and control of the land. This idea had a revolutionary pertinence, as the political struggles of monarchy and Parliament were, at root, about access to and control over at least the means of life and at best wealth.

Winstanley agreed with the Levellers in arguing that kingly rule was based solely on the institutionalised greed of a powerful few, who through force of arms had conquered the territory and held its resources for themselves against the rest of the nation's populace. The legal system, the tithes it imposed, the enclosures it supported, the punishments it inflicted on the commoners who transgressed the property rights of the few, showed that 'England' was no more than 'a prison, the varieties of subtleties in the laws preserved by the sword are the bolts, bars and doors of the prison; the lawyers are the jailers; and the poor men are the prisoners' (Sabine 1941: 57). Like the Levellers, Winstanley argued that if the political goal of the war was to be liberty, its conclusion could come only with the overthrow of the entire legal system and by returning the land to the community. This alone would establish a common wealth. Here Winstanley's programme differed from that of the Levellers, for he saw the economic implications of this idea of a common wealth – a common ownership and use of the land which would point to a collective governance of the territory and all its resources . . . 'government of the earth' (Sabine 1941: 537).

There is, in this argument, the seed of a further argument about the effect of privatisation of resources. In Winstanley's language, it is framed as a consideration of the virtue of common preservation versus the vice of self-preservation. The self-interested pursuits of 'individuals' who 'seek their own preservation, Ease, Honour, Riches, and freedom in the earth . . . and regard not the Peace Freedom and

Preservation of the week and foolish among bretheren' (Sabine 1941: 537) are 'the root of the Tree of Tyranny' in which 'bondage tears and sorrows and poverty are brought upon many men . . . indeed this tyranny is the cause of all wars and troubles and of the removal of the government of the earth out of one hand into another as it is, in all nations' (Sabine 1941: 537).

Winstanley had little sense of economics and could not fill the gap between the initial claim that private property stimulates social unrest and potentially political crises, and some kind of proof of this outcome. The missing information, the account of the ways in which private property could be used to systematically manipulate scarcity, create artificial values, control access to the means of life and the distribution of goods, was filled three hundred years later by Karl Marx. Nevertheless, at this point, Winstanley's connections between private property and social inequality, and his perception of inequality as the cause of social unrest, conflict and possibly war, were shown to have a strong basis in fact. In contrast to the Levellers, Winstanley had mounted the beginnings of a potentially robust argument against the socio-economic order of his time.

DISCUSSION POINTS

1 Winstanley asks his contemporaries to throw out their fear, aggression, self-love and partiality. Is this asking them to deny fundamental and unchangeable parts of human nature?
2 Winstanley has been criticised (as were communists later) by commentators for his lack of a rational or scientific analysis of the benefits and problems involved in establishing and maintaining a communist polity. Such criticisms raise the question of how a science of society (social science) could provide the *ethical* grounds for any political order of life.

The Levellers and nationalism

As we have seen, the arguments between the Levellers and the Cromwellians for the future of the republic were underpinned by the notion of being the people's representatives. One of the points at issue was the notion of who exactly the people were. All those involved in the debates would find common ground for an answer in the idea of the Christian people of England, but this answer itself hides within it some tensions which are core to democratically governed polities.

The confusions indicated the serious conceptual flaws in their understanding of what a sovereign community of free-thinking English individuals could be. While it was strong on emotive symbolism, the Levellers' argument confused the vital point about what exactly constituted membership of the community.

There was little clear agreement about the quality an individual needed to possess to qualify as fully rational and thus fully capable of operating as a citizen. For example, did the fact that rational individualism was tied into the Puritan notion of a true Christian mean that the beliefs of atheists, Jews or Muslims put them beyond rational argument and thus excluded them from citizenship? Typically for the times, there was 'a total silence about women's political rights' (Crawford in Mendle 2001: 197). Women were often considered (by powerful men) to lack the capacity for reasoned judgement required for full citizenship. Did this prejudice eat into Levellers' conceptions of the people?' Did such a tight conception of rational individuals deny political rights to the many people within the nation state who were Christian men? (Most Independents and many Levellers believed this to be right.) Such a belief at worst would leave significant elements of the social community open to potential hostility and violence.

Perhaps the defining quality for membership was Englishness (many Levellers thought so. In many of his writings John Lilburne voiced a popular sentiment when he railed against foreign impostors pretending to be English) in which case foreigners in general would lack rights and be open to violence. A different interpretation could claim that membership of the community sprang simply from being in the country and being a rational, free-thinking individual. William Walwyn argued for this very cosmopolitan idea.

Underpinning all these issues is the point that collective self-rule stands in an uneasy tension with the ideal of individual liberty. In the Puritan Debates, this took the expression of the tension between the notion of a self-ruling Christian collectivity and the Puritan advocation of the liberty of the free-thinking individual. This tension manifested itself in the factional disputes about who was truly Christian and who was not, among the many sects. Not all the self-proclaimed Christian groupings were considered Christian from a Puritan perspective. Many independents had their doubts about Anglicans and Presbyterians, and most could not cope with the idea of allowing Catholics any rights at all (Cromwell shared with the great Puritan thinkers Milton and Locke – two men famous for their advocation of toleration – an opposition to Catholic rights). Very few Puritans would include non-Christians into citizenship – Jews and Muslims, for example. Indeed, many Puritan sects sought to exclude other Puritan sects from citizenship.

All these issues are products of a perennial question for any and all political communities: 'Who are "the people"?' The need for an answer to this question is especially important to a republic, and is also particularly urgent for a polity in radical dispute with itself.

For seventeenth-century debaters mired in the confusions of the multi-interpretations of Christian theology, the relatively easy and superficially unifying non-religious concentration on nationality provided an attractive way of determining who was to be included or excluded from the citizenship of the new republic.

Oddly, nationalistic thinking was particularly attractive to Levellers, since it provided a distorted conceptual framework through which they could channel their sensitivity to the clear cultural and political divisions between themselves and the aristocracy. Nationalism provided the Levellers with a means to express common prejudice against the aristocratic minority with whom they were in conflict. Aristocratic landowners and the lawyers who maintained their property rights were dismissed as 'Normans' – outsiders and enemies of England's 'natural Saxon' people. To understand how this was so, we need to pause to consider the nature of nationalist thinking in general.

Nationalism

Although societies exist materially as economic and social entities, there is a level of human existence at which collectivities imagine themselves into being and regard themselves and their economic and social activities in a mystical fantastical light as a unique people of destiny. Nationalism is a classic way in which such imagined transformations have taken place. Nationalist consciousness incubates and reproduces vital mythologies which revolve around the stories of an imagined community. The mythologies are stories but not only stories; they are stories with a purpose – they tell their listeners something significant about their existence as members of a community. The myths tell stories that appear to reveal or explain how and/or why the listener's identity is part of a greater collective identity. They tell how this identity came into being; perhaps they tell or hint at their purpose and destiny. The hero of the story is the people themselves, that is, the collectivity struggling and enduring as one – as a nation.

For the listeners, the sense of their own self becomes inextricably linked to their membership of the collectivity: their own key features are the features common to and definitive for the collectivity's members. Their individual birth is a part of the continuation of the collectivity and thus their future is the next instalment of its adventures. Ultimately, the contours of the myth are designed to direct the individual listener to understand that their existence is a continuation of the story of this collective hero.

In nationalist imaginings of collectivity, the collectivity is not a mere aggregate of individuals brought together by biological circumstance and economic necessity; it is a community. The nation's members share in a communion – a merging of their individual identities in a bonding whole greater than its parts. This whole has a uniqueness and destiny which corresponds to its unique situation in time and place. The nation is bound together by the culture and economy of its collective existence, which also maintain its umbilical link to the territory from which it extracts the means of life and upon which it carves out its own special existence.

The persuasive power of such imaginings lies in the fact that although they are fantasy-filled they are not simple fantasy; they fantasise upon historical relics. They take up and use the fragmented and partially understood remains of an actual past and impose meanings upon them by giving them significant roles in the mythical story of the nation. The less well understood the relic, the more significance it will be given by myth-makers. For example, in English nationalism, the little understood Stonehenge, the vaguely recorded exploits of King Arthur and the mysterious amalgam of actual and mythological personages that come together in Robin Hood are all loaded with mythologised significance. Richly embellished stories tell of their vital contribution to the story of the imagined English community. They endure over generations as iconic symbols of Englishness and thus contribute over centuries to the continuation of an actual and definable English collectivity. Perhaps more powerful to the nationalist mythologisers are those people and events which have left a greater degree of factual evidence and are better known for what they were. In current times, the London Blitz functions in this way. These are still subject to mythologising (the Blitz has been mythologised into the story of 'plucky little Cockneys' as the epitome of solid and enduring Englishness) and, because they carry a baggage of certifiable proof, they can be used with even more effectiveness as elements of the myth of the nation. In this way, the myth of the Saxon English was developed and used by Levellers to express their discontent with the creaking class system of seventeenth-century England.

For the seventeenth-century English, the historical veracity of the Saxon kingdom and the subsequent Norman invasion gave a persuasive power to Levellers' claims that the class division of lords and commoners was a division of Saxon English and Norman oppressor. Although the claim was based on vague and simplistic mythologising of the Saxon mode of life and the fruits of the Norman Conquest, it was given apparent substance by many enduring relics of the Norman Conquest. The aristocrats were in many cases descendants of Norman Knights. The feudal legal system which enforced the property rights of the aristocracy was not only written in Latin, but the legal transactions which so often deprived commoners of access to land or trading rights were commonly conducted in arcane Norman French – a foreign tongue to all but lawyers at that time. Not surprisingly, retrieval of Anglo-Saxon culture was a feature of the seventeenth century. Milton typified 'a long preoccupation with old England past' (and excelled in its reinvention – strong echoes of Saxon epic poetry are to be found in *Paradise Lost* (Ackroyd 2002: 88–89). This revival represented an attempt to return to pre-Roman pre-Catholic culture, to reveal an older more authentic English world, standing proudly against Roman Catholicism and Scottish Presbyterianism. It was a world of the imagination to be sure, but it was a world that seventeenth-century English Protestants could imagine and claim to belong to.

Nationalism in Leveller discourse

The Levellers hallmarked a core element of English nationalism when they argued that the 'natural' Saxon culture of England had been subordinate to the foreign imperialist culture of the Normans. Lilburne, in his influential pamphlet *The Causes of Regal Tyranny Discovered*, appealed to common sensibilities and mythologies when he recounted how 'William the bastard Conqueror' overturned the Saxon order and gave the land to his fellow Normans 'who he made Dukes Earls and Barons for helping him subdue and enslave the free nation of England' under 'the iron Norman yoke'. 'In those days', he declared, 'it was a shame even among Englishmen to be an Englishman' (Brailsford 1961: 129). This common sense of aggrieved Saxon Englishness gave evocative power to his claim that the current nobility were 'the lineal issue' of those original Norsemen, 'Robbers rogues and thieves' (Brailsford 1961: 129).

In classic nationalist style, the Levellers then argued that the personal faults of the monarch, the inequalities of wealth and power within their society, and the entirety of its legal and political structure, could be traced directly to the Norman Conquest and thus was the fault of untrustworthy foreigners. The monarch was a descendant of a robber baron, 'the lords are but as intruders thrust upon us by kings' supported by 'shamelessly, cheating hackney lawyers, being worse than the devil' (Sabine 1941: 632). The appeal for democratic reform was framed in nationalist tones, as an appeal to the House of Commons as representatives of the Saxon English people to overthrow the Norman lords: 'We desire you to free us from their negative voice, or tell us that it is reasonable we be slaves' (Brailsford 1961: 96–97). The petition for economic reform was framed as a demand to undo 'That the ancient and almost antiquated badge of slavery, *viz*, all base tenures by copies, oaths of fealty, homage, fines at the will of the Lord, etc. (being the Conquerer's marks upon the people)' (The Army's petition, 3 May 1648 – Brailsford 1961: 440).

This nationalism – a secular form of identification – was by necessity entwined with the dominant Protestant culture. The lords were, by definition, an affront to God's law because, according to the Scriptures, 'All men being alike privileged by birth, so all men were to enjoy the creatures alike without property one more than the other, all men by the grant of God are free, and every man individual, that is to say no man was to lord over his own kind; neither to enclose the creatures to his own use, to the impoverishing of his neighbours' (Sabine 1941: 611). The lords' 'sinful' behaviour was manifested in their enclosing of common land into private estates: 'man following his sensuality became a devourer of the creatures, and an encloser' (Sabine 1941: 611). The King was especially devilish: the 'tyrant', the 'chief encloser called Lord of the Manor', and his laws 'were not of God's institutions at first, but . . . arose from the Heathens, *viz*. those that lived after their own beastly lusts' (Sabine 1941: 611–612). It follows from this claim that lords

> do live out of Gods way and in rebellion to his laws because they live without a calling and so are idle . . . wasters . . . vermin in a commonwealth . . . and by their own law should be put into a house of correction and made to work. . . . They are rebels against Gods command, for saith he, *In the sweat of thy face thy shall eat thy bread*: By *thou* is meant all mankind, none exempted.
>
> (Sabine 1941: 633; italics in original)

The politically analytic substance of these tracts is heavily compromised by the religious polemic. The arguments against unequal distribution of wealth, the potential argument against the idea and fact of private property and undemocratic rule are buried under a mountain of Puritan disdain for 'idleness', while this disdain is itself sung out in a racialist tone. The Saxon English, they claim, are fair, honest and free, the Norman French are deceitful, power-hungry and land-grabbing . . . and, for those who sought religious proof for their secular pudding, Catholic at root.

Perhaps, sadly, what we see here is an example of the self-creation of an imagined community. In subsequent centuries, burying good liberal arguments for economic welfare, and accountable government, under overly robust self-righteous and sometimes xenophobic language has become the commonly approved and practised mode of argument for many newspapers and commentators contributing to English public debate.

While the intensity of socialist feeling varied among the membership of the Levellers and among the Levellers' spokespersons (Walwyn and Overton were more socialist than Lilburne) and their nationalism was even less well defined, when we look at their final demands for a post-war settlement we can see some small signs of the dreadful outcome that often attends the merging of the two ideologies. The defeated Royalists were stamped as Normans, 'foreigners' with Catholic tendencies, and doubt was cast on their rights to anything at all within the nation state. The nationalist reasons for taking their property could be extended to expelling them from the polity altogether in an act of ethnic cleansing. Fortunately, the Levellers' liberal temperament dampened this spiky xenophobic tendency and the settlement's terms did not exclude the royalists from equal rights as citizens of an English republic (Brailsford 1961: 536–537). One wonders if the republican government's liberalism would have held sway over their nationalism had the Levellers' ideology become their blueprint for action.

Conclusions

The Levellers' arguments were directed by the theological thinking common to the time, but the political dimensions of their situation shaped their concerns. The movement was an elemental part of the struggles to establish a new type of polity, and their arguments contributed to the efforts to determine the grounds of political conduct, the terms of political allegiance and the formal structure and process of power. At the level of constitutional debate, their activities and arguments brought forth ideas and presented conundrums that remained relevant throughout the later history of the modern world. The core problematics addressed were the location and working process of national sovereignty. The questions raised included: 'What is the source of political authority in post-theocratic states?', 'Is the modern state's function to enable the self-governance of national communities?', 'Is the national community identical to the populace of the territory or do special conditions pertain?', and 'What mechanisms are necessary for the legitimate use of power by the state – must it be fully democratic, or do special conditions for full participation (such as property rights or specialist knowledge) pertain?'

Within this debate, the two big ideas have had a vibrant resurgence in the previous two centuries. The argument for mass democracy in Britain was revived with full force by the Chartists and achieved final success in the early twentieth century, while nationalism has constantly resurfaced throughout the twentieth century, sometimes with a beneficial effect such as in the establishment of the Republic of Ireland and sometimes with disastrous outcomes, such as in the creation of Nazi Germany and in the more recent destruction of Yugoslavia.

The Diggers' arguments and activities introduced the communist challenge to the emerging liberal capitalist order of the Western world and, in doing so, reveal the very basic strengths and weaknesses of communist politics. The strength of Winstanley's arguments lay in their moral and practical dissection of the failures of societies built on the principles of self-interest. This strength is consistently displayed in later communist political theory, taking its full-blown and most powerful form in the nineteenth-century writings of Karl Marx. The weakness of the Diggers' project stemmed from their inability to establish a practical working alternative to the principles of property and trade. Indeed, the slightly comical picture of a few dozen men being physically carried from the land and locked into nearby public buildings by angry local landowners conjures up the basic mix of romanticism and futility that beset much communistic activity prior to the Russian Revolution of 1917. Crucially Winstanley's thought lacks a developed sense of the ways and means in which political power is built up and maintained, and may be used effectively to create new orders which can service a propertyless community of equals. This lack remained a constant in communist theorising until the early twentieth century when the Bolsheviks, having captured the Russian state, were forced to take on this problem as an urgent and practical necessity.

Revision notes

1   The Levellers were a loose anti-Royalist, pro-democracy movement rooted in the Protestant communities of yeoman farmers, urban tradesmen and minor merchants. They had overlapping concerns with the landowning Protestant elite who dominated Parliament, but significantly disagreed with this elite about the possibility of creating a fully democratic political order in the UK.

2   The Levellers' power was rooted in their numbers within the New Model Army, but the Army was also the source of the parliamentarian landowning elite's power. Thus the debates in the Army – notably the Putney Debates – reveal to us the detail of the democratic and counter-democratic arguments at work within the parliamentary forces at the time.

3   The Levellers' analysis of the sovereign source of power initiated the English ideal of democratically sourced authority for governmental action. It also signposted nationalist notions of the sovereignty of a national 'people'.

4   The Diggers were distinct from the Levellers in that they were communists. The Digger manifesto called not only for parliamentary reform, but for a reform of the entire socio-economic order to establish agrarian communes producing and consuming the means of life collectively.

Bibliography

Ackroyd, P. (2002) *Albion*, London: Chatto & Windus.

Berens, L.H. (1961) *The Digger Movement*, London: Holland & Merlin Press.

Brailsford, H.N. (1961) *The Levellers and the English Revolution*, London: Cresset Press.

Mendle, M. (ed.) (2001) *The Putney Debates of 1647*, Cambridge: Cambridge University Press.

Sabine, G.H. (1941) *The Works of Gerrard Winstanley*, New York: Cornell University Press.

Further reading

Christopher Hill (1972) *The World Turned Upside Down*, London and New York: Penguin, offers a highly accessible and informative contextualisation of the Levellers' and Diggers' activities and arguments.

Michael Mendle's *The Putney Debates of 1647* is a set of essays by a range of notable academics discussing the significance of the events at Putney.

John Plamenatz (1992) *Man And Society*, Vol. 1, London and New York: Addison Wesley Longman, Chapter 6, entitled 'Divine Right absolute monarchy and early theories of the Social Contract' is a valuable exploration of the discourse of legitimate power during the seventeenth century and is useful supplementary reading for this chapter and for the chapters on Milton, Hobbes and Locke.

Thomas Hobbes

Leviathan is the greatest, perhaps the sole, masterpiece of political philosophy written in the English language.

(Oakeshott 1946: 223)

Life and times

Thomas Hobbes was born on 5 April 1588 and lived to the grand old age of 91. He was born prematurely, apparently because his mother was alarmed by the news that the Spanish Armada was approaching England (Aubrey 1982: 152). Such a traumatic entry into the world was, in fact, quite appropriate given the chaos that surrounded the rest of his life. For Hobbes, a shy man, had to contend with a period that was probably the most violent and bloody in English political history. Perhaps it was the struggle of matching his natural timidity to a social and political environment that was out of control which brought out the genius of the man. By all accounts he was not predisposed to be one of the greatest political philosophers of the modern age. He was born into rather undistinguished *petit bourgeois* surroundings, the second son of a vicar of Westport near Malmesbury. Biographers and commentators generally seem to hold a rather poor view of his father, one critic calling him 'incompetent and unlettered' (Macpherson 1968 :15).

It is not entirely clear where such writers get their evidence from but it must be supposed that they are generally pleased that the poor soul passed away before he could have much influence on young Thomas' tender mind. His care passed to a very rich uncle who ensured that Hobbes received a fine education, becoming an outstanding scholar of Greek and Latin before going up to Oxford University at the age of 14 to study classical literature and theology. After graduating from Oxford at the age of 20 he secured a prestigious post as the tutor, and later secretary, to the son of William Cavendish, first Earl of Devonshire. Hobbes was inspired by his position. He had become bored by the strictures of university life, and by following the accepted traditions of education. He thirsted after newer forms of knowledge and was keen to develop ideas of his own. The Cavendishes gave him a great deal of security and freedom to develop his thoughts. Under different circumstances he would probably have been content to live apart from the practical world, fighting only the conflicts of philosophy and reason for the rest of his life. This luxury was not open to Hobbes, as it was insecurity, fear and conflict that dominated the political landscape of seventeenth-century England.

Hobbes in context

Throughout Hobbes' life the social, economic, religious and political conditions of England were undergoing a profound transformation. England was moving from a traditional community based upon status and land to a society based upon instrumental contract and the market economy. Hobbes was an early observer and a participant in the remarkable story that saw the rise of modernity. His classic text of political theory, *Leviathan*, was, on one level, an attempt to make sense of the epochal change that was altering the very foundations of the way in which people thought of themselves and acted out their daily lives. During his lifetime European societies began to exhibit the first significant manifestations of the Enlightenment. In particular a monumental shift was taking place regarding human identity. Prior to the revolution of thought that the Enlightenment brought about, human beings generally took their identities from communities (clans, tribes, villages and so on) to which they belonged. However, Enlightenment philosophers, perhaps most famously Descartes, had argued that it was, in fact, the *individual* who ought to be the starting place for understanding the world around us. This seems so commonplace to us now that we can barely think of understanding ourselves in any other way. The entire edifice of Western discourse is predicated on the basis of individuality; yet this has not always been the case. Think of Socrates who would rather commit suicide than face exile from Athens. Why? The reason was that by leaving his community he would be a non-person, a man without an identity. That for him was a fate even worse than death.

KEY CONCEPT

The Divine Right of Kings

Jacques-Bénigne Bossuet (1627–1704) reinforced medieval notions of kingship in his theory of the Divine Right of Kings, a theory which argued that certain kings ruled because they were chosen by God to do so and that these kings were accountable to no person except God. The origin of this concept extends far back into European, Middle Eastern and Northern African history. However, Bossuet was reacting to an extreme situation and carried this argument to extremes. Not only did God bestow power on certain monarchs (and he argued that his king, Louis XIV of France, was one such monarch), but the bestowal of this power legitimated autocracy (rule by one person). The King ruled by virtue of God's authority; therefore he should be obeyed in all things. No group, whether they be nobles or a Parliament or the people, have a right to participate in this rule. To question or oppose the monarch was to rebel against God's purpose. This doctrine of absolutism came to a bloody end following the French Revolution of 1789–1792 and the beheading of Louis XIV of France.

When Descartes declared, 'I think therefore I am' he was signalling the shift in thinking of ourselves in traditional terms to one that we may recognise as quint-essentially modern. By placing the only sure knowledge of the world that we have firmly in the hands of individuals, Descartes had helped to provoke a revolution regarding the very nature of existence. This pushed against the ideas of the dominant and socially powerful Catholic Church. Catholic theology understood being a Christian as a duty. If you were born into a Catholic community you were automatically a member of the faithful, an association under the eye of God. If you turned away from that community you would be committing a grave sin (and God's punishment would befall you). In other words, there was no choice. By Hobbes' time the terms of individualism had grown to the degree that the Catholic Church faced a challenge from the emergence of Protestant sects which began to argue that serving God was an act of will or individual choice. Furthermore the basis of religion was the individual's relationship with God. There need not be any communal association, even less a constituted authority or church, which had to act as an intermediary between the individual and God. Religion was becoming personal and the forsaking of worldly for spiritual values a matter of rational choice.

The events which explicitly shaped Hobbes' attempt to confront the transition that he was living through were the constitutional conflicts of the 1640s. These turned into a ferocious civil war. The English civil war was, in many ways, a graphic portrayal of the epochal shift from traditional to modern society. Political conflict erupted between supporters of absolute monarchy and supporters of parliamentary liberties. The Parliamentarians were challenging the traditional notion that authority ought to reside with the monarch who owed his position to God. Authority, in this sense, came under the notion of the Divine Right of Kings. This view (that God had ordained and chosen royal rulers) was one that had prevailed throughout the Middle Ages. It corresponded to the idea of a *Great Chain of Being*. The principle of Divine Right left no choice as to who was to rule; this was God-given, inviolable, unchanging, eternal. However, this idea began to lose legitimacy in a world that was being demystified by the philosophical ideas of the Enlightenment which had as its central tenet the idea of individual free will and choice.

The civil war ended in 1652, but it and its aftermath preoccupied public life until the settlement of 1688, known as the 'Glorious Revolution', which instituted a constitutional monarchy. Hobbes did not live to see this relatively peaceful outcome to the decades of instability and insecurity that he had experienced. His chief work, *Leviathan*, was published in the last year of the war and, as Hobbes tells us, it was 'occasioned by the disorders of the present time, without partiality, without application, and without any other design than to set before men's eyes the mutual relation between protection and obedience of which the conditions of human nature . . . require an inviolable observance' (Macpherson 1968: 728).

Hobbes' method

Hobbes' method is many-sided and a complex interweaving of various intellectual positions, both traditional and modern. Those who merely situate Hobbes as a realist (or Machiavellian) and the author of a 'science' of politics over-simplify the dynamics of his method. Furthermore, like most of us, Hobbes was confused; or at least, he was overwhelmed with choice. A highly educated and cultured man, he was aware of a wide range of diverse methodologies. His genius, in fact, was his attempt to tie together the methods of the past with those emerging in the present. In so doing he created a view of political understanding that was to last well into the future.

Hobbes' project was an audacious and ambitious one. His aim, no less, was to place the understanding of human existence and relationships within the context of the new discoveries of thought and science. Writing as he was during a period of unprecedented revolution, this is no surprise. The revolution in which he was caught up was not only on the battlefields. As noted above, radical innovations were taking place in science and philosophy. However, that being said, this is real life, and real life is rather more full of 'greys' than 'blacks' and 'whites'. Hobbes' time was, one can say, 'not quite modern'. His education had been a classical one that had tutored young men of distinction for generations, stretching back to the Middle Ages. It ought to be remembered, then, that previous intellectual currents also influenced Hobbes' thought. His 'master-concepts' of 'Will' and 'Creation' derived from the Judico-Christian tradition, even though under his employment these notions became secularised. Furthermore, without the established Christian beliefs in spiritual autonomy and freedom, modern ideas of the individual would scarcely be possible. In order for the foundation of political thought that we have in Hobbes to emerge, it is necessary to understand that it presupposed Christian eschatology. In addition to the general impact of the traditional Judico-Christian discourse of the times, Hobbes was also influenced by late scholistic nominalism as well as the rhetorical tradition of the Renaissance (Johnston 1986: 35).

Nominalism, in philosophy, was a theory of the relation between universals and the particular which was popular in the Middle Ages. It ought to be contrasted with the medieval philosophical notion of realism. This is rather ironic because Hobbes is closely associated with, indeed is seen as one of the founders of, *modern* realism. This is particularly the case in the area of international relations.

DISCUSSION POINT

In modern international relations theory Hobbes' 'state of nature' is taken as a symbolic way of representing the state of competition that persists between nation states in international politics. A school of modern 'realism' developed around this notion that nation states are the basis of understanding global politics and that their relations are based purely upon instrumental gain. In other words, classical realism assumed that conflict and self-interest (that is, national interest) was the 'Realpolitik' of international relations. Why do you think about this proposition? Can Hobbes' 'state of nature' be used to analyse contemporary international affairs?

In medieval philosophy, however, realism represented a position taken on the problem of universals and was closely tied to an idea regarding the position of God in the human world. The most popular theory of realism in the medieval period followed authors such as St Thomas Aquinas. He held that universals exist only in the mind of God, as patterns by which he creates particular things. A problem with realism arises because in order to perceive a particular object as being of a certain kind, say a table, realists would argue that we must have a prior notion of table. Does the kind of 'table', described by this prior notion, then have an existence independent of particular tables? Nominalism says that it does not, that it is just a name for a group of particular objects. In other words, nominalism is the doctrine which argues that general or abstract words do not stand for objectively existing entities and that universals are no more than names assigned to them. Nominalism went on to influence materialist and empirical philosophy in modern thought.

KEY PEOPLE 1

Thomas Aquinas (c. 1225–1274)

Aquinas was both philosopher and theologian. His aim was to establish compatibility between the Christian faith and reason. His two best-known works are the *Summa contra Gentiles* and the *Summa theologiae*. These are dense texts dealing with fundamental questions, such as the existence of God. Although in some ways a modern and highly original thinker, his metaphysics were grounded in Aristotelian thought. The influence of his work remained during Hobbes' time.

When it is said that Hobbes was influenced by the scholastic nominalist tradition it means that he was convinced by the argument given above. If Hobbes had not accepted this position but adopted that of medieval realism, he could not possibly have developed the kind of secular political theory that is contained in *Leviathan*. So from what may appear as a rather abstract philosophical argument, there are very important consequences for Hobbes' work and, indeed, for the whole liberal tradition of political thought.

The term 'scholastic' is used before nominalism because in the philosophy and theology of Western Christendom in the Middle Ages virtually all medieval philosophers of any significance were theologians; their philosophy is generally embodied in their theological writings. There were numerous scholastic philosophies in the Middle Ages, but basic to all scholastic thought was the conjunction of faith and reason. This meant the use of reason to deepen the understanding of what is believed on faith and ultimately to give a rational content to faith. It was in the course of applying reason to faith that medieval thinkers developed and taught important philosophical ideas not directly related to theology. Again, it is important to note that Hobbes' secularism stems from this point. But it is also important to remember that while the scholastic tradition turned Hobbes towards a rational understanding of human experience, it was still tied in some way to theology. When we look at *Leviathan*, God has not completely disappeared; far from it. For example, the whole of Part III discusses a 'Christian commonwealth' at great length. Hobbes begins with a discussion of the principles of a 'Christian politiques' (Macpherson 1968: 409), and from this point on ties politics and theology closely together in terms of justifying his position.

The way in which Hobbes does justify his position is also important. Hobbes was an enthusiast in the art of writing and arguing. For him the rhetoric was as important in political discourse as the content of the ideas that were being expressed. Those who see Hobbes as a rather dry writer of a rational political theory miss the importance of rhetoric in his work. The effective use of language may be seen in the chapters on the 'Christian commonwealth'. Here he manages to bring together the popular language of the Bible with the new scientific method of argument that he was developing.

'Accordingly where-unto, our Saviour himself expressly saith, (John 18.36) My Kingdome is not of this world' (Macpherson 1968: 514). This example illustrates how in one sentence Hobbes sought to justify his argument in theological, rational and rhetorical means. He uses the Bible to insist that there are 'two worlds', one which God rules over, the other which is ruled over by man. In this sense *Leviathan* is a work of art, an extremely clever way of using theological language, and the figures of speech of the day to make an effective political argument. *Leviathan* stands as a great piece of rhetoric in this sense, a persuasive argument that has lasted generations and is of great influence, regardless of its theoretical, philosophical and even practical flaws.

The aspects of Hobbes' thought must not be set aside when assessing his overall method. Hobbes, indeed, was desperate to be a truly modern man, methodologically speaking. However, like all of us, his education and the context of thought influenced him during his time. He was betwixt and between the medieval scholastic tradition and the modern scientific revolution. There is little doubt that Hobbes adopted ideas of the scientific revolution and attempted to apply them to a systematic analysis of human existence. Such a project may be discerned in the three treatises which preceded *Leviathan*. These concerned geometry and physics (De Corpore), individual physiology and psychology (De Homie) and the artificial state (De Cive). Although Hobbes' enterprise was to pursue a 'scientific' explanation, the science involved was, of course, the conception of science of Hobbes' own times. This was totally under the spell of the ideas of geometry, and has long been superseded by quite different conceptions.

In concordance with the scientific principles of the day, Hobbes used motion as a pivotal point throughout his analysis. These laws of motion operated in a way derived largely from the deductive system of geometry. Macpherson (1968: 25–26) argues that Hobbes followed Galileo's 'resolutive-compositive' method. This demanded resolving political society into motions of its parts (the individual) and then resolving their motion to hypothetical simple forces which could be shown to explain them. This method is purely formal, requiring no appeal to empirical evidence. Sabine (1973: 457–458) points out that geometry was the pre-eminent mode of scientific enquiry in the seventeenth century and, consequently, the most legitimate. Its influence was clearly visible in the writings of Descartes. Sabine asserts that Hobbes' method 'differs little' from the Cartesian approach (Sabine 1973: 458).

It is true that both authors start from the certainty of the self. However, this alone is not sufficient to justify Sabine's view. As we have seen, Hobbes' influences went well beyond a merely scientific analysis. Moreover, his metaphysics were fundamentally opposed to those of Descartes. Hobbes held to a monist notion of being; that is, he argued that matter affects mind, making men mechanisms of cause and effect. Men were at the mercy of the material and natural world. Descartes believed in an interaction whereby mind also affected matter. This gave a greater degree of autonomy to the individual to be able to conquer nature. In this sense their metaphysics set their views of human nature apart. As we shall see, Hobbes was sceptical regarding man's ability to overcome his own natural characteristics and earth-bound struggles, whereas Descartes conceived of men as a great deal more autonomous and effective upon changing the circumstances that they found in their world.

KEY PEOPLE 2

René Descartes (1591–1650)

Descartes is often regarded as the founder of modern philosophy. He was also a mathematician. His aim was to formulate a new starting point for philosophical investigation, and to use modern scientific methods to devise a metaphysics for the modern age. His famous assertion, '*I think therefore I am*' (known as the *cogito*) was the basis upon which he built his philosophical system. Descartes argued that knowledge of the existence of the self, the 'I', was the only sure, certain starting place for asking philosophical questions. As such, he situated the individual at the centre of human concern. This broke with the traditional Aristotelian philosophy that took existence to be based on human beings being part of an object whole. In other words, Descartes was influential in providing the theoretical basis of individualism, from which the political ideology of liberalism developed.

Both Macpherson and Sabine are among the authors who emphasise that Hobbes' thought was based upon the development of a 'science of politics'. From this standpoint they argue that Hobbes' method was a failure. However, as stated above, this is clearly a reduction of the manifold parts that make up Hobbes' method. As well as the medieval legacy and the scientific revolution that no doubt influenced him there is yet another area to consider. Michael Oakeshott has maintained, most notably, that the philosophical base of Hobbes' work and the role of contingency throughout his method are also important. Oakeshott has argued against seeing Hobbes as a scientific systematiser. It is Hobbes' system of philosophy that ought to be viewed as giving coherence to his thought. What is important in his method is the way he links philosophy to reason, and the specific character of reasoning as Hobbes sees it. Oakeshott maintains that for Hobbes, philosophy is the world as it appears to reason and, in general, it appears as a world of cause and effect. The mechanistic element in Hobbes' work derives not so much from his adoption of the scientific method of geometry, as such, but the way this was applied to his philosophy. The scientific element in Hobbes' work gave his rather complex system of thought a degree of rationalism. Oakeshott is critical of this aspect of Hobbes' work, but he does see it as only an 'aspect', not the entirety of his ideas. The use of scientific concepts in a philosophical system undermines it. This is because Hobbes moves continually between a vision of politics that is based on experience and one that is based on artificial, 'hypothetical efficient' (according to Oakeshott) notions. In other words, by introducing scientific method into his philosophical system Hobbes confuses theory and practice in his work.

Oakeshott's interpretation of Hobbes' method has received a mixed reception. Many have interpreted his ideas as overly creative, or even fanciful. However, if we take it that a key element of Oakeshott's analysis is to highlight the degree of contingency in Hobbes' work, as opposed to its secure 'scientific' basis, then it may be seen that other authors have agreed with his proposition. For example, Wolin (1961: 257–262) has discussed the use of language in *Leviathan*. He maintains that

Thinking about Hobbes' method, is it possible to construct a theoretical model that promises certainty? And then all you have to do is apply it to day-to-day political practice? Can politics be perfected in this way? What are the problems with translating theory into practice?

Hobbes understood that the political order not only involved institutions of power, the law and so on, but also a system of communication. He therefore attempted to set clear meanings to the concepts of political language (e.g. justice, rights) via the artificial definition of *Leviathan*. This brings us back once more to the place of both nominalism and rhetoric in his work. Wolin highlights the intended polemical effect of *Leviathan* at the time he was writing. This text was addressed to the public at large with the goal of shaping opinion in favour of shaping a rational polity. The context of Hobbes' thought, the upheaval of the times, needs to be remembered even when discussing his method. The way in which he brought together the legitimate schools of philosophical, theological and scientific knowledge to the questions of his time was the genius of the Hobbesian political imaginary.

Hobbes on human nature

Leviathan opens with an account of man that depicts the human mind as epi-phenomenal. However, a debate reigns as to how far this initial characterisation persists after the first nine chapters (Warrender 1957: 91–93). Suffice it to say here that, in general, Hobbes had a weak sense of the self. This is what another author has conceptualised as a 'passive human identity' (Hollis 1977: 33). Such an interpreta-tion fits into the above discussion which relates Hobbes' method to Descartes. However, this relatively weak notion of self in his work remains paradoxical in the light of his individualism. On the one hand, Hobbes has been seen as a founder of modern individualist liberal polities. Yet in philosophical terms he underdevelops the idea of what an individual actually is, and how autonomous individuals are from the strictures (and structures) of their environment and social institutions.

The influence of geometry and the deductive reasoning of cause and effect may be seen most forcefully in Part I of *Leviathan* where Hobbes writes 'Of Man'. The sense of being in motion with him, as we read him, is an unmistakable part of engaging with the text. For Hobbes, man is a creature of sense. The human mind receives sensations that give rise to his receptive powers. These receptive powers are images, imagination and ideas which memory can recollect. From the faculty of recollection man derives prudence, a natural wisdom endowing him with foresight. Out of his receptive powers comes man's emotions or active powers that concern his endeavours: desire and aversion. Hobbes gives these attributes of humankind a predominant emphasis. In this way he indicates that man is, above all, a passionate rather than rational creature. Furthermore, the accent is on desires. He seems to consider man's aversions, especially to death, as axiomatic. Those things which man desires he loves, Hobbes says, he calls 'good'. Objects of aversion he hates and calls evil. As different men love and hate different things there can be no objective good or evil. The end-product of man's emotions is 'felicity'. This is the never-ending succession of man's desires. The means of acquiring felicity is power, which becomes a desire in itself to ensure future security.

'And thus it follows that I put for a general inclination of all mankind a perpetual and restless desire of Power after power, that ceaseth only in death' (Macpherson 1968: 161).

It is in the very act of 'willing' these things that human individuality becomes established. Hobbes describes felicity only in terms of the individual will. There cannot be any communal 'felicity' within his way of thinking. Here is the founding moment of Hobbes' assumption that the individual is the basis of society. Man's virtues are the thoughts and actions serviceable to the pursuit of felicity. Concurrently, defects hinder this pursuit, especially pride and vainglory.

Hobbes' description of man's nature has led Strauss to conclude that Hobbesian man is a 'political hedonist'(Strauss 1952: 129, 170). Yet it appears that this idea is a little misconceived given what Hobbes actually states. Hobbes is not interested in generalising about human ethics. His discussion of these areas of human nature is predicated on the back of his view that human beings, ultimately, are just trying to survive. It is the idea of self-preservation that informs his view of human emotions, not a psychological examination of the moral malaise of modern man. Furthermore, although Hobbes is interested in constructing a model of man, he makes no moral judgement about man's nature: 'The desires and other passions of men are in themselves no sin' (Macpherson 1968: 187).

In this sense Hobbes is a modern. He takes the human condition as separate from the kingdom of God and argues that man acts in accordance with the experience that he finds on earth. An earth that God gave him, maybe, but still a world where morality is not dictated from above but originates in the reality of human existence. Hobbes is exhibiting the characteristic of toleration for which the classical liberal tradition is known. This is a tradition that has been criticised by those who maintain that the emphasis on individual 'felicity' does create evil in the world, and that only some kind of communal 'felicity' can make the world a more just place. Rousseau, through his concept of the 'general will', was one such theorist who challenged Hobbes on this basis. He argued against what he saw as the concept of the autonomous individual in Hobbes' thought. Importantly he claimed that man was a product of social institutions. Hobbes had not recognised the importance of social structures in shaping man's desires and aversions, even his moral values. By arguing this case (see Chapter 6) he revealed an absence not only in Hobbes' theory but also in the whole social contract approach. Firmly embedded in the tradition of Rousseau, Macpherson argues that Hobbesian man was a product of a 'possessive market society'. However, it may well be the case that Macpherson stretches the point too far by insisting that man is *only* the product of his social environment. As Johnston points out, in terms of the rhetoric tradition the identification of man as a rational egoist may be seen as a model used by Hobbes to agitate against the reality of the non-rational character of man (Johnston 1986: 37).

Fast forward

> **Go to Chapter 4** for Macpherson's argument about 'possessive market society', where it is discussed in relation to Locke.

The state of nature

There is a radical conflict between man's nature and his natural condition. The recognition of this is the prerequisite for the establishment of civil society. The natural condition is one stripped of all social being, an apolitical situation, a state of nature. This is, for Hobbes, a hypothetical state. It never existed as such. Its purpose is to serve analysis, to stand in contrast to political society. Thus it is a timeless realm, not prior to civil society but the symbolic order into which a society, ripped apart by disagreements, might fall. It does not take much imagination to realise that here, in his concept of the state of nature, Hobbes was drawing upon the chaotic potential of the English civil war. In relation to his methodology, Hobbes' state of nature serves the rhetorical, philosophical and scientific aspects of his work. First, it pertains to the actual circumstances of his time, a potentiality that all his contemporary readers would recognise, a fear many of them might also carry. Second, it is a quite sophisticated philosophical notion. It is an analytical tool that has been devised in a rational manner and may be situated within his system of thought. Third, it maintains the deductive steps that Hobbes is using, carrying the reader through his geometric 'scientific' analysis from the discussion of human nature through to the actual construction of the desirable polity.

In the state of nature, Hobbes maintains that every man has a right to natural self-preservation and an absolute freedom to do as he wills. Freedom is defined, in keeping with classical liberalism, purely negatively. It is mere licence. Paradoxically the state of nature, which at first appears to be a place of such great freedom for individuals, becomes the site for a challenge to the individual pursuit of 'felicity'. When each individual is unshackled by rules, laws or institutions the human condition turns into a '*war of all against all*'. The certainty man has of obtaining his desires is, precisely, nil. In the state of nature individuals, regardless of their physical capabilities, possess a roughly equivalent strength and cunning, so none can be secure. There is consequently great fear in the state of nature, especially the fear of violent death. It is this prime emotion which purges pride, illuminates man's natural prudence, and literally knocks him to his senses. The sense that it provokes is 'reason'. This is the foundation upon which the modern polity will be based. Hobbes is maintaining that fear (particularly fear of death), insecurity and self-preservation has an overwhelming effect on man in the state of nature. So overwhelming that it leads to civil society via the laws of nature.

Unlike prudence, Hobbes is indicating that reason is an acquired skill. It is an innate capacity of man but it is not one that every man uses to the same degree and skill. When man, as a whole, does exercise it, he comes to realise that the pursuit of 'felicity' is threatened by the continual competition of the state of nature. This realisation becomes the basis for the 'articles of peace'. The truths associated with right reason are the laws of nature. However, as Oakeshott has argued, it is something of a misnomer to call the truths of reason the laws of nature. They become so only once embedded in the commands of God or the civil sovereign. When they exist in the minds of men they are constituted as 'theorems'. Again, this indicates that Hobbes' view of human nature is quite sophisticated in the sense that human beings are portrayed as having a great many potentialities (including being potentially violent, selfish, irrational and other negative attributes) which different circumstances will contrive to bring out. Hobbes maintains that what humankind will be is dependent upon their external circumstances. Hence, if the social environment is an ordered and rational one, the human potentialities that will be provoked will tend to be more pacific.

 Fast forward

Go to Chapter 7. It was not until the time of Burke that modern historical method became established.

The social contract

Once men have reason enough, fear will compel them to see the absolute necessity of establishing a rational polity under a single sovereign so that 'commodious living' is assured. The social contract is the vehicle by which Hobbes seeks to explain how man moves from a state of nature to civil society. Note that, once again (as in the case of the state of nature itself), Hobbes is not saying that there was an actual contract that was signed by all men sometime in history! Not only would this be absurd, it would also require an understanding of history that Hobbes did not have. Modern historical method did not really develop until the time of Burke (see Chapter 7). For Hobbes the contract was a notional contract, a vehicle for expressing the way in which men mutually consented to leave the state of nature, construct civil society and 'will not to will'. The agreement of the contract is a key point in Hobbes' thought, the moment when men enter a sociable existence and undertake political obligations. They agree to transfer their natural rights via civil society to a sovereign authority. Most importantly this act is one of transference rather than renunciation. Men cannot stop being what they naturally are. The potential to 'will' again as they did in the state of nature remains. But a rational choice has been made due to the paradoxical un-freedoms of the natural condition. The fact that this is 'transference' is established in Hobbes' work through the notion of authorisation. The sovereign is taken to be a representative of the rights of the individual members of civil society (not of a unity of interests). He receives all men's natural rights and is therefore authorised to will in place of their separate wills.

Fast forward

Go to Chapter 6 to see how Rousseau was a social contract theorist with a difference! Hobbes and Locke used social contract theory and came to liberal conclusions. Rousseau, however, used social contract theory to develop a theory of collective democratic politics.

In authorising the sovereign, individuals become obligated to the ruler's law and to pledge themselves to use all their strength and power on his behalf. Because the contract goes against the grain of all human passion, man's obligations can only be ensured by an external force; one that is self-imposed, but it is still an external authority. This is the power given to *Leviathan*.

For Hobbes, then, civil society is a purely artificial association arising from the social contract. This point of view was in quite sharp contrast to the pre-modern notions of 'The Great Chain of Being' and the 'Divine Right of Kings' which took civil society to be a natural order ordained by God. The radical departure of Hobbes was to deny this long- standing claim and to show the artifice behind the construction of modern nation states. Furthermore, it is not God who constitutes the state. It is constituted as a social sphere only through the existence of the sovereign power. This goes against the arguments of Locke (see Chapter 4) and Rousseau (Chapter 6), who follow Hobbes in the social contract tradition. One of the most important reasons why Hobbes maintains that social order comes from without rather than from within is his view that man's nature cannot be fundamentally altered. Unlike for Rousseau (and later Marx; see Chapter 9), man's nature is not perfected by the establishment of the social but accommodated by it. Nor is civil society the site for man's salvation. Such an idea would be inconceivable to Hobbes given the ceaseless character of 'felicity'. The benefit to man's soul of living in a civil society under political authority is rather a limited one. It provides the circumstances for a peaceful existence, no more, no less.

Civil law is defined by the will of the sovereign. *Leviathan* creates the distinction between justice and injustice, right and wrong (as far as this world is concerned). No law may be deemed 'unjust' as all rulings are passed with but one intention: the preservation of the peace. One of the sovereign's most important duties in this respect is to establish laws of property. It is only by virtue of delimiting property rights that men are able to claim ownership. This is opposite the state of nature where no man's property (including his own life) is secure. This is one of the great advantages of the rule of law and it is central to all liberal political theories.

Fast forward

Go to Chapter 4: Locke's ideas are often studied alongside those of Hobbes. This is because he too was a social contract theorist, an Englishman influenced by the constitutional changes of the seventeenth century and a founding father of liberalism.

As well as being the definer of the law, *Leviathan* also enforces it. The sovereign is authorised to place subjects before a court if they breach his rules. This right to punish is founded upon the sovereign's own natural right. In this way Hobbes avoids the suggestion that subjects will their own punishment, an issue that was to be problematic for Rousseau when he declared that men ought to be 'forced to be free'.

The *Leviathan*, then, is a constituted authority which men voluntarily, through use of their reason, decide to assent to, giving up day-to-day political power for the sake of a peaceful existence. In the end that is what we all want, isn't it? A quiet life! Well, early liberal thinkers seemed to think so. It may seem, from the description thus far, that as *Leviathan* both defines and enforces the law it is an authoritarian authority, albeit self-imposed. The sovereign, on the face of it, might institute an absolutely regulated society, one where subjects obeyed his every command. In this way Hobbes' *Leviathan* might surely be replicating the Leviathan of the Bible, a monster which symbolised the power of evil.

DISCUSSION POINT

Should morality play any part in politics? If we accept Hobbesian man as naturally competitive and self-interested, then should politics simply be a means to contain this competition? Should we expect political leaders to act more morally than the voters, given that their nature is the same as everybody else's?

However, such a view as this would be a perversion of Hobbes' intent. He would have been aware that, ultimately, the symbolism of *Leviathan* was used in the Bible to show how evil is always defeated by the power of good. There are a number of ways in which Hobbes indicates that freedom of the individual will be protected. First, the subject always maintains a 'true freedom'. He is under no obligation to accuse himself if he breaks the law. Second, Hobbes states that individuals have a right to protect themselves if *Leviathan* fails to do so. Should such a situation arise, the purpose of *Leviathan* would have failed and men would be thrown into a state of nature. Third, the sovereign is instituted to maintain the peace, but like all men (because after all, whether *Leviathan* is a monarchy or a republic, the sovereign will be a man) he endeavours to preserve himself and pursue 'felicity'. His prudence will indicate to him that this is best achieved through minimal government. There exists, then, for Hobbes a large 'silence of the law' where men are as free in civil society as they are in the state of nature. 'In all kinds of actions by the laws permitted, men have the liberty of doing what their own reasons shall suggest, for the most profitable to themselves' (Macpherson 1968: 264).

Finally, the second law of nature (that men must allow others as much liberty as they would allow themselves) dictates that individuals are guaranteed a basic equality. The sovereign must dispense justice evenly if men are to accept his rule. All the above points highlight why it is that Hobbes is seen by many commentators as a founding father of the liberal tradition.

Liberalism and democracy

For Hobbes, a human being is an 'individual', not in the sense of his self-consciousness but in the activity of 'willing'. From birth to death the individual as imagination and will constitutes an amazing unit. The relationship to other individuals is purely external. We are unique and discrete beings. The recognition of 'individuality' by Hobbes is, of course, in no sense a moral obligation but a 'fact', a philosophical and scientific postulate. While these individuals may be collected together (e.g. in a nation state), and made to represent one another, they can never compose a whole, a 'collective', as such. Their individuality can never be lost. Natural man is the stuff of civil society and Hobbes was concerned that whatever else modern civilisation turned out to be it had to be capable of accommodating these individuals without the destruction of their individuality. Otherwise humanity faced ruin.

Hobbes was clearly no democrat. There was no such thing as the 'people', no 'general will' or 'common good'. In *Leviathan* he advances a number of arguments to support the view that monarchy is the most appropriate form of the institution of sovereignty. However, in principle, the Hobbesian system may be used to justify democratic forms of government. The intellectual window of opportunity that Hobbes opened up, which allowed ideas regarding liberal democracy to grow, stems largely from his views of representation. By placing the source of representation in the authorisation of *Leviathan*, Hobbes, for the first time, put forward the idea that individuals could devise a representative authority. This was a departure from the traditional idea that only God could be represented (in the monarch). Hobbes' perhaps unwitting democratic move was to illustrate how it was possible for people to be the foundations of authority through a social contract. Such ideas may be discerned in various representations of the people's acts across the world. This idea became part of the notion of modern democracy and, of course, gave rise to different models of representation across nation states.

For the readers of his day there was an ambiguity in Hobbes' work regarding the ultimate form of good government. This led his contemporaries, of all political persuasions, to condemn him. The republicans obviously took him to be a monarchist. The monarchists condemned him both because he appeared to recognise the possibility of other forms of government, and because his recommendations in favour of monarchy bore no relationship to their own. Hobbes clearly did not follow the traditional monarchist view regarding absolute right and an 'absolutist' style of ruling. It may be said that the fact that Hobbes was accepted by neither political faction of his day was a mark of his intelligence and genuine desire to construct a coherent polity. He may well have believed that the monarchists claimed too much for authority and the republicans too much for liberty. For him, genuine authority could only derive from an act of the will of whoever is obliged. Similarly, real liberty ought not to be so destructive as to have no boundaries and to endanger the whole society. Such a tension, between the rights of the state and those of the individuals, is one that liberal states continue to live with to this day. Without being himself a liberal (merely historically this was not possible), Hobbes has become one of the leading theorists of this school of political thought.

Summary

Hobbes' ideas along with those of John Locke constitute the key features of classical liberal political theory. They may be summarised as follows. The individual is the basis of human society, and this is true in the state of nature and civil society. Entering civil society is a rational choice. It is an act of individuals freely willing and constructing this form of society. In this sense political communities are artificial associations. Political obligations arise as a consequence of the social contract that individuals voluntarily enter into. This contract obligates each individual to preserve the sovereign authority and abide by the law. In return, government ought to give a large degree of personal freedom. Government ought to be minimal. Civil authority must guarantee individuals freedom to form voluntary associations of their choosing (religious, economic or otherwise). The state provides and maintains a set of rules which enable subjects to pursue their own various ends.

The character of the political in Hobbes' *Leviathan*

Hobbes reconciles equality of justice with inequality of wealth, status and education. These are not taken to be potential areas of conflict because the range of inequalities derives from areas other than those relating to the political circumstances of members of *Leviathan*. Hobbes clearly distinguishes the parameters of the political. This is of central importance. It was recognised by Carl Schmitt, often called the twentieth-century Hobbes, and adopted to his theory of 'decisionism' (Schmitt 1996). A view such as this could not exist today, where social issues are of paramount importance to political decisions. However, this point does raises important questions regarding the character of what Hobbes takes as the political (in other words, what is politics?). The manner by which the political is delineated by Hobbes makes it questionable whether Hobbes' 'mortal God' could be sufficiently capable of binding a political community and, consequently, able to enforce a single will. Civil society for Hobbes is completely artificial, it has no internal regulating force (no 'community' or culturally binding source). It is also entirely dependent on an equally artificial sovereign. This makes the bond between ruler and ruled rather weak. According to Wolin this gives rise to a 'fatal contradiction' in Hobbes' theory. He allowed that private property constituted a form of private power and that sovereign power relied on the private power of members of civil society to enforce his rule. However, while the sovereign was dependent on private power the ability to compel subjects to enforce the law was minimal. Hobbes recognised this problem and devised a language of unity to bring subjects and sovereign closer. Yet it remains that no strong source of obligation unites them. Wolin concludes that Hobbes is naïve to assume that in a world of egoists there would be no conflict between individuals and the sovereign, and all that was necessary to erase the tension between public and private ends was the establishment of a 'publicly instituted ego'.

This criticism rests upon the assumption that *Leviathan*'s authority derives, essentially, from its powers of coercion. This view may be mistaken. As pointed out above, Hobbes' *Leviathan* does not institute an authoritarian polity but minimal government. Furthermore, the conclusion that Hobbes' political community was theoretically weak is one that is possible to reach only by rejecting what is the most discussed topic in *Leviathan*, namely religious and spiritual matters. Oakeshott argues that Hobbes has a civil theology which is an essential part of his conception of political community and accounts for the necessary 'glue' which binds ruler and ruled. No distinction is made between natural, rational and God's law. All the laws that relate to the conduct of men are, in the end, to be found in the Scriptures, and in this way they become laws. The Scriptures are acknowledged to be an arbitrary selection of writings. They are nothing but interpretation, and interpretation is a matter of authority. In the state of nature interpretation is an individual act but when men move to civil society they transfer their natural right to interpret the Scriptures with the rest of their natural rights to the sovereign. All authority in political society rests with the sovereign, including spiritual authority. The political community is therefore a Christian commonwealth. Sovereign interpretation of the Scriptures is equivalent to God's law. The idea of a Christian commonwealth adds a new sanction to its subjects' obligations, uniting the political community under God's law. Thus religious belief had a great practical application for Hobbes.

Hobbes' notion of political community arises from his analysis of civil society as pure artifice, and this requires an external authority to give it cohesiveness. This does not necessarily exhibit a weak sense of political obligation if one allows for Hobbes' civil theology. However, what may be said to be put into question by the way that Hobbes defines the boundaries of the political is the very status of 'political community' in his theory. That is, it is arguable whether a political community, as such, can be identified in *Leviathan* at all. The members of civil society appear, for the most part, as apolitical. Their only real political act is to establish *Leviathan* in the first instance. The only other political involvement that Hobbes allows individuals in civil society is to reject the sovereign should he fail to protect their security. However, given the strong religious bond obligating subjects to the ruler's law, the freedom allowed by the 'silence of the law', and the awareness that Leviathan may take up the sword against any transgressions, it appears that revolt would be unlikely. Of course, this is precisely what Hobbes was aiming for. The contract serves to obligate both the subject's right and power to act politically. He is to submit to the will of the sovereign in all matters that are deemed politically relevant. Furthermore, if one accepts Hobbes' mechanistic notion of human nature, as given in the first nine chapters, this takes away man's potential to be an autonomous political being. What all this suggests is that in *Leviathan* we have the expression of an anti-political text *par excellence*.

Revision notes

Hobbes' political thought contains the key features of classical liberal political theory. They may be summarised as follows;

1   The individual is the basis of human society. This is true in the state of nature and civil society.

2   Entering civil society is a rational choice. It is an act of individuals freely willing and constructing this form of society.

3   Political communities are artificial associations.
4   Political obligations arise as a consequence of the social contract that individuals voluntarily enter into. This contract obligates each individual to preserve the sovereign authority and abide by the law.
5   Government gives a large degree of personal freedom. Government ought to be strong but minimal.
6   Civil authority must guarantee individuals freedom to form voluntary associations of their choosing (religious, economic or otherwise).
7   The state provides and maintains a set of rules that enable subjects to pursue their own various ends.

Bibliography

Aubrey, J. (1982) *Brief Lives: A Modern English Version*, ed. Richard Barber, Woodbridge: Boydell.

Flathman, R.E. (1993) *Thomas Hobbes: Skepticism, Individuality and Chastened Politics*, London: Sage.

Hollis, M. (1977) *Models of Man: Philosophical Thoughts on Social Action*, Cambridge: Cambridge University Press.

Johnston, D. (1986) *The Rhetoric of Leviathan: Thomas Hobbes and the Politics of Cultural Transformation*, Princeton, NJ: Princeton University Press.

Macpherson, C.B. (ed.) (1968) *Leviathan*, Harmondsworth: Penguin.

Oakeshott, M. (ed.) (1946) *Leviathan*, Oxford: Blackwell.

Sabine, G.H. (1973) *A History of Political Theory* (4th edn), London: Holt, Rinehard & Winston.

Schmitt, C. (1996) *The Concept of the Political*, Chicago: Chicago University Press.

Strauss, L. (1952), *The Political Philosophy of Hobbes: Its Basis and Its Genesis*, London: Chicago University Press.

Warrender, H. (1957) *The Political Philosophy of Hobbes: His Theory of Obligation*, Oxford: Clarendon Press.

Wolin, S.S. (1961) *Politics and Vision: Continuity and Innovation in Western Political Thought*, London: Allen & Unwin.

Further reading

Since *Leviathan* was first published there have been countless editions by a range of publishers across the world. From these there are two particular editions that are well known and are recommended reading. C.B. Macpherson places Hobbes firmly in his historical setting. He also interprets Hobbes' ideas and intent in relation to his own socialist ideological perspective. Michael Oakeshott interprets Hobbes philosophically rather than ideologically and is concerned with showing the coherence, or not, of Hobbes' system of thought.

Further reading of Hobbes' own work would include (1983) *De Cive: The English version, entitled in the first edition Philosophicall rudiments concerning government and society*, Oxford: Clarendon Press.

A wide selection of Hobbes' writings are presented in a useful reader: R.S. Peters (1962) *Body, Man and Citizen*, London: Collier-Macmillan. In addition, a useful encounter with Hobbes' ethics may be made with D. Boonin-Vail (1994) *Thomas Hobbes and the Science of Moral Virtue*, Cambridge: Cambridge University Press, and M. Oakeshott (1975) *Hobbes on Civil Association*, Berkeley: University of California Press. For extra reading on Hobbes in context see J. Mitchell (1993) *Not by Reason Alone: Religion, History, and Identity in Early Modern Political Thought*, London: University of Chicago Press.

John Locke

[H]e that will not give just occasion to think that all government in the world is the product only of force and violence, and that men live together by no other rules but that of beasts, where the strongest carries it . . . must of necessity find another rise of government, another original of political power.

(Second Treatise of Government)

Locke's theories have had a profound and enduring influence throughout the history of the modern Western world. Today, two distinct strands of Lockean influence still run through our modern consciousness. Locke's philosophy of knowledge, embodied in his *Essay Concerning Human Understanding,* fired the scientific rationalism of the modern age, while Lockean political theory, best captured in his *Second Treatise of Government*, remains a foundation of liberal democratic politics. There is no overt logical connection between these two strands of Locke's writings and, although the *Essay Concerning Human Understanding* remains a recognised classic in its field, it is the political works alone which concern us. Of these, the *Second Treatise of Government* – and the three letters on toleration – remain foundational texts in the development of liberal thinking. When you read these works you will see that they contain a bundle of ideas tied into an argument that, at times, is overwhelmingly familiar to anyone with an ear for political talk. Locke's articulation of the concept of private property – revolutionary in its time – is now commonplace, as is his conception of a separation of legislative and executive powers within the state. His argument for religious toleration has, with a little logical extension in the hands of subsequent thinkers, become the bedrock for the notion of cultural toleration essential to multicultural pluralist societies that make up the modern Western world. Taken up (along with Montesquieu) as an icon of liberal consciousness by the founding fathers of the USA, Locke's ideas have been spread globally in popularised form. However, his status as an icon of liberalism belies two significant facts. The first of these is that his most influential work – the *Second Treatise of Government* – expresses the thoughts of a political activist writing for a particular time and place (England in crisis in the seventeenth century). If it is the case that 'the purpose of Locke was to justify the English Revolution of 1688', as W.S. Carpenter has claimed in his introduction to *The Two Treatises of Government* (Locke 1924: v), it is questionable whether it is appropriate to treat Locke's work as a universal set of principles. For this reason, we have to consider whether his ideas provide an appropriate basis for the conduct of political life in the modern Western world. Having said this, Locke's *Second Treatise of Government* is clearly a work of political philosophy. It attempts to deal with the universal principles of the human condition, focusing on the ethical basis of power in a world where humans must do politics to survive. As John Plamenatz has argued, Locke's political writing is not simply 'an apology for a particular form of government' (Plamenatz 1992: 331).

This issue leads into the second fact, which is that many political theorists today do not consider the arguments in the *Second Treatise of Government* to be the most coherent articulation of the principles of liberal democratic government. So, despite Locke's enormous reputation, we find that, in addition to considering the historical significance of his writings, we must examine the internal coherence of his argument.

Liberalism

This term 'liberal' has to be used with care, as it can be applied to the full range of political approaches within mainstream democratic politics. It originates in the concept of liberality, which means generous allowing, and has come to be associated with the idea of letting things run freely. By the eighteenth century, this idea had become incorporated into a political argument by influential theorists such as Adam Smith and Tom Paine. They argued that, contrary to the practice of many rulers, the state should let social and economic arrangements take care of themselves wherever possible. The state's role was to strongly enforce minimal laws designed to protect the individual's opportunity to express their opinions and beliefs, and to develop their economic prospects. Two key elements of this philosophy – now known as classical liberalism – were provided a century before by John Locke. These were that each individual has a natural right to make and use private property, and to use their mind and body as they think fit, within broadly defined limits of equal opportunity for every individual. A key element of this philosophy (also provided by Locke) is the notion of toleration. For individuals to be able to express themselves freely, they must all be tolerant towards each other's different modes of self-expression.

In later centuries, the idea of equal opportunity, mixed with a growing perception of social causes of inequalities, has led to the development of arguments for greater state activity – specifically for state programmes of economic and cultural 're-balancing'. These notions, while liberal at root, are at odds with the minimalism of classical liberalism. In recent times they have been attacked by the ' New Right', who take the principles of classical liberalism as the blueprint for their 'neo-liberal' politics. This neo-liberalism is associated with Thatcherism in the UK and the right-wing Republicanism of Ronald Reagan and Newt Gingrich in the USA.

In considering Locke's political theory, and the commentaries upon it, we shall see that issues about which Locke was arguing in his works are entwined with issues derived from the importance of Lockean ideas, as translated by those who followed him into principles of political systems. And all the time we must wrestle with the conundrum: 'Do we treat Locke's ideas as historical artefacts – useful only for the insight into how people used to think? Or perhaps we should see them as ideas which are being misapplied in our modern world and outside of their time and place, or, again, as ideas with the capacity to outgrow their time and place of conception?'

The glorious revolution

The British monarchy was restored in 1660 after the dictatorship of Oliver Cromwell had come to its end. The first new monarch was Charles II, who, in a compromise with

continued

Parliament, was allowed to rule provided he kept his Catholic sympathies quiet. Initially he was supported by an overwhelmingly Royalist Parliament. This support gradually subsided as his absolutist and Catholic tendencies became more pronounced. In 1685 he was succeeded by his brother, James II, who quickly converted to Catholicism and overturned legal restrictions on the Catholic population of Britain. He also began to build alliances with Catholic foreign powers, notably the French monarchy, who had long been hostile to Protestant parliamentary Britain.

In 1688, Parliament revolted against James' rule and invited the Dutch Protestant, Prince William of Orange, to take the Crown. William's reputation as governor was matched by his reputation as a soldier. Within days of his arrival in November 1688 his forces were bolstered by thousands of English Protestants. James' generals deserted him, and he fled to France. King William agreed to a new constitutional settlement in which monarchic powers were reduced and those of Parliament increased. This agreement established the constitution arrangement which, much modified in Parliament's favour, exists in the UK today.

Locke and the English revolution

Locke's life runs through a period of great upheaval in English political life. He was born in 1632, a little more than a decade before the English civil war ripped through every layer of England's social, economic and political life, and he wrote his great works in the shadows of the struggles for power culminating in the glorious revolution.

Locke's class and party were set from childhood. He was born into a family which converted their trade into an entrepreneurial business. His father, from a staunch family of tailors who, like many members of the fast growing middle class, was a Puritan, left the business to become a lawyer, and then joined the Protestant parliamentary army against Charles I's aristocratic forces. Locke's political existence began when he was sent to the prestigious Westminster School. Here the two main strands of his adult life began to take distinct form. We see the beginnings of Locke the scholar; at Westminster he studied for a scholarship to Oxford University. We also see the beginnings of Locke the political thinker and actor, for, throughout his time at Westminster, he had to deal with the strongly royalist leanings of his teachers and fellow students. The school itself is within hearing distance of the site of King Charles I's execution, which took place in 1649 while Locke was still there. (The moment echoes through Locke's political writings in the many references to the bottom-line right of free individuals to execute those who violate their life, liberty or estate.) At Oxford, Locke became attracted to the growing practice of experimental science, and by studying to be a medical doctor he allowed his interest to develop in a practical and career-oriented manner. It is one of those quirks of fate that led him in this guise to meet, treat and cure Lord Shaftesbury in 1666.

Shaftesbury was soon to become one of the most influential and powerful men in British politics, and this moment of fate propelled the scholarly Locke into political life. He became a close friend and a key adviser to Shaftesbury, who in turn became leader of the parliamentarian defence against Charles II's attempts to return the state to monarchic absolutism. Locke was radicalised by Shaftesbury and his ideas moved from a Hobbesian conservatism (recorded in his writings on toleration written in 1660–1661) to the radical liberalism expressed in the *Two Treatises of Government* published in 1689. He was also embroiled in an intense and dangerous power struggle, which culminated in 1683 in a failed coup attempt by Shaftesbury and his associates, followed by a state purge in which most of those captured by the King's forces were executed. Locke escaped in 1683 to Holland, where he lived in exile for six years under a false name. During this period, his political sensibilities were kept sharp, as continued attempts by the Crown to have him extradited to England reminded him of his precarious position. He also witnessed the arrival of many Huguenots, escaping the religious intolerance of the French absolutist King Louis XIV. Furthermore, the condition of exile and the causes of this condition were thrown into stark relief by the practices of Locke's hosts, the Dutch liberal nonconformists, 'who were puritan in matters of conduct as they were tolerant in matters of belief' (Cranston 1957: 233). The combination of over-powerful monarchs and religious fanatics hounding people out of their homes clearly affected Locke's thinking, as is evident in the letters on toleration written while in Holland. The theme of the over-mighty state is also central to the second treatise, published shortly after Locke's return from exile in 1689. It is not clear if he wrote this while in Holland or before (Locke was so worried about being identified as the author that he had the works published anonymously and refused to admit authorship, even in the years after the Catholic monarchy had been overthrown). In either case, it is a powerful tract against absolutist monarchic power.

Whether as an *agent provocateur* in England or as a writer on the run, Locke's production of a work which so challenged the monarchic state of his time provides a serious reason to regard his works as the writings of an activist working against the powers which threatened his religious and political identity and his personal existence. This in itself does not preclude treating these works as also having insights into the political condition generally and therefore having something useful to tell us today. Neither do the theological arguments that at first sight seem to provide the means (and, in the first treatise, the ends) of his political argument. Like us, Locke's audience would see that politics – the use of power – involved ethical issues. However, unlike many people today, they could not conceive of a secular basis for ethical conduct – by and large people understood their world in religious terms. Locke as a Protestant was very religious, and he attempted to articulate a religious understanding that set out the rightful terms and conditions for the use of power. Yet Locke's Protestantism was fuelled by scientific rationalism and he was also concerned to establish practical means for establishing a working political order. So, while the political claims are set out in religious terms which may not persuade modern secular minds, this religious understanding is underpinned with rationalist terms of universally applicable principles for building and maintaining a workable polity of free-thinking individuals. It is therefore possible to consider Locke's arguments as both of his time and also relevant to ours. This possibility becomes a necessity when one takes into account the incorporation of Locke's ideas into the fundamental structure of the constitution of the many liberal states that populate the modern world.

Locke's political theory

In Locke's time, political power and the religious edict did not come apart in practice nor, to most minds, did it come apart in theory, but Locke understood that, whatever the source of power, different types of power exist, and a distinct sphere of politics can be recognised. He also recognised that arguments concerning the proper form and scope of government could be built from an analysis of the fit of political activity into the general conditions of human endeavour. As we shall see below, he presents an argument for an ethical and practical system of government, which is derived from a perception of the uneasy relationship that humans uniquely have with their natural environment.

Locke argued that God has created a special set of conditions for human life. The conditions are manifest in the relationship of the human mind and body to the natural order of the world. He pointed out that, at a basic level of experience, our understanding of what is real corresponds to factual truth: there is a relationship between the logic and mechanisms of our cognitive processes and the logic and mechanisms of the world outside us. There is also a relationship between our practical action and our environment – we have the physical capacity and unique dexterity to be able to convert our environment into a purpose-built design. We can understand the world and we can change it to our design.

God has a purpose in giving humankind this gift. The purpose becomes clear when you follow through the implications of possessing these abilities. Humans have the ability to think of the principles of how things work. To understand how they work is the basis of being able to make them. What is also needed is the physical power to break up the order of one's physical environment and the dexterity of hand to shape its broken parts into newly designed objects. This unique dexterity, Locke noted, is possessed by humans and, combined with their reasoning powers, enables humans uniquely among all of the creatures of the earth to act into their environment and restructure it. Only humans can design and make an artificial environment. For a religious man it is not hard to see a God-given reason for this special power. It is part of a greater design. Locke recalls from the Bible God's words to Adam as he casts him from the garden of Eden: '"As long as thou livest shalt thou live by labour" and, "In the sweat of thy face thy shall eat thy bread", these words were not spoken personally to Adam, but in him, as their representative to mankind, this being the curse upon mankind because of the fall' (Locke 1924: 32). But Locke suggests that this destiny is not as bad as it seems. We are, by nature, creative artisans and traders. We must make our world, we must shape our destiny. So God gives us the liberty to create our own destiny to some degree, and the destiny we choose to make will show God the character of our being, so that he can judge us.

One does not have to be religious to see that Locke makes a point about the uniquely human capacity to radically alter our environment, nor to see that this ability expresses a uniquely human power of governance. We are placed in a political relationship to our world. The precise nature of this political relationship is rooted in the way in which we work upon our world – the way in which we convert it from its 'God-given' natural state into man-made possessions. For Locke, the political condition of human life springs out of our production of private property.

Private property

Property, says Locke, originates in each individual's 'own person' in their natural possessions. It lies first in 'the "labour" of his body and the "work" of his hands' (Locke 1924: 130). (This second category, being distinguished from mere physical labour, implies that the mental energy used in generating ideas is as much a property as the physical energy used in their application.) Through labour and work, this energy is passed into the natural environment, even as it changes it into artificial products. For example, by cutting up a tree and redesigning its parts into furniture, a person destroys its raw natural state and imposes an artificial form upon it. The mental energy of the person is embedded in the form of the crafted objects –the form of a chair, for example, is the idea (design) imposed on to an object. The physical energy of the craftsmen is embedded in the new shapes and textures of the wooden objects by their labour – the rubbing, pulling, bending and cutting of the wood. The creator and the natural elements are combined in the artificial form of the new objects, and so the objects mark out the presence of their creator in the world in the form of territory: 'look', says the artisan, 'here are *my* chairs; I built them'. Locke puts it this way: 'the labour that was mine, having removed them out of the common state they were in, hath fixed my property in them'(Locke 1924: 130). Making things out of nature makes them the property of their maker and the property marks out their maker's terrain in the world. 'His labour hath taken it out of the hands of nature where it was common . . . and hath thereby appropriated it to himself' (Locke 1924: 131). So the artisan can say, 'As these chairs are mine, I get to say who can and who can't sit in them'.

DISCUSSION POINT

Locke's argument introduced into political thinking a now familiar brand of Protestant individualism. He emphasised the individual's ability to transform the world with action, and he focused ethical considerations on the responsibilities each individual bears for the outcome of their activity. A question raised by this approach is, 'Does the focus on the individual preclude proper consideration of the social factors involved in shaping individuals and their economic and environmental condition?'

The uniquely human combination of the ability to think abstractly and to apply abstract thought to actual conditions through creative work enables people to abstract themselves from the immediacy of the present. We can, and commonly do, think about what we have experienced and how we have acted in the past. We can also imagine what we might do in the future. For Locke, the common ability to conceive of possible futures is highly significant. With the means to redesign the environment and to think ahead to what environment we would like to live in, the imagined future becomes a realm of possibility, a realm of what might be done. It is therefore a realm of choice. When humans see their environment, they see potential; we can create and destroy the elements of our environment. Once this is made clear, it is also clear that acting from the present towards possible futures requires ethical judgement. To be human is to use your mental and physical abilities to change your natural environment and create an artificial one. When undertaking this task, humans have to make judgements about what should be created or destroyed. So we see how it is that Locke argues that possession of these powers puts us on the spot (to his mind God gave us the powers precisely to put us on the spot) – we *have* to make moral choices about what we do and how we act.

The state of nature

For Locke, the power to make property gives us governance over the environment and places us in a moral position with regard to our actions. These are two of three key elements of Locke's presentation of the political order of life. The third vital element is the relationship of individual humans to each other.

Locke sets out his understanding of this third element by employing a popular theoretical device of his time; he explores how humans might interact in a state of nature. As we have already seen, in Locke's conception of the natural human condition, we address our environment as individuals; each converts nature into their own private property and each exploits all they encounter for their own ends, converting it into private property. If this is so, logic dictates that this is how individuals would treat each other in a state of nature. Individuals would seek to exploit other individuals as they do everything else in nature. The question Locke sets himself, then, is whether people in the state of nature would seek to rip each other from their natural condition and make them into private property by enslaving them.

At first sight, it may seem that Locke's logic would lead him to follow Hobbes into the 'war of each against all' thesis, but he does not. Slavery 'is nothing else but the state of war continued' and the state of war – a struggle between men for 'absolute power' (Locke 1924: 125) over one another – is the opposite to the state of nature, for 'the state of nature is a state of equality wherein all the power and jurisdiction is reciprocal' (Locke 1924: 118). So how can it be that mutual hostility drags people out of a state of nature, while the desire to exploit and use one another will characterise human relations in the state of nature? Locke's argument rests on the notion that a sense of communality derived from a common understanding of each other's aims and needs civilises the desire each person has to use others for their own ends. Humans are equally endowed with mental ability to understand the principles that govern how things work, and the physical capacity to work their environment to suit their needs. So the state of nature is 'a state of equality . . . there being nothing more evident that creatures of the same species . . . born to the same advantages of nature and the use of the same faculties, should also be equal amongst one another' (Locke 1924: 118). It is so evident that in the state of nature people will see it; they will understand that this equality is their common condition and usually they will respect each other's independence. This idea contains within it the suggestion that people naturally recognise other people's individuality. People can recognise each other's ability to reason and act for themselves and so will be inclined to tolerate the different modes of individual expression.

For evidence, Locke points to how humans behave 'in a state of nature' in the seventeenth century. 'The promises and bargains for truck, etc., between . . . a Swiss and an Indian in the woods of America are binding to them . . . they are perfectly in a state of Nature with reference to one another' (Locke 1924: 124). Their natural condition is not simply defined by their environment. It is true that being in an uncivilised, undeveloped place provides the context of a state of nature, but their natural condition is also expressed by the fact that when in such an environment they do not go to war against each other, but instead truck and barter. Humans are *naturally* inclined to truck and barter; they are sociable, they trust each other and they recognise the value of each other's products. An individual can see the creative labour involved in other people's work and can also judge the value that the product of that work may have for them. This enables people to barter – that is, to swap their produce. Locke notes that bartering signifies that the participants have an agreed standard of value, and such an agreed standard allows the introduction of money: 'some useful thing that men might keep without spoiling, and that, by mutual consent, men would take in exchange for the truly useful, but perishable supports of life' (Locke 1924: 139–140). Money exists in the state of nature and enables the construction of complex socio-economic relations. Money promotes the spread of property beyond what is made to what may be exchanged. It becomes possible to buy another's labour with money that equals the product of one's labour. Money therefore enables individuals to extend their ownership of property through other people's efforts. This situation is not exploitative in Locke's eyes. It is the product of agreement which is expressed in the form of a contract. One person (A), who has, through a combination of luck, judgement and/or superior skill, produced more property than another (B), may make a contract with B to employ him as a wage labourer. A takes the product of B's efforts as his own, while paying B an agreed sum in proportion to B's labour. This is not an argument which seeks to build a foundation for the individual's rampant exploitation of everything and everyone they see. The state of nature is governed by natural law, which sets specific limits on the exploitation of resources (including human resources).

It is the law of nature that each person is able to think for themselves and to make property. In a natural situation, it is right and proper that they do so. They therefore have a natural right to do so. However, the law of nature sets a limit on the use of natural elements for conversion into property: in the state of nature, anyone who took fruit or made meat from animals and then let them rot without use 'offended against the common law of nature and was liable to be punished' (Locke 1924: 135). The law of nature, says Locke, tells the individual not to take what he cannot use. Greedy appropriation of natural resources wastes nature without purpose and deprives others of the opportunity to use it productively. (Note that in Locke's picture money gets around this restriction because it is a means to gather up and save surplus wealth without restricting others' access to natural resources.) This economic law shows that the natural right to make property brings with it a duty. This is the duty not to infringe others' natural rights. One is bound not to destroy others' capability to think for themselves, and to produce and use property. In this way, the economic law extends beyond its own economic dimensions to set out a principle of mutual toleration. The quantity and quality of an individual's property are the expression of that person's unique engagement with the world. As such, property magnifies the differences between individuals, being the means by which individuals express the quirks of individual taste (such as dress sense, or sense of humour) and deep-seated (spiritual and philosophical) beliefs. 'The State of Nature has a Law of Nature to govern it, which obliges every one, and reason which is that law, teaches all mankind that being all equal and independent, no-one ought to harm another in his life, health, liberty or possessions' (Locke 1924: 119). So, although some individuals are more successful than others and gather more property, there is a form of natural equality between them that operates through an agreed standard of behaviour based on mutual toleration. All people recognise their natural equality and exhibit a common natural morality, 'for truth and keeping of faith belongs to man as man, and not as members of society' (Locke 1924: 124).

KEY CONCEPT

Toleration

Tolerating is enduring against pressure. In human terms, this means putting up with something or somebody which you would prefer to have removed. There are three categories of reasons for wanting something or somebody removed: (1) it annoys you, (2) it offends you, (3) it threatens you (it is possible to feel annoyed, offended and threatened by the same thing).

If something actually damages you, it is by definition beyond your tolerance.

What are the reasons for tolerating things? There are two sets of reasons for doing so. The first set of reasons is pragmatic. It may be that you cannot actually get rid of the thing or person that is upsetting you. Or it may be that you can get rid of it, but it is strategically advantageous not to do so. The second set of reasons is ethical. It may be that you can have something or somebody removed, but you believe that it would be morally wrong to do so.

Despite Locke's belief in the natural sociability of people, it is clear that his state of nature is not a straightforwardly harmonious status quo. The fact is that humankind is at odds with nature. Unlike other species, the human species is not settled in the Garden of Eden. Even in their savage state, humans are always at odds with the natural cycle, which they break up and use in the creation of an artificial world – the human world. In Locke's Christian mindset this fits neatly with the biblical story of God's curse on Adam. Humans' everyday struggles with their natural condition re-enact the day God had to 'turn him [Adam] out of paradise "to till the ground"' (Locke 1924: 32). It is possible to leave the biblical reference points behind and still join Locke in noting the irony of the fact that natural human activity constantly propels humankind out of the natural order and sets us at odds with it.

Civil society

The civilising of individuals' desire to exploit each other takes the state of nature some way towards producing a naturally civil society, but Locke argues that such a society would be unable to maintain the status quo and would collapse into a nasty state of lawless conflict, without the artificial help of man-made law and a government to enforce it. To survive, natural society must alter into civil society; that is, a society in which the principles of natural law which brought it into being are artificially reinforced by humanly designed government and law enforcement agencies. So the natural human condition requires the creation of what we would recognise today as the basic elements of a state. Considering that Locke's natural society is full of the functional elements of a peaceable social life, it may appear odd that he reaches the conclusion that it is unsustainable. However, it is also not hard to see that the activities of production, barter, contract and property building in the state of nature would establish social relations that may require political governance. Locke argues towards this conclusion in the following way. The state of nature is 'a state of perfect freedom' in which individuals can 'order their actions and dispose of their possessions as they think fit within the laws of nature' (Locke 1924: 118), but 'it is not a state of license' (Locke 1924: 119). In the state of nature, the laws of nature set limits to human conduct. However, as Locke has shown, nature, and thus the laws of nature, can be trampled on by humans, and there are reasons why, on occasions, some people might trample on those laws. There are, argues Locke, two functional flaws in the natural order which propel people out of it into a state of war with each other. First, the creation of disparities of wealth creates the temptation for the less well-off individuals to ignore the natural rules of conduct and engage in various forms of theft. Second, there is no natural body which imposes or interprets the law, so each individual comes to know the law of nature through the use of their own mind, and each person has to enact its principles independently. They must do so, because nature leaves them to it, and they do it because nature empowers them. It is both necessary and right, and expresses the fact that 'in the state of nature every individual has the executive power of nature' (Locke 1924: 123) in regard to their own property. So each individual has the final judgement involving any aspect of the condition of their property – which consists of their own ideas, body and everything they have made from them. This power extends to the right 'of every man . . . to punish' (Locke 1924: 121) anyone who violates their property in any way, even to the point of execution.

The difficulty, Locke notes, is that 'self-love will make men partial to themselves and their friends; and, on the other side, ill-nature, passion and revenge will carry them too far in punishing others'. So our knowledge of natural law is framed by opinion and distorted by bias, and this prejudiced form of knowing can easily reduce people's willingness to be tolerant of others. The difficulty here is not so much that people may make wrong judgements, as Locke believes that in the end 'the Lord the Judge shall judge' (Locke 1924: 127). The difficulty is that the equality of their differing judgements will destroy the natural social order (Locke 1924: 123). When individuals' activities affect each other (or affect each other's 'life liberty and estate' as Locke would have it), as they quite often do, each person tends to favour their own odds. Each seeks to enforce the law of nature as they see fit. So, 'nothing but confusion will follow' (Locke 1924: 123). What is worse, such confusion can rapidly descend into a state of war, as individuals accuse each other of crimes against the law of nature and attempt to enforce punishment. This situation can easily lead disputing parties into violent conflict. In such situations, bias and passion combine to overpower reason, people fall out of the state of nature and become 'noxious creatures' (Locke 1924: 125), locked into 'a state of enmity, malice, violence and mutual destruction' (Locke 1924: 126).

Locke believed that, sooner or later, people in the state of nature would see that they must move out of this state. Being rational, they would understand how this degenerative process works, and perceive that if they did not act to preclude it, each and all of them would be reduced to an unhappy violent animality. Being naturally sociable and reasonable, these people would be willing to compromise their natural powers for the piece of security which would allow them to pursue the activities of production, trade and use of their private property. As each and all recognise each other as equals, such a compromise would logically take the form of a mutually binding agreement – that is, a contract to set up a public body which enforces the natural law by artificial (i.e. humanly made) law. To set up such a body, the contract would require each individual to surrender their power to judge and punish those who violate their property rights to a competent and disinterested third party. Locke calls this third party 'the magistrate', but, having the power to judge and punish, it is empowered with the basic functions for ruling over a society. In fact, Locke's 'magistrate' is a very basic kind of government, and for this reason the social contract instantly moves society out of its natural condition and into a 'political or civil society' (Locke 1924: 154), which Locke, stressing the economic base of society, also calls a 'commonwealth' (Locke 1924: 182–183).

People cannot live together simply in nature; they need a man-made, that is, an artificial environment, and the principles which govern it and mechanisms that work it must be humanly designed. There is nothing in the natural order that ordains a natural system of rule. To be sure that the natural law is obeyed, people need man-made laws and systems of law enforcement to protect them. 'God' says Locke, 'sets him (Adam and through him all human-kind) to work for his living, and seems rather to give him a spade into his hand to subdue the earth than a sceptre to rule over its inhabitants' (Locke 1924: 32). We are not by nature kings of a given world. We are the artisans who must graft to create a world for ourselves: we are the designers of this world, but our choices are not endless. Our world is the environment we must survive in; it must be safe, and it must allow us to work, build, make property and trade with one another. Thus Locke brings us to the question, 'What shape, then, must this world be, what mechanisms are necessary to make it click its moving parts in a coherent, functioning self-supporting whole?' The answer Locke gives to this question is that the shape of particular governmental systems can vary – 'they can be democratic, oligarchic, or monarchic' (Locke 1924: 182) – but whatever type of state exists, it can only do so rightly and successfully if it is derived from the consent of the individuals it governs, and if it continues to function with their consent.

Civil society and the state

The function of the state is to enable civil society to exist. Civil society modifies natural society by replacing individual self-governance with common consent to a governing body established in the social contract. Locke argues that the contract is a way in which individuals hand over their power to the state without surrendering their life liberty and property to it. When people contract to set up the state, they do not *give up* their powers to judge and punish; these are what makes them human (for Locke, these powers are God-given and only God can take them from a person). Individuals

---

 Rewind

Go to Chapter 2 to see how this argument is still used against Hobbesian-style demands for complete protection of citizens by an absolutely powerful state.

---

can, however, *entrust* these powers to another. This is what they do when they empower the magistrate to act on their behalf. The state is trusted by the citizens (for that is what they become on making this contract) to use their powers fairly, and to use them for the citizens' benefit rather than for the state's own advantage. In this way, Locke uses the idea of trust to bridge the gap between the necessity for individuals to have the powers of judgement and punishment which define them as humans, and the necessity for them to give these powers to the state. Underpinning this idea of trust is the concept of consent. The social contract, which establishes civil society and the state, comes into being only when the contractees agree to it. In the same moment, the consent of the contractees locks them into the political order. Once they have consented to the arrangement they have contracted into, and, like any other contractees, they are obliged to stick to the terms of that contract or prove a good reason not to do so. However, Locke is aware of the tendencies of governments to serve their own ends. Anyone who sits in the seat of government is subject to the 'great temptation to human frailty', which is the tendency 'to grasp at power' (Locke 1924: 190). Consent therefore should also provide a means for the dissatisfied individual to withdraw from civil society. A mechanism for registering ongoing consent (or withdrawal of consent) must be established, so that citizens who believe that their rights are violated can say they no longer wish to participate. For this reason, Locke argues for the process of regular voting on the membership of the government by the property-owning individuals who make up the citizenry. This mechanism establishes the principle of the citizens' right not to obey a government to which they refuse consent. Its vote is a protective device to ensure that the state does not ride roughshod over the citizens who provide its enormous powers. Locke acknowledges that there will be those who do not vote. They would include children, non-citizens, people who are eligible to vote but are not interested in doing so, and those who are eligible but who do not understand the system of power and are too nervous to state a view. These people, he argues, give tacit consent. That is, by using social facilities (even simply walking on the pavements), and by not saying 'no' to government directives, they show willing, and so they passively register consent. Those who do not wish to give consent to the state must leave and go elsewhere.

DISCUSSION POINT

Locke's notion of tacit consent raises the problem of the relationship between the state and those who do not vote. Have those non-voting people really given consent? If not, how can they be said to have an obligation to obey the state?

Toleration and the state

In setting consent as the bedrock of the political order, Locke ties the ideal of consent into a practical and ethical argument for a tolerant state, since a state which does not tolerate the activities of its citizens would not get their consent (and an intolerant state would not be interested in getting the consent of those upon whom it sought to impose its will).

Locke's argument for a tolerant state is not only an ethical argument. He is not only setting the conditions for the state's legitimacy (its moral right to exist), he is also arguing, on practical grounds, that without consent a state cannot use power well, nor hold it for very long. He has in mind here the religious intolerance, and particularly the intolerance, of the Catholic monarchies of Europe towards Protestants which had led to war across Europe and to civil war in the United Kingdom. His argument, however, may be applied with only minor modification to the issue of toleration of cultural difference in general and so remains highly relevant to the politics of our pluralistic societies today.

The ethical part of his argument works in this manner: God comes to different people in different ways: people interpret their human condition in different ways, and act on these interpretations in different ways. Thus different customs and practices are developed. These practices do not necessarily challenge natural law (we might say here that they threaten other humans' existence) and, if they do not, there is no need to challenge them. In fact, such a challenge violates their natural right to think things out for themselves and to design their own order of life. If there is one right way, God will let us know when we meet Him. It is not a matter for secular powers to deal with. Any state that tries to impose one interpretation of the human condition on unwilling citizens is acting immorally and is therefore illegitimate. It has no right to exist. The citizens have a right, and in fact, a duty, to overthrow it.

The practical part of his argument lies in his warning that any society in which the state attempts to impose a particular belief system on members who do not believe it will exist only as long as those members cannot publicly reject it. Even if these people are terrorised into obedience the state will be at risk, for people will secretly harbour their beliefs (you cannot stop believing something just because you are told to), and at the first opportunity proclaim them publicly. People will always attempt to protect their beliefs and their world, for their beliefs will be integrated into the customary social economic practices that shape their world. Thus internal dissent and the constant potential for civil uprising and war weaken intolerant states. Tolerant states will rest easy on the strengthening support of the diverse groups within the society they protect. The ethical and practical parts of the argument combine to show that government from consent overcomes the tendencies of natural society to fall into conflict and it provides checks on the tendency of the state to override the citizenry. In this way, Locke makes tolerance and consent the twin foundations of the political order which maintains civil society.

Locke's argument for toleration is regarded as the strongest part of his political theory. In combination, its two strands – tolerance between individuals (as the ideal 'natural' situation) and state tolerance of citizens' diverse subcultural modes of expression – have the strength of combining a coherently argued ethical stance with the pragmatic outcome that tolerant societies are peaceful and easy to govern. Yet Locke's argument also sets limits on toleration. He argued that Catholics could not be tolerated. At the time, English Catholics identified more strongly with their religion than with the Protestant English state, which they saw as an enemy power. They were, Locke noted, not only intolerant of others when they had power, but, having lost power, they were also willing to act against the state in the interest of foreign (Catholic) powers. No state, Locke argued, can securely maintain its integrity while allowing such dangerous elements to work against it from within.

DISCUSSION POINT

Two points that are clear from Locke's argument are: that no state can tolerate consistent subversion, and that the liberal state cannot easily tolerate the intolerant. These points are highly relevant in today's multicultural liberal societies, many of which are home to people who are not particularly impressed by liberalism, and some of whom work against it. Are liberal societies that incorporate people who are opposed to liberalism working in the interests of liberalism?

The limited state

Locke's concern is not only with the ethical basis of the state, it is also with its practical viability. This is clear from the amount of space he gives over to analysing the mechanisms that drive it. Consent provides the principle which legitimates the state (gives it an ethical basis in rights), but the practical workings of the state–civil society relationship depend on having the correct functional workings in place. Locke analysed the function of government in an exploration of the dimensions of state power over the citizens, which, he pointed out, is a source of potential dictatorship over the citizens. To stop such a situation being possible, limits need to be placed on governmental power. It is this line of thinking that brings Locke to his presentation of the notion of separable governmental powers, each of which could be parcelled out to differing state bodies that would then counterbalance each other, and so ensure that a monopoly of lawmaking and law enforcement in one body could not happen.

Locke argues that there should be a distinct *legislature*: a body whose function is to make the law that will codify the natural rights of the citizens. Locke fully expects legislative decision-making to be an ongoing business rather than a one-off constitutional framing of the natural rights of the citizens in binding law. Practical experience of the lawmaking process shows that it does involve making complex decisions around ongoing problems. Such power placed in the hands of any person would be dangerous to the citizens, as all people are biased in their own favour and anyone given the power to enforce their opinion as law would be open to corruption; they would 'suit the law . . . in its making and its execution, to their own private advantage' (Locke 1924: 190). For this reason, Locke argues, two restraints should be placed on the legislature. These are as follows:

 Fast forward

Go to Chapter 5 where you can see that the idea is fully developed into 'the separation of powers' thesis by Montesquieu in the eighteenth century.

1   *The powers of selection and recall*: The power to legislate is 'given by the majority to one or more persons only for the duration of their lives, or any limited time' (Locke 1924: 183).

'When it is reverted to the community they may dispose of it anew into what hands they please' (Locke 1924: 183). In this restriction we can see an element of democratic control. The majority of citizens elect and de-select their representatives, but it is unclear whether it is only property owners who constitute the majority of the citizens. The question that lurks unanswered in Locke's presentation is, 'Does the citizenry include property owners only, or does it include propertyless people?'

2   *They are limited to making law*: To ensure that the lawmakers do not act as dictators, the enforcement of the law – that is, the execution of the law – is to be carried out by a separate body, namely the *executive*. The executive should be a separate body to the legislature, so that its members have the opportunity

to treat the members of the legislature objectively. It is only with this distance that the executors of the law could treat the legislators in the same manner as all the other people in society: that is, as citizens obligated by their consent to the governmental system to obedience to the laws. Thus only with a separation of legislative and executive powers into separate bodies can the state check the powers of those who occupy it as rulers.

DISCUSSION POINT

The separation of powers has now become a central feature of the American constitution and the constitution of many other liberal democratic states. It is notorious for creating legislative gridlock, which itself expresses the problem of locating sovereignty when the state is effectively split between competing parties. Is the full separation of powers, with its constant potential for constitutional crisis, a necessary feature of a liberal state?

Commentators: interpretation and legacy

Eighteenth-century interpreters such as Thomas Paine and the USA's founding fathers read Locke as a pioneer of democratic thinking, and the founder of the notion of a property-owning democracy. The democratic principle of consent through voting has become established as a foundational principle of liberal government, as has the notion of property ownership as an important – if not necessary – condition of membership in civil society. However, it remains unclear what precisely Locke understood as government by consent, and it remains unclear what he meant by a commonwealth of property-owning individuals. The ambiguities within his presentation of these ideas produce a number of issues about the theoretical coherence of his argument and also about the practical coherence of the Lockean system of government – and of those elements of liberal-democratic government constructed with reference to Locke's ideas and practised in subsequent centuries. These issues occupy the greatest part of the critical commentary on Locke's work.

A telling contribution to the issue of consent is made by John Plamenatz (1992). He points out that when Locke's argument is looked at in the light of its historical context, it is highly likely that the argument for government from consent was intended to ring-fence the sphere of acceptable types of government. It suited Locke well to set out terms which meant that democracies and constitutional monarchies could be included as legitimate forms of government, but the kind of absolutist monarchy practised in France and aimed at by the monarchs of the United Kingdom could not. However, Locke's argument moves from a mode of consent which is found only in clear positive expressions of agreement to a catch-all notion of consent – in which simply being in the state's territory gives the state the right to take control over all aspects of one's life. This shift in the meaning of consent does not necessarily destroy the logical coherence of Locke's argument, says Plamenatz, but it does mean that by the end of his argument, the idea that consent expresses a genuine assertion of citizens' wishes and acts as a check on the state's power is spent. As a consequence the presentation of the unique legitimacy of government by consent fails to serve his ends.

Property, civil society and democracy

C.B. Macpherson (1962) and J.D. Mabbott (1973) have detected fundamental flaws in Locke's notion of property. Both note that money circumvents the limitations on gathering property which Locke claims lay in natural law, not only allowing for some individuals to hoard more than they need, but also allowing for the argument that an individual may own the produce of another's labour. Mabbott points to the 'infamous passage' in which Locke writes, 'the turf my servant has cut . . . (has) become my property' (Mabbott 1973: 148), to show that Locke's 'labour theory of property' is undermined by inclusion of 'unearned income', which allows Locke to assume the natural status of two economic classes – the propertied master and the unpropertied servant. Because property owners buy the labour of the servant, they own all the servant's produce. Macpherson notes that in making this claim, Locke slips from using 'property' to mean 'life, liberty and estate' – something everyone has – to meaning possessions acquired through productive labour or through exchange. This latter sense excludes those who have no possessions other than their body and mind. Thus the questions arise: are the propertyless not to be seen as protected under the terms of the social contract? Are they excluded from civil society? Macpherson notes that Locke knew that the majority of people in England in his time were propertyless in the ordinary sense of the word, and that he wished to exclude them from the political equation. It is known that it was a common assumption among political theorists and practitioners of Locke's time that the non-propertied existed outside civil society, and, in support of Macpherson's thesis, Locke's casual references to servants, and to other wage earners, all indicate that he did not believe that the majority of the population could be the 'majority' of citizens who elect the legislature. If this is indeed the case, his development of the notion of tacit consent may be seen as a means of arguing that those without property – and thus lacking the right to check government power – had an obligation to obey the state by the simple fact of being there and not leaving.

Conclusion

What the critical commentaries reveal to us is that Locke's theory is not an argument for a fully representative democratic government. Despite his popular reputation as the founding theorist of modern democratic government, democracy itself was not the great goal of building limited, self-checking and constitutionally regulated government. The *Second Treatise of Government* is also entitled 'The true end of Government', and Locke declares in it boldly that 'the great and chief end' of government, 'is the preservation of property' (Locke 1924: 180). For Locke, liberal democratic government was a political system which could and should be designed in service of what he saw as fundamental, God-given, human rights – the rights to express oneself in creative production of property, and to express oneself in the free exchange and use of that property.

Revision notes

1   Locke is writing about the key political issues of a time when the British Isles were disunited by conflict between monarchy and Parliament, and overlapping conflict between Catholicism and Protestantism. The key points of contention that derived from this context were: (a) the legitimacy of monarchic rule, (b) religious intolerance, and (c) the legitimacy of state imposition of religion on the populace.

2   Locke's conceptions of private property and the individual as the primary unit of moral responsibility and practical action have become bedrock principles of liberalism and are strongly associated with capitalism, but it is not accurate to present Locke as an advocate of liberalism or capitalism. Liberalism was not a recognised political category. It was not possible for Locke to perceive the development of capitalism, since key features of its development, such as steam power and electricity, lay in an unimaginable future.

Locke and Hobbes

Similarities

1   Hobbes and Locke both see the state as the necessary agency for the maintenance of civil society.

2   Both theorists draw the legitimacy of government from the covenant of the people made in a social contract.

3   Both theorists see the function of the state limited to service of civil society.

Differences

1   Locke sees the state of nature as a coherent social organisation, whereas Hobbes sees it as a formless state of chaos.

2   Hobbes sees the state as the only possible location for order and therefore for legitimate power. Locke sees the all-powerful state as a threat to the social order which precedes it and which it ought to serve.

3   Hobbes seeks to show that the power to exercise decisive government is best placed in a single sovereign body. Locke seeks to build defences against concentrations of power within the state through the separation of powers and democratic accountability.

Bibliography

Cranston, M. (1957) *John Locke: A Biography*, London: Longman.

—— (1987) 'John Locke and the Case for Toleration', in S. Mendus and D. Edwards (eds) *On Toleration*, Oxford: Clarendon Press.

Dunn, J. (1984) *Locke*, Oxford: Oxford University Press.

Locke, J. (1924) *Two Treatises of Government*, New York: Everyman.

Mabbott, J.D. (1973) *John Locke*, London: Macmillan.

Macpherson, C.B. (1962) *The Political Theory of Possessive Individualism: Hobbes to Locke*, Oxford: Oxford University Press.

Plamenatz, J. (1992) *Man and Society*, Vol. 1 (rev. edn), London: Longman.

Further reading

Your initial reading of Locke will probably focus on the *Second Treatise of Government*, which comes as a single volume from many publishers. A good version is Blackwell's (Oxford, 1966, 3rd edn) with an introduction by J.W. Gough. For comparisons with Filmer, you will need both Treatises. A commonly available edition is *Two Treatises of Government* (New York: Everyman, 1994), edited by Mark Goldie.

For an informative introduction to Locke you cannot do better than John Dunn's *Locke* (see Bibliography above). It combines brevity and accessibility with an informative overview of the major ideas and issues.

Help with critical analysis of the central ideas in the *Second Treatise* may be found in John Plamenatz's *Man and Society* (1992).

An interesting study of Locke's place in the tradition of social contract theory is provided by Carol Patemen's *Sexual Contract* (Cambridge: Polity Press, 1988), which explores Locke's implicit exclusion of women from the initial social contract.

Part II

REASON AND REVOLT: THE FRENCH REVOLUTION

Montesquieu

I have laid down the first principles and found that particular cases follow naturally from them; that the histories of all nations are only consequences of them; and that every particular law is connected with another law, or depends upon some other of a more general extent.

(*The Spirit of the Laws*)

Montesquieu achieved fame in his lifetime with two very different works. The first was the brilliant satirical novel, *The Persian Letters* (1721), which contrasts the absurdities and liberties of Parisian social and political life of his time to the despotic regime of an imagined Persian seraglio. The second work was *The Spirit of the Laws* (1748), a social scientific analysis of socio-political orders of life. Since this time, he has enjoyed the status of a 'great thinker' in the Enlightenment pantheon. What is unusual, however, is that the reasons given by commentators for his high standing as a social and political theorist have never been consistent. In fact, they are often at odds.

His contemporaries – the '*philosophes*' of the French Enlightenment and many British Enlightenment thinkers – considered him to exemplify their ideal of civilised man, creative writer and philosophic sage. By the end of the eighteenth century, however, it was his work as a political theorist which inspired the greatest praise. His ideas held high currency among the French revolutionaries, and, perhaps most notably, his constitutional discussions, which overtly praise the British parliamentary constitution, had a direct and lasting influence on the construction of the new American Republics. It was this direct influence in the development of Anglo/American constitutional politics which set his subsequent reputation as a liberal-minded constitutional theorist in the English-speaking world. This century, his reputation has ultimately rested on the doctrine of the separation of powers: the famous argument that the three core functions of the state – making laws (the legislative function), executing the law (the executive function) and upholding the law (the judicial function) – should be given to separate bodies in order that each body may check the power of the other and in so doing build a power-checking device into the state. This doctrine is now presented to college students worldwide as the core idea in Montesquieu's constitutional theory, and the backbone of the liberal state, and in this move, Montesquieu's status as a 'father of liberalism' is enshrined.

However, in this century, his reputation has also been revised, with the key elements of his reputation – his liberalism and his clarity as a theorist – coming into question. Some commentators have presented a historicised picture of Montesquieu as a conservative aristocrat who developed the separation of powers thesis not as a liberalising measure, but as a weapon against the modernising tendencies of the French monarchy in the 1700s. Others claim that Montesquieu's work is too confused in its structure and at the level of ideas to warrant the status of greatness that has become attached to it over the centuries.

Furthermore, in 1892, a whole new approach to Montesquieu was initiated by the sociologist Emile Durkheim, who argued that Montesquieu's greatness did not lie in his constitutional theory, but in his establishing the first principles of sociology – a theme which has gained much ground since. Today, Montesquieu's writings are being reassessed by specialists in critical theory who see in them a theory of the erotics of power and an insight into the social construction of identity. As is always the case when looking for guides to past theorists, we find many guides to Montesquieu, each one presenting us with their own interpretation of his works and his aims.

In the particular case of Montesquieu, consideration of his work with reference to his life and times is fascinating and fruitful. First, the story of his reputation as an author, as it evolves through his life, suggests an enigma at the heart of Montesquieu's enduring reputation as a great writer of the Enlightenment. Second, by contextualising the themes which run through his writings, within the context of the major themes and issues dominating French society during his times, we begin to unravel some of the mysteries of Montesquieu's writing and establish a consistent socio-political set of concerns.

Montesquieu's life and writings

Throughout his life, Montesquieu was able to live well. He was an aristocrat with a large income from vineyards in Bordeaux. Although he inherited a position as 'President' in the regional judicial body, he sold this and liberated himself to do purely intellectual work in his chateau near Bordeaux. Here he surreptitiously worked as an amateur scientist, writing various papers (none of which were particularly notable), and as a political theorist, in which vein he produced a reasonably well-received work on the greatness and the decline of Roman political society (*Considérations sur les Causes de la Grandeur des Romains et de leur Décadence*). The bulk of his labours, however, was devoted to a massive project of scientifically informed political theory, which was eventually published as *L'Esprit des Lois* (*The Spirit of the Laws*) just three years before he died. This work surprised his contemporaries, as the enormous success of *The Persian Letters* had seemingly ensured Montesquieu's public reputation as the author of orientalist fantasies. The originality and daring scale of *The Spirit of the Laws* made his reputation over again, yet it did so in a scientific and serious format which was seemingly at odds with the fantasy writing of his early years. What he left were two great works written twenty-seven years apart: one a slim volume containing a funny, cutting and lightly erotic fantasy story; the other a huge tome containing a self-consciously serious analysis of cultural and political practices throughout history and across the globe. Thus his reputation at his death was slightly at odds with itself.

KEY CONCEPT

Orientalism

Orientalism has become recognised as a European (and later 'Western') cultural construct, expressing a fascination with the culture and politics of the non-European world while simultaneously revealing a significant degree of ignorance about the realities of this world. The fascination with the Orient began in the early eighteenth

continued

century with the huge popularity of fictional travel stories portraying a largely imagined world in which 'Eastern' empires were dominated by strange religions, usually defined as 'Mohammedon', and unenlightened by science and rationalist philosophy. Typically, Oriental societies were defined by the unfettered power of the rulers, with arcane rituals of slaughter and enslavement, and were run through by rampant eroticism in all areas of life. Montesquieu's *Persian Letters* was one of the most popular Orientalist fictions and it contributed greatly to the establishment of long-held European prejudices.

For readers of his works since, this slightly confused twofold reputation is one of the reasons that the task of interpreting his aims is particularly difficult. In addition, Montesquieu's interest in science, Orientalism, politics and society led him to address a huge range of subject matters. When reading his books, it seems at times as if he writes about everything and anything he can think of, and uses any style of writing he finds attractive at the time. For this reason, it is hard to see what exactly he is aiming at, what points he is trying to make, and what method of analysis he is trying to use in making his points. It is only when his work is placed in the context of his times that an interconnectedness of themes and issues begins to emerge.

KEY EVENT

The French Enlightenment

The Enlightenment is a term used to present a period of time in the history of Europe in which philosophy and the arts were vitalised by the introduction of modern scientific technologies and methods. The discovery of modern scientific principles enriched an ongoing reappraisal of ancient pre-Christian philosophical and artistic activities originating in the Renaissance. The common thread from the Renaissance to the Enlightenment is the rejection of the ideas and methods which had dominated Christian Europe from the beginning of the second millennium. However, where the Renaissance looked to a time before Christianity for inspiration, the philosophers of the Enlightenment proclaimed confidently that this was a new post-Christian age in which understanding was shown the way to truth by the light of science. The Enlightenment is commonly carved into three elements – Scottish, French and German – which cover slightly different historical and intellectual ground. Here we consider only the French Enlightenment.

Context

What at first sight seems an unlikely combination of speculative and fantastic fiction with scientific rationalist analysis takes on a greater coherence when viewed in the context of late seventeenth- and early eighteenth-century France. The times were driven by the ideals and aims of the French Enlightenment, and the political/religious struggles to establish or maintain the social and political structures which were integral to the emerging monarchic state of France. While the French Enlightenment was driven by optimism, it was located in a theatre of political, theological and socio-economic uncertainties. The ideas and their situation not only expressed the rapid changes from the preceding Catholic-aristocratic dominated *ancien régime*, but also expressed the unpreparedness of those involved to establish an alternative to it. It was a period lurching towards cultural and political crisis. All such crises are marked out by the uncertainty within the orders of life, which threaten the identities of those living within them, and such uncertainties marked out the crises of the *ancien régime*.

KEY PEOPLE

Absolute monarchs

French absolutism reached its apex with Louis XIV, who claimed that the King alone was the ultimate decision-maker – that is, sovereign power – within the state's domain. In claiming authority for this supreme power, Louis, like his forebears and those who would follow him in the powerful Bourbon dynasty, relied on claims set out in a highly influential doctrine that the monarchic state was an element of a universal order prescribed by God. This argument, known as 'the Divine Right of Kings', was never fully accepted by other powerful groups in French society and the monarch's claim to absolute power was always more of an aspiration than a fact. After Louis XIV, the monarchy became increasingly embattled as the Nobles of the Sword, the oldest and most powerful segments of the aristocracy, attempted to reassert their power, and the economically and intellectually powerful Bourgeoisie began to flex their political muscles. The monarchy's final demise came with the execution of Louis XVI in the French Revolution.

From the seventeenth century to the French Revolution of 1789, the politics of Europe was dominated by crises. The old continental political order which had held sway for several hundred years was in serious decline and potential new orders were struggling to take its place.

The old continental order was run through with the intellectual and moral mores of Catholicism and dominated by the Catholic Church, in tandem with its secular support, the Holy Roman Empire. Since its inception in AD 900, the Empire had gradually reduced in size and power, and by the seventeenth century the old continental political order was breaking up. Out of varying alternatives vying to replace it, one pretender was emerging as the strongest. This was a collection of centralised, relatively secular governments ruling over national territories. Nowhere was this more evident than in France, where the Bourbon dynasty, growing in power and confidence, moved to monopolise authority and power into a system of absolutism.

Montesquieu's public life corresponded with the middle period of the absolutist era. This period, known as 'the Regency', followed Louis XIV's death and was a relatively calm and superficially confident time in France. The nation was not at war and its political order appeared to function in a pragmatic and unideological way. To Montesquieu's contemporaries, the monarchic system appeared to be safely entrenched and, even with the benefits of hindsight, it is a time that is often portrayed as the calm before the revolutionary storm at the century's end. This picture is very simplistic. In fact, the rule of the monarchs was but briefly if ever absolute. Even by the 1720s, French socio-political and economic life was already racked by the uncertainties which culminated in its eventual collapse.

The process was, however, rife with tensions between sectional social group-ings. In France, this took the form of conflicts between the aristocratic class, who dominated the regional *Parlements* and sought a regionalised system of power, and the monarchs, who sought increasingly to centralise power in their person. It also included an emerging new socio-economic class – the bourgeoisie – who were slowly coming into economic power as the economic system became more reliant on trade and banking (Ogg 1965: 246).

The entangled details of these long-term processes obscured them to those involved (no doubt it is the same in the present). Political participants could perceive only part of the whole. Many concentrated on the religious conflicts which attended the growth of various forms of Protestantism and the fracturing of Catholicism, without perceiving fully the significance of the underpinning economic and regional features. For example, a long-running conflict between the Huguenots with the nominally Catholic monarchy was addressed in almost purely religious terms, yet the Huguenots were a powerful socio-economic grouping in Languedoc, Dauphiné and Burgundy (Ogg 1965: 258), and were therefore a regional block on the mon-archy's attempts to centralise power. Similarly, the monarchy's dispute with the Jansenists expressed regional and class conflict, since Jansenist power resided in the Bourgeois deputies of the Paris *Parlement* – a body which was to play a vigorous part in the downfall of the monarchy. In addition, France's economic system, built on a system of speculation designed by John Law (a Scottish financier who was for a time finance minister for France), collapsed in 1720. Not only did this collapse cause economic stress within France, but it also had a great effect on the establishment of colonial enterprises. Money became worthless; wealthy people were bankrupted; disorder was evident.

The uncertainties of French political and economic life were stimulated further by France's growing contact with non-European cultures. In the late seventeenth century diplomatic relations were opened with many Eastern countries. In 1717, Peter the Great of Russia paid a state visit, as did an array of variously dramatic and exotic ambassadors (some of whom were impostors). In addition, the translation of the Koran into French, and a flood of works offering a mix of genuine travel documen-tation and orientalist fictions, stimulated a general fascination with 'oriental' people and culture.

The discussions which expressed this fascination also highlighted a growing sense among the French literati and *philosophes* that theirs was only one social culture among a vast range of possible and actual modes of human living. This realisation stimulated general questioning of French and indeed European norms and values,

 **Fast forward**

Go to **Chapter 6** for further information on the *philosophes*.

creating a general undertow of cultural uncertainty working beneath the flood-tides of optimism of the Enlightenment. Such uncertainty was mixed in with and largely hidden by the enthusiasm of the *philosophes*, believers in the sure progress of human civilisation through the use of scientific rationalism towards certain knowledge. Insightful observers, including Montesquieu and Voltaire, took note that the *philosophes'* faith in progress through science was not matched by evidence of its success; categorical and provable truths remained difficult to establish in economic and political life, and cultural uncertainty remained ever-present. Experience, it seemed, could not be so easily understood, nor the truth so easily plundered.

Montesquieu in context

Underneath its confident exterior, early eighteenth-century French society exhibited many uncertainties – uncertainty about how to understand common experience, uncertain socio-political orders of life, and uncertainty about the cultural identities of those living. These uncertainties provide Montesquieu's great themes and are explored through his exposure of the relativism underpinning the general cultural crisis. In *The Persian Letters*, this exploration begins with the fictional adventures of two Persian travellers in Paris. The story is told through a series of letters supposedly sent by the fictitious travellers to their comrades in Persia. Through the letters, Montesquieu exposes both the distinctive qualities and the absurd rituals of French socio-cultural and political life. Satirical insights lacerate French pretensions to cultural and intellectual superiority. The opera, politics, modes of fashion, and romantic and sexual practices are all discussed in tones of amazement, amusement and anthropological objectivity which only a stranger from a foreign land could deliver. Although the letters are full of references to the events of the time, the economic crisis, the visits of Eastern dignitaries, and the debates of the *philosophes*, there were few among his contemporaries who recognised that the author was mapping out the condition of crisis of his time. Retrospectively, it is easier to see that his insights are not only witty insights into superficial social problems, but also reveal the fault-lines and disorders of the *ancien régime*. In such light, *The Spirit of the Laws* may be treated as an attempt to set out a prescriptive formula to deal with the crisis tendencies exposed in *The Persian Letters*.

The Spirit of the Laws is both historically significant, and significant in the development of theoretical analysis of politics. Theoreticians are interested in Montesquieu's insightful analysis into the possible conditions of political existence which are, roughly speaking, set out as the possibilities for establishing and maintaining workable and ethical orders of social life. Historians are interested in the huge influence which his prescriptive writing had on the founding fathers of the USA and the French Republic. Of course, the entwining of the historical and theoretical in the moment of the work's creation, and in the following moments in which it was read and propagated by his admirers, ensures that the two dimensions are of equal importance in considering the work's overall significance. If we take them together, we might see how the work laid grounds for the constitution of a new order – a modern liberal nation state out of the crumbling *ancien régime*: a way out of the inertia of crisis.

Montesquieu's social theory

Montesquieu's novelty as a political theorist stems not only from the way he attempted to develop his political presentation through the use of a social scientific method-olology, but in the way he sought to provide his readers with a scientific manual of political possibilities.

In the introduction to *The Spirit of the Laws*, he wrote, 'I have laid down the first principles and found that the particular cases follow naturally from them; that the histories of all nations are only consequences of them; and that every particular law is connected with another law, or depends upon some other of a more general extent' (Montesquieu, trans. Nugent 1949: lxvii). In this statement he set out the basic scientific position that all claims to general truths must be applicable to particular examples (the empiricist element of his method), and all explanations of examples must be made in terms of general principles (the rationalist element of his method). He was claiming, in *The Spirit of the Laws*, that this position enabled genuine objective insight into the workings of socio-political orders of life.

In addressing this claim to an audience of people who are only beginning to explore the science of political understanding, Montesquieu is revealing his percep-tion of the relation of the theorist – who must be objective and impartial – to the practitioner who is involved in their political situation. He was indicating how the political theorist and the politician have different relationships to the political world.

This relationship may be seen through the handy analogy of gardening: in every garden, a thousand flowers may bloom; some are weeds and need plucking out; others can become wild or grow out of shape; these need pruning before they too turn to weeds. Gardening is an art form; the gardener creates his vision from the uncertainty of the burgeoning beds. As in any art, he must employ a degree of practical judgement; gardeners need to know their garden and each individual flower, but to really gain control over the garden – to create it, to nurture it and to shape it as it grows – they need more than just a practical knowledge. They need to know the types of plant they are dealing with and they need to know the scientific principles of gardening. In Montesquieu's vision, the politician is the gardener and the theorist is the provider of the scientific guide to gardening.

In *The Spirit of the Laws*, Montesquieu is providing a scientific categorisation of types, along with a scientific account of the principles which make them grow and the conditions under which they can become corrupted. He was aware that his theory could be used by political actors as a scientific guide, to manage the uncertainties of their particular circumstances. He was also aware that to be scientific and not merely speculative, its theoretical content had to be developed from reliable factual information. So he gathered all the data which he could get hold of on the diverse social orders across the globe and accounted for in history. In doing this, he was attempting to construct an empirically based social science.

Despite this aim, he began *The Spirit of the Laws* with a traditional attempt to found the discussion of politics on a speculative account of human nature. To be human, he wrote at the start of *The Spirit of the Laws*, is to be timid, driven by 'fears and apprehensions' (Nugent 1949: 4) and therefore to need security, to want pleasure and therefore to desire stimulating goods, to be inquisitive and creative and to need the liberty for self-expression. But to be human is also to be corruptible, especially by the desire for pleasure, which can lead to excess and laziness, and by fear, which can lead to subservience and/or violence (Nugent 1949: 5). He stresses constantly that the elements of human being can work against each other: 'The human spirit is contradiction itself' (Montesquieu, trans. Betts 1973: 85). The desire for pleasure can override the fear of danger and lead to disaster, as exemplified in his time and ours by the dangers of disease involved in unprotected sex (often the act of those expressing their passion of the moment), and of wanton spending leading to poverty and its attendant woes. So there is an art in achieving human happiness. It depends on achieving a balance of parts. Some individuals prioritise security and restrict pleasures that bring danger, while others will give greater rein to pleasure and live a more risky existence. So it is with human collectivities. Societies order themselves with regard to these elements and the balance is everything: get it wrong one way or another and that society will corrupt and fail. But getting it right is very hard; human nature is an explosive mix, a constantly contradicting set of impulses. Societies have to govern and direct their members' impulses with a clear perception of what is involved, and to develop the skills and technologies to manage the elements.

A central task which Montesquieu set for himself in *The Spirit of the Laws* is to review the technologies of governance – social modes of behavioural training, as well as the machinery of state – as they are used to meet human needs by governing human impulses. Montesquieu set about his task enthusiastically. Aware that the governance of human societies is carried out within a vast and highly diverse range of environments, from those who live in deserts to those living near the frozen poles, he gathered up all the powerful images and information flooding into Europe from other parts of the world. *The Spirit of the Laws* quotes copiously from travel writings of the explorers of Japan and China, Persia and Russia. All the information he could acquire is organised into a complex jigsaw which, once put together, presents an intensely rich and quite fantastic picture of the diversity of human culture, custom and practice across the globe. With this Montesquieu presented a powerful case for cultural relativism. He showed that a vast and dazzling array of cultures exists across the world and that although many are very strange to the European mind of his contemporaries, they are not necessarily less valid than the European social model. For, though basic human requirements are common to all, they are shaped differently by the different circumstances in which people live across the globe and throughout history. Different norms and values, customs and practices, are good for different types of people. Who they are, and how they meet their needs and deal with their desires is expressed collectively in the customs and practices of their social life. It is their national spirit – their '*esprit général*' (Nugent 1949: 292).

Montesquieu's scientific approach becomes very clear when the detail of his social relativism is examined. He reaches his conclusions through a novel attempt to assess the influence of environmental factors, humans' needs and desires, and their creative activity in shaping social customs and orders of life. To our eyes, his work appears at times to be a clumsy discussion of climate and racial types. At points it appears comically crude and hopelessly racialist. After experimenting on frozen sheep's tongues, he concluded that the nerves of 'northern' people are so frozen that they have no feelings, that 'you must flay a Muscovite alive to make him feel' (Nugent 1949: 223). In such places, he argues, it is necessary to employ brutal methods to get anything done. In hot climates 'people's animal senses are over-stimulated while simultaneously mind is overpowered, there is no curiosity', and 'indolence constitutes the most happiness' (Nugent 1949: 224). Such places will be dominated by super-stition, have little economic power and are commonly governed by religiously based elites. At other times, Montesquieu manages to concoct subtle and sensitive insights into the varied cultural modes of producing the needs of life and imposing on them deeper significance of expressions of collective identity. For example, in discussing the holy status given to cattle in the Hindu regions of India, he takes something completely strange and probably incomprehensible to most Europeans of his time and renders it sensible. Meat and milk are vital to health, and scarce in the Indian climate. The religious custom of treating cattle as sacred shows that the significance of cattle as life-providing instils respect in the relationship of humankind to the beast. Far from being perverse, it is entirely reasonable. It is part of the *esprit général* of Hindu peoples; their way of surviving relatively happily and with a strong sense of their fit into the natural world. Because Montesquieu was a deist – that is, he believed that God is the creative force and will manifest in the design of nature, not a person in the Christian sense – he would have seen the Hindu custom as spiritually nourishing. He took something which appeared perverse and incomprehensible to the European mindset and showed it to be a good way to be human. In this example, along with many others, Montesquieu shows his contemporaries that there are many ways of achieving a relatively happy, healthy and secure life.

DISCUSSION POINT

When reading old political texts, it is not unusual to find particular ideas which today we consider as enlightening, developed from general arguments framed in terms which we find unacceptable. This is the case with Montesquieu's social theory. The 'good' ideas on cultural difference and relative truth are developed from a general argument which is built upon racialist ideas and Orientalist prejudices. Most importantly, the good ideas appear to be a logical progression from the bad general arguments. The question to be considered, then, is whether it is possible to separate the good ideas from the bad argument – to keep the former and drop the latter. What are the implications if this cannot be done? If it can be done, what is the method to be applied?

Montesquieu's political theory

Despite its relativism, Montesquieu's is not an 'anything goes' philosophy. The bottom line for judging whether a social order is acceptable is not whether any other society's customs are similar to European ones, but whether they attend to people's basic human requirements – for security, and for a degree of stimulating pleasure. As these requirements sometimes work against each other, meeting their demands, while simultaneously directing their effects away from incoherence, collision and catastrophe, is an art – the art of producing and maintaining practical and fulfilling modes of living (customs and practices). This art is the activity of constituting and governing a social order of life. It is what we call 'politics', and Montesquieu's point is that, contrary to the arguments of the absolutists of his time, it is necessarily riddled with uncertainties. In addition to the art of balancing potentially opposing impulses, political government is made more difficult by the unique circumstances imposed on the society to be governed by its particular environment. The practical needs and problems faced by each society will be unique, and the overall diversity of needs among various societies makes a single method of government impossible. The spirit of each people provides the fertile bed from which each political culture must grow, so one will find as many different polities as there are different societies. None of these are perfect, but those political systems that work do so by reinforcing the features of social life that enable the society they govern to endure. These features are those that meet the human needs of social members to a degree they find acceptable. Those that fail to meet these basic human needs cause dehumanisation and misery, and, since they violate the fundamental principle of all social life – the collective establishment of security and a modicum of happiness – they must eventually collapse in catastrophe. This is not a simple categorisation into good and bad socio-political orders. Montesquieu, possibly with one eye on the French monarchy of his time, argues that the imperfections of systems which appear to be working well create the potential for them to grow out of shape, to become lawless and to turn into catastrophic failures.

To develop this analysis from an empirical base, Montesquieu set about working through the vast array of social cultures in the world up to his time, sifting out the range of variation which is compatible with human security and well-being. As a means of imposing some conceptual order on the huge amount of information which he gathers, he develops a categorisation of types, made in terms of their working principle and their corruptibility. The types are republics, monarchy and despotism. No actual polity matches these models exactly, since they are abstracted from the many actual polities he analyses. As such they are intended to represent the distilled principles of the types of system which he found operating in multiple variations across the world. In distilling the principles of types of polity Montesquieu's aim was to dispose of the confusions produced by the wide variations in the history and geography of the many polities observed, and to expose both the basic continuous principles which drive the socio-political orders of life, and the features which corrupt them.

The comparison of republicanism and absolutist monarchies in *The Spirit of the Laws* shows that they both have tendencies towards the elimination of all forms of difference within the body politic. At the theoretical level, both models are presented as the answer to tensions created by the many differences which are commonly found within social orders of life. In his presentation of both models, he returns continuously to the way in which such tensions are perceived by republicans and monarchists as the pernicious source of social, economic and political uncertainty. Thus both models are anti-pluralist, and, in exploring the failings of both models, Montesquieu also made a case for viewing pluralism as the life-blood of the ethical and enduring polity. Its opposite is the condition of despotism: a hellish scenario, lacking laws, order, and any degree of security or freedom.

Republics

Montesquieu's approach to republican orders of power is deceptive. Presenting an ideal type, he enthusiastically discusses the means by which republicanism includes its members in a condition of virtuous and equal participation in public affairs. But gradually, the flaws in the ideal are revealed through a step-by-step introduction of malformations in *actual* republics.

Montesquieu argued that since the Romans' conceptualisation of political community as *Res Publica* (literally, the public thing), republicanism has been rooted in one fundamental idea. This is the idea of the republic as a single political identity, whose body (the body politic, defined as the state) is no more or less than the activities of its constituent members (the citizenry), whose heroic enterprise – the building and maintenance of a collective order of life – is their virtue. Thus, says Montesquieu, the principle of republican life is a common commitment to the collective, inspiring the quest for excellence in citizenship. In the tradition of republicanism, this is termed (political) 'virtue' and is the ethical basis of citizenship. This virtue is not of the Christian, Islamic or Judaic kind; it is rooted in the Romans' notion that human excellence is achieved only through active membership of the body politic (*Res Publica*). Republican virtue lies in learning and practising the skills required to keep the polity going. As the ethical life of the citizens is developed by participation in public (that is, political) life – they have little or no moral identity beyond their active membership of the republic, their judging and active self – the best part of what we would recognise as their distinct personality – is derived from political life. Thus the individual identities of the citizens and the identity of the republic are integrated. They do not separate. Displays of independence or individual interest are vices. All activity is aimed at the public good, which is at one and the same time the good of the citizens and the good of the state: 'public employments are attestations of virtue, depositions with which a citizen is entrusted by his country, for whose sake alone he ought to live, to act and to think; consequently he cannot refuse them' (Nugent 1949: 67).

Montesquieu saw the influence of Plato in the republican tradition's desire for total and unbroken unity of the citizens and the state in a single political identity. Plato, the author of the very first work in the tradition (titled *The Republic*), believed that every political constitution had a perfect form which existed in a metaphysical (above the physical) realm of ideas. Montesquieu saw this notion expressed in repeated attempts throughout history to impose the constitution of an ideal republic on to a whole range of different socio-political situations. Using the examples of ancient Sparta and Rome, Montesquieu argues that traditional republican society, aiming to eliminate all insecurities within the body politic, required full commitment from the citizenry. Anything less than this commitment, any attempt to find happiness in private activity such as family life or commerce, was seen to fracture the collective and challenge the public monopoly of space and time. Republicans saw that pursuit of private interests sowed the seeds of competition and the potential for combat. The insecurity of each and all, driven by the combative relationships of individual self-seekers, can, and frequently does, manifest itself in the family, and in economic activities. Therefore, to stop the family and the market bringing uncertainty into the social body, they would be eradicated or at least subsumed into the greater public whole. The emotion, passion and creative drive of the citizens would be directed and driven by love of the republic: 'As such love requires constant preference of public to private interests, it is the source of all private virtues; for they are nothing more than this very presence itself' (Nugent 1949: 34). By overriding the private spheres of life, and eradicating all the difference and diversity expressed and encouraged within them, the Platonic republic seeks to negate all sources of uncertainty, by merging individuals into one homogenous body.

The instability of republics 1: Commerce

Montesquieu points out that these attempts to exclude any uncertainty from political life eventually create disaster, for the abstract ideals of the virtuous republic cannot match the particular requirements of the actual society. Each society undertakes the necessary activities of family and market life in unique conditions, and each develops its own unique mores and customs for coping with the uncertainties which such activities produce. This 'way of life' underpinned the society's *esprit général*. Republicanism, he argued, ignores the particular environmental conditions which frame social and political activity and so ultimately runs up against the particular purposes of people's practical daily social and economic activities. The idealism of the republic undermines the society's *esprit général*. So while it appears to provide a perfect political order in the abstract, in actuality, republicanism carries features which attempt to rip societies from their roots.

People root into their environment through the customs of daily life, especially the customs and practice of trade and commerce, since these are the social expression of people's working with their environment to modify it, to exchange its parts to meet the needs of life, and to produce luxuries.

Commerce is not simply a way of meeting needs. It is the expression of human diversity which is fundamental to social life, and it is the home of a society's manners. The diversity of social membership is economically expressed in trade, which enables different and potentially conflicting needs to be met in as near as possible mutually satisfying arrangements. Good manners must be developed in the service of successful trading; it is necessary to be polite, to establish common ground for trade. It is useful to be nice to obtain contracts. Thus, while self-interest – a source of social uncertainty – is nurtured, it is contained within the bounds of practical possibility. Further, while commercial relationships are imbued with the potential for conflict, a commercial discourse is one in which common interests and feelings are constantly expressed. People say, 'It's nice doing business with you' and suchlike. Friendship, the grounds for genuine communality – a communion of individuals expressing their intentions and feelings while taking care to pay regard to the intentions and feelings of others – is easily developed. Public manners, which are shaped by commerce, in turn shape the *polite*ness which is the *polit*ic of everyday discourse, and the substance of the everyday existence of the *polity*. At its core, everyday polite, commercial activity 'produces in the mind of a man a certain sense of exact justice, opposite on the one hand to robbery, and on the other to those moral virtues which forbid our always adhering rigidly to the rules of private interest and suffer us to neglect this for the advantage of others' (Nugent 1949: 317). Commerce provides the means to a more extensive communality built on fine-tuned practical judgement, a culture of exchange which combines economic with aesthetic judgement, and as a result develops the participants' taste, and includes the diverse needs and tastes of the participants in a general culture of the community. Taking these points together, Montesquieu has made the case that the pursuit of private interests through commerce drives the economic and cultural heart of the politically astute and fundamentally *civil* society.

One final point he makes is that commerce is the social expression of people's working with their environment; commercial manners design a social morality which fits with the particular goods and limits of their local environment. This is significant in the light of Montesquieu's interest in the fit of socio-political orders to their natural environment. The arguments seem to indicate that he believes that, while all social morals tend to appear right in the context of their own culture, some are objectively right because they fit functionally with limits imposed upon human activities by what we would call environmental considerations.

The instability of republics 2: Warfare

In addition to the economic issues, republicanism rips societies from their geopolitical roots. As a tightly knit body, republics will have clear-cut boundaries – a tight membership corresponding to clear territorial borders. This places them in tension with outsiders, who may try to trade or make politics with them, and also makes them a highly visible target for attack, so a problem of size and locality emerges. 'If a republic be small, it is destroyed by a foreign force; if it be large, it is ruined by internal imperfection. . . . The evil is in the very thing itself, and no form can redress it' (Nugent 1949: 126). For this reason, Montesquieu argued, republics display a tendency to expansion which creates warfare that often ends in their own destruction. He makes his case through an account of the spread and collapse of the Roman Empire. The Roman republic began as a small republican city state surrounded by barbarians. In order to protect itself and the virtue of its citizens it expanded into the barbarian zones, civilising those it conquered by including them as Roman citizens in the widening Roman territories. The republic expanded ever outwards and eventually the bulk of Roman citizens were not from Rome. The principles of the republic they must protect from barbarians were not related to the *esprit général* of their indigenous, non-Romanic culture. They had never seen the Rome they fought to preserve; they had weak emotional and cultural links with it, so they fought as conscripts or mercenaries, not as fiercely caring virtuous citizens, and they began to lose their battles. In this way, the Roman republic lost its roots in Roman society, lost contact with the actuality of its *esprit général*, and collapsed. In summary Montesquieu wrote, 'Is it not strange but true to say that virtue itself has need of limits?' (Nugent 1949: 150), suggesting that if the republic is to survive, then virtue, the ideal of republicanism, needs to be checked by recognition of practical circumstances in which republicans find themselves operating.

DISCUSSION POINT

Montesquieu's analysis raises the question of whether it is necessary to compromise all or many of our political ideals to establish workable political systems. It also begs the question of whether it is possible to compromise any political ideals, or whether compromise reduces ideals to mere aspirations to be traded off against achievable goals.

Monarchy

There can be little doubt that in discussing monarchies, Montesquieu was aiming his analysis at the political actors of his own time. Not only in France, but throughout Europe, monarchy was the dominant mode of governance. Yet the actual condition of monarchies varied. In England the power of the monarch was checked by Parliament, in Spain the King had an absolute power which was constrained only minimally by the Catholic Church, while in France absolutist pretensions remained constrained by defensive campaign of the aristocratic *Parlements* and the judiciary (nobles of the robe). The ideal type of monarchy as presented by Montesquieu may be seen as a distilling of the principles of organisation common to the various European monarchies. The ideal type, he claimed, shows that monarchy works as a system of governance due to two elements: (1) its driving principle of honour, and (2) the moderation of this principle by the powerful checks on monarchic power made by the aristocracy. In the courts of all great monarchies, the drive which dynamised activity was the court members' pursuit of personal power, wealth and, above all, glory. The encapsulation of these within a system of honorific positions – knighthoods, dukedoms, earldoms and so on – enabled a hotbed of power struggles to exist within the aristocratic class, without open conflict dissolving the court into a war of each against all. Honour is intimately related to glory. Honour is achieved by being seen to do the right thing, and, in a society in which militarism and grandeur were highly valued, being seen to do great things in battle and being seen to have a magnificence of person were a vital means to progress in the court's hierarchy. In court, the hierarchy of honour gave a context for each individual's status, which was preserved through mannered customs of courtly behaviour. The honorific language and titles provided a space of politeness which, even as it enabled individuals to trade subtle threats or make propositions, covered the *realpolitik* of their jousts for power with the cloak of civility. This basic deceit created a situation in which many powers working for their own ends checked each other, and so prevented the concentration of power into the hands of any one person. Thus while the monarch retained dominance, he did not achieve absolute power. Here Montesquieu shows that honour is bound by rules of engagement, which gives a powerful checking role to those who would use it formally, such as a Parliament or judicial body.

Despotism

To Montesquieu's mind, despotism appears less as a type of political constitution than a condition of anti-constitutional politics. In despotisms there is no law, only personalised power, arbitrary force, and as a consequence, a Hobbesian state of fearful uncertainty.

Rewind

Go to Chapter 3 for further information on Hobbesian 'state of nature'.

The term 'despotism' is derived from ancient Greek, in which it was used to denote the power of the patriarch (father) over his family. As this original usage indicated, despotic power is not rule-governed, but is an expression of customary power directed solely by the ruling individual's desires. Arbitrary, personalised, and lacking foundation in laws which regulate the ruler, despotic lawmaking is nothing more than an expression of the ruler's whims, as is the process of judging crime. With no means to know what will be considered lawful and unlawful from moment to moment, and without means to counter the power of the despot, the people live in fearful anticipation of the despot's next decision. He can, it seems, use them as he will or destroy them on a whim. But the despot himself lacks power to be in total control. He cannot be everywhere, so he has to have lieutenants to govern those who live across the territory. Having no legal framework to work with, the lieutenants will each act as little despots, imposing arbitrary rule which they fearfully hope fits the will of the despot. The people fear the lieutenants, who fear the despot. The despot, who is but one man ruling through fear, fears the people, as he knows they can rise up against him if he fails to control them. This in turn makes him reliant on his lieutenants, and so he has reason to fear that they may turn on him also. In despotic regimes everyone keeps their heads down, and so on the surface, despotic societies can seem peaceful and calm, but 'this . . . cannot be called a peace; no, it is only the silence of those towns that the enemy is ready to invade' (Nugent 1949: 59). In despotic societies everyone is a potential enemy of everyone else and life-threatening attacks are always imminent.

Discussion of despotism is the one constant which runs through all Montesquieu's writings, and it serves as a motif – a signpost saying this is where we go if we lose sight of how good politics works to serve our humanity. In precise terms, despotism is posited as the opposite of moderate, or more precisely, moderated government. Monarchies and republics, on the other hand, are presented as two types of moderated government. In monarchy, the power of the state is moderated by the internal check between aristocracy (in both its military and judicial functions) and the monarch. In republics, the power of ruling is governed by the people, who are directly involved or at least formally represented within the state. Unlike despotism, which is a dark and lurking presence in the world, these moderated governments are to be considered as building blocks for working and ethical political systems. However, both monarchies and republics have in them the constant potential to corrupt into despotism: 'the danger is not when the state passes from one moderate to another moderate government, as from a republic to a monarchy, or from a monarchy to a republic; but when it is precipitated from a moderate to a despotic government' (Nugent 1949: 114–115). The development of the Roman Republic into an empire exemplifies how this corruption can take place. At the point of transition, it became too remote from its localised origins to be the community it represented, too large for popular governance, and too driven by the need for conquest for the establishment of civil conditions; it became subject to the arbitrary and self-serving rule of generals who made themselves into emperors.

In monarchies, as in republics, the potential for corruption lies in the principle that drives them, for the quest for glory which is driven by the principle of honour may upset the delicate balance of power it produces. If the checks produced by the balance of aristocratic and monarchic power are lost to an overwhelming monarchic power, the activities of the state become a lawless expression of the monarch's power. Thus the monarchy 'is corrupted when ... the prince ... puts, like the Roman Emperors, Medusa's head on his breast' (Nugent 1949: 114). What is lacking is failsafe checks on the tendencies of the types of moderated political systems in operation to dissolve into despotism.

Montesquieu stresses the irony of the fact that in both monarchies and republics the desire to eradicate difference and uncertainty in the pursuit of security has often led to total uncertainty and insecurity. For this reason, he sets out an alternative system which is rooted in what is now seen as the liberal perception of liberty. Liberty, says Montesquieu, is a legally constructed space where the individual diversity which provides the economic and creative vitality of any society may be expressed in a situation of complete security. This idea is not entirely novel and its author expressly states that it is derived from (though also modifying) the liberty of English citizens, as framed and protected by the English system of constitutional monarchy in place at the time.

There is great power in Montesquieu's vision of despotism. Strong echoes may be seen in the portrayals of the collapse of the empty and lawless systems of Eastern Europe in the 1990s, perhaps most impressively in the decline and fall of the USSR after decades of despotic rule by fearful and lawless dictators. In other cases, visions of despotic fear and lawless rule have been conjured up to portray the political situations in states such as Argentina (during the Falklands War), Iraq (under Saddam Hussein), and Iran (particularly under the rule of the Ayatollahs). However, it should be noted that all these societies are not only anti-liberal, but that they are also the traditional targets of Orientalist prejudices (Iran is the modern state of Persia – the location of Montesquieu's fictitious and influential portrayal of Oriental despotism). The question then arises as to whether the power of Montesquieu's notion of despotism is the power of an insightful analysis into the common failings of non-liberal political systems, or the power of emotive anti-Oriental prejudices to blind us to the reality of each distinct political situation. It is possible, of course, that it is a confusing combination of political insight and cultural prejudice, in which case we have to ask if the two elements can be separated to enable the insights to be used free of prejudicial bias.

Liberty and the rule of law

Liberty in Montesquieu's time was strongly associated with republicanism, but Montesquieu stresses that republicanism lacks the means to provide it in any enduring form. He pointed out that in republican usage, the term referred to a collective space produced by mutual support and collective activity which provides the condition for the well-being of each and every member. He then argued that this notion of liberty is incoherent. The original goal of any political organisation, he argued, is the security of each and every one of its members. Security is intimately connected to liberty, for 'the political liberty of the subject is a tranquillity of mind arising from the opinion each person has of his safety' (Nugent 1949: 151). Yet, in republicanism, the glorification of the idea of excellence through communal participation comes to override the original primacy of security. Republican virtue, abstracting the value of human conduct from that of maintaining security, opens the door to insecurity. Therefore republicanism is unable to produce enduring liberty. In the case of monarchies, the fact that lands are connected to titles distributed by the monarch ensures the fundamental security obtained from control of one's life-supporting resources is not a right but a privilege. Furthermore, the safety of the monarch's subject is always at risk from the demands of combat which a society committed to honour and grandeur promotes. No matter how powerful or benevolent the monarch, an enduring liberty cannot be guaranteed in a monarchic system. Only a peaceful life civilised by friendship and trade can give enduring liberty. Thus government must be committed to maintaining and protecting civil society, and as people driven by their conflicting impulses cannot be trusted to keep that commitment, a sure-fire system which maintains civil society and endures regardless of the people operating it must be developed. This idea lies at the core of Montesquieu's famous notion of the separation of powers.

The separation of powers

Montesquieu's examples show that all states need an in-built device to check their tendencies towards growth into private economic and family spheres, and to tendencies towards corruption, both of which end up destroying the liberty zone which we call civil society. In this light, the separation of powers may be seen as an anti-despotism device. This is how it works: Montesquieu sets out three basic powers of government: executive ('that of executing the public resolutions'), legislative ('that of enacting laws'), and judicial ('of trying the cases of individuals'). 'There would be an end to everything, were the same man or body . . . to exercise those three powers'

(Nugent 1949: 152). By 'everything' he means liberty and security, and therefore human well-being. Therefore the three powers have to be divided and used as checks upon each other. So, for example, if the lawmaker passes a law which gives the state all the property of every citizen, the executive could refuse to put the legislation into action, and the judiciary would find the legislation contrary to the rule of law and reject it. Here, the rule of law operates as the first of two fundamental checks which ensure and express the liberty of the citizens.

Montesquieu was aware that if the law was to act as a check on the ruler and not merely be an instrument of his or her will, then positive law must be founded in the universal and regular principles of natural laws. Natural laws, as they are seen working in the biology of the world and in the physics of the universe, express the 'necessary relationship between things'. For political law to be grounded in natural law it would have to express the necessary relations between the ruler and the citizenry. Like the law of gravity which dictates that everything released into the earth's atmosphere must eventually fall to the ground, the natural law of politics dictates that only legislation which expresses the necessary relationships between humans – that is, works for mutual security, and the general condition of individual liberty – can maintain a functioning socio-political order. Natural law is not only an ethical standard with which a judge can check actual legislation, it is also a practical check, since, as despotism shows, if the rules are no good the system will not work.

The second fundamental check on the corruption of the state is the democratic control of the legislature. Montesquieu argues that the liberty of all members depends on their having the means to check legislators who may seek power over them at their expense. They alone know how exactly legislative plans will affect them in their daily lives, and so, to protect themselves and their condition of life, they should have the power to vote on such plans, and to check that once agreed they are executed properly. In short, every citizen needs a stake in the system of governance; something they can hold on to and use in their defence from time to time. A system of elected representatives gives the citizens a channel to have their needs and to a lesser degree their opinions expressed in the legislative process. It also provides something, or someone, they can get their hands on, give a good shaking and even throw out of office if they feel abused. As we who live in liberal democracies know, our ability to vote out governments provides a constant background to the deliberations and activities of politicians, and from time to time electoral defeat has dramatically halted overbearing executives in their tracks. It is important to note that Montesquieu's liberalism is offset by some elements of aristocratic elitism which some commentators (see below) detect running through the arguments within *The Spirit of the Laws*. Presenting a widely held view of the time, he argued that though the commoners elected members to the legislature these members did not dominate it, and that was how it should be. The pro-active role of drafting and designing legislation should go to the nobility. This was because, on the one hand, most ordinary people were not capable of dealing with the complexities of legislating, though they could respond intelligently to legislative plans which affected them. On the other hand, the interests of the nobility were tied into the interests of the nation. The wealth of noble families, for example, constituted a large portion of the national wealth and so in a sense the noble's private wealth was directly invested in the economic state of the nation. Nobles also had special training in judicial functions, as Nobles of the Robe, in diplomacy, as members of the court, and in internal politics as Members of Parliament. To give them only the same voting rights and functions as ordinary citizens would have been to wrongfully reduce their value and place legislation into the hands of people who would be likely to make a mess of it and, in so doing, threaten the security of the state.

DISCUSSION POINT

The notion of a special aristocratic stakeholding no longer applies, but the underlying idea that an elite of legislators is needed for strong and rational leadership is still popular. Part of this idea is rooted in the notion that the masses are too uneducated or thoughtless (or both) to be trusted to make laws. Does this argument provide an insight into today's political society or is it an inherited prejudice against ordinary people?

From the perspective which is concerned with placing theorists into contexts, the most pressing themes running through the vast range of commentaries on Montesquieu's work are concerned with his status as a social theorist and his status as a political theorist. Put simply the two main issues are, 'Is he a founding father of sociology?', and 'Is he a founding father of constitutional liberalism?' We shall now explore the arguments which claim that the answers to these questions are 'yes', and weigh them up against the opposing arguments. The riposte to both of the 'founding father' debates lies in a single line of argument which presents Montesquieu as a conservative thinker. He is conservative, it is argued, in two senses: first, in the sense that his concerns and methods were those of a traditionalist political thinker as opposed to a ground-breaking sociologist, and second, in the sense that he was a political conservative as opposed to a radical liberal thinker.

Montesquieu: sociologist?

The presentations of Montesquieu's work as sociology began with Emile Durkheim's *Montesquieu and Rousseau: Pioneers of Sociology*, in which the 'father of functionalism' attempted to show how his sociology actually was 'fathered' by Montesquieu. More recently, it has been significantly developed through the claims of such theorists as Ernest Cassirer (1951) and Raymond Aron (1968), as well as Montesquieu 'specialists' such as Alan Baum (1979) and Werner Stark (1960).

The first strand of Durkheim's argument is that Montesquieu initiates new sociological *methods* of examining socio-political orders. Pinpointing Montesquieu's mixing together of abstract theorising on the general rules of social existence with the empirical examination of particular social formations, Durkheim writes, 'Since these rules are established by new methods, they differ greatly from those of earlier writers on politics, who formulated types supposedly transcending all considerations of place and time and suitable to all mankind' (Durkheim 1960: 17).

The methodology Durkheim has in mind is *The Spirit of the Laws*' novel empirical collation of the varied range of physical and cultural conditions encountered by human societies (what Durkheim would call 'facts') and their effective determination of possible political orders of social life (Durkheim 1960: 474–529). The second strand of Durkheim's argument is that Montesquieu 'derives the laws (of political life) from the "nature", not of man, but of the social organism' (Durkheim 1960: 21). The 'nature of man' and its fit into the natural order in general is in fact a continuing theme of *The Spirit of the Laws* and Durkheim's claim is overstated, but it is not simply wrong within the discussions of climate, culture and the political power. *The Spirit of the Laws* does offer a conception of social processes shaping the possibilities of political organisation, and it invites the reader to see such processes as the expression of natural laws. On this basis, Durkheim's claim that Montesquieu's theory is substantively functionalist looks good. Montesquieu's theory does contain elements of a sociological methodology and it does express sociological interests in the external factors which determine political life. What is more it is possible to see hints of functionalist reasoning. For example, there is an implicit functionalism expressed in Montesquieu's argument for checking monarchic power by the nobility. He wrote that if the aristocracy had their political power reduced to that of the commoners, 'the common liberty would be their enslavement and they would have no interest in supporting it' (Nugent 1949: 155). In this statement he indicates that aristocratic power is good not because of any abstract rights due to the aristocrats, but for the very functionalist reason that aristocratic power is good for the functional stability of monarchic society. The general sociological principle being indicated here is that situations and institutions which contribute to the inclusion of all the diverse parts of a social order into the political process are good precisely because they integrate all the parts together into a functioning social order, which is the classic and core functionalist idea.

However, before we can join Durkheim in celebrating Montesquieu as a proto-functionalist, we should note that there are significant problems with his analysis. In attempting to use Montesquieu's work to provide a traditional authority for the functionalist position, Durkheim simultaneously ties *The Spirit of the Laws* into the functionalist project. The question that this approach begs is how could, and why would, an eighteenth-century theorist be involved in a twentieth-century attempt to build an empirical science of society? Once this question is raised, so does the worry that the concerns of the one making the interpretation have forced an artificial shape on to the interpreted text. That there are real grounds to worry becomes clear on looking further into the issue, since the clear lines of an apparent link between Montesquieu's work and functionalism begin to break up almost immediately. Even among those who see Montesquieu as a sociologist, there are those who doubt his functionalist credentials.

As presented by Ernest Cassirer, Montesquieu's 'new method' shapes an entirely different type of sociology. Cassirer says, 'One can say of Montesquieu that he is the first thinker to grasp and to express clearly the concept of the "ideal-type" in history' (Baum 1979: 100). Use of ideal types is a method associated with the sociologist Max Weber, and it is a very different methodology to that outlined by Durkheim. In Weber's method, the ideal type provides a theoretical construct 'formed by the synthesis of a great many . . . more or less present, and occasionally absent, concrete individual phenomena'(Baum 1979: 102), and it is this which gives an ordering sense to the empirical information, even though the empirical information provides the evidential support for his theoretical assertions.

Montesquieu's method often meets Weber's criteria. We have seen how, by use of the traditional but previously loosely defined categories of republics, monarchy and despotism, he builds ideal types which 'are not merely aggregates of accidentally acquired properties, but . . . were, so to speak, pre-formed, the expression of a certain structure' (Cassirer 1951: 210).

The fact that two very different types of sociology may be found in Montesquieu's work indicates that there is a problem in locating a coherent and constant sociological method. The problem is exacerbated by the fact that quite often in his work Montesquieu uses the methods and categories of the philosophic tradition which dominated political thinking up to his time and so is not consistently sociological throughout.

It is at this point that the argument against interpreting Montesquieu's work as sociology takes effect. Even as the first claims for Montesquieu as sociologist were being made, the case for Montesquieu the traditionalist philosopher was set out in M. Levin's *The Political Doctrine of The Spirit of the Laws: Its Classical Background* (Sparks 1999: xxxvi), in which the author set out in detail Montesquieu's use of the ideas and arguments of the ancient Greek and Roman philosophers. We have seen some elements of Montesquieu's traditionalism in this chapter. For example, we saw that Montesquieu perceived human problems to derive from human nature. What is sometimes obscured by concentration on his relativism is that he consistently argues that, regardless of the diversity of cultural expression and social orders of life, all human interaction derives from this nature, and is expressed in political relations. Here we see a traditionalist whose concern is to establish and secure the place of 'man' in nature, and the nature of 'man'. This concern dominated traditional political theory and set it apart from modern social science.

In recent times, Thomas Pangle has argued that, although the concern with social order and cultural values made Montesquieu's work novel within the tradition of political theory at that time, its conceptualisations of 'society' were politically underdeveloped and thus 'notions of the "social" and "society" played a secondary role in his study' (Pangle 1973: 45). Following a careful exposition of Montesquieu's concern with human nature, and the equally traditional concern with the source and dimensions of natural law, Pangle concludes that 'Montesquieu is in accord with the tradition of political philosophy as opposed to modern sociology' (Pangle 1973: 45).

DISCUSSION POINT

The fact that in some parts *The Spirit of the Laws* uses traditional philosophical concepts or methods, and in other parts appears to operate very different sociological methods does create difficulty with claims for Montesquieu as a sociologist, but does it not also reinforce the picture of him as a precursor of sociology?

Montesquieu: liberal or conservative?

Early in this century a fierce debate erupted between the political historians Mathiez and Carcassonne as to whether Montesquieu's work was an argument for the conservation of the monarchy by buttressing it with a constitutionally strengthened aristocracy (Carcassonne), or whether it was a reactionary defence of aristocratic power against the modernising monarchy (Mathiez). The precise details of that debate are of no concern to us here, the point being that both historians, in their own way, sought to show that Montesquieu's concerns were with the power struggle between his class and the monarchy. The underlying implication of *both arguments* was that liberal readings of *The Spirit of the Laws* separated the work from its context in the struggle for power within the *ancien régime* and so were profoundly off the mark.

Methodologically the suggestion is that liberal interpretations effectively separate the issue of the meaning and value of the text as a piece of political theory from its historical value. Politically the suggestion is that the liberal interpretations of Montesquieu misunderstand the principle he was advocating and that their constitutions which claim to derive from his principles are in fact built on sand. Carcassonne's reading of *The Spirit of the Laws* in particular has become very influential. He suggested that the principle of the separation of powers could be best described as a formalising of the traditional check on the monarch's power by those whose long-held familial control over much of the French land, including its use for production and the livelihoods of those who work it, gives them a vested interest in the well-being of the common people and the protection and good use of the country's terrain. In short, he claimed that Montesquieu is advocating a balance of governmental power by an elite motivated by *noblesse oblige*. In support of this argument, we have already seen evidence that Montesquieu was inclined to present the aristocracy as a special force within the polity. In addition, it is hard not to read the final sections of *The Spirit of the Laws* as a defence of aristocratic power. Carcassonne points out that the final parts of the work refer to a hot theoretical debate of his time in which ideologues of the monarchy and of the opposing *Parlements* attempted to establish the origins of the French monarchy's power and the rights of the aristocracy in relation to it. Sticking to his method, Montesquieu gathered together all available documentation to show decisively that the origins of both lay in the warlike conquest of the Romanic civilisation by the Franks, and that from this time the King and his warrior nobles had governed together through an edgy, sometimes combative, but always mutually checking balance of power.

The method of contextualisation does point up the shortcomings of ahistorical readings (and in doing so delivers a blow to cruder presentations of Montesquieu as a sociologist), but it does not preclude the possibility of producing a historically tenable liberal interpretation.

Pangle shows how Montesquieu's argument may be read as a simultaneous defence of aristocratic power, and as an argument for limited government, individual liberty and free trade without confusion or incoherence. He writes: 'first, he (Montesquieu) wishes to preserve the balance of powers and principle of honour that makes the nation "moderate". Second, he wants to preserve the charms of the French way of life. . . . Third, he wants to extend the beneficent influence of commerce through a type of commerce that is in harmony and dependent on that tasteful aristocratic tone; he hopes to persuade French to move towards English commercial politics within a French context' (Pangle 1973: 290). Strikingly, the greatest difference between English and French society of the time was the absence of a strong and assertive middle class in France, while in England, the aristocracy was not so numerous nor, since the English civil war, so powerful as in France. It would make political sense (as well as serving Montesquieu's class interests) to apply the general system of checks and balances to the particular French situation so that the aristocracy performed the checking power which in other societies might be controlled by other social groupings.

Fast forward

Go to Chapter 6 for details of class structure in French eighteenth-century society.

Two points may be made here. First, Pangle's analysis points to the way in which a historically informed analysis of an actual situation of political crisis can perceive the principles from which a rectification of *that* crisis may be derived, *and* from which many other imbalances of power may be rectified or precluded. Second, the ability of Montesquieu to weave a conservative case for aristocratic power out of a liberal design for limited liberal democracy and conservative elitism are more entwined than many will allow. It is notable that the British Houses of Parliament upon which Montesquieu modelled the social construction of his new model of government embodied within it a tri-part division of social classes into commoners (House of Commons), aristocracy (House of Lords) and monarchy until the end of the twentieth century. In so doing they exemplify the ease with which conservatism can blend with liberalism.

Conclusion

The Spirit of the Laws is notoriously lacking obvious structure. Summarising the response of many, Becker called it 'a book of disconnected reflections' (Baum 1979: 106). Sabine, rather more aggressively, wrote: 'there is not in truth much concatenation of subject matter and the amount of irrelevance is extraordinary' (Sabine 1963: 556). The jumbled character of *The Spirit of the Laws* is probably due in part to the untested novelty of his general approach. Montesquieu signalled that with *The Spirit of the Laws* he believed himself to have pioneered a completely novel approach to political study when he described the work as 'a child created without a mother' (Pangle 1973: 235), and *The Spirit of the Laws* exemplifies pioneering work which is often confused and muddled, since the pioneer – the one who goes first – has to mark out a map from a strange, confusing and unmarked environment. Pioneers usually go astray and make clumsy errors. The pioneer still produces novel and world-changing outcomes; even errors such as Columbus naming the Caribbean islands the 'West Indies' come to mark out lasting changes in the order of things. Although inevitably marked by confusion and error, pioneering works become historically and socially significant. Such is the case with Montesquieu's work which has (at least) a twofold significance. First, it lays before us a problem of understanding at the heart of social science: that the relativity expressed in the diversity of people's modes of life appears to deny the universality of reason, yet such diverse social orders of life can only be understood through the application of an overarching universalistic rationality. The difficulty can be put shortly and bluntly in the form of a paradox: 'The truth is that all truth is relative.' It is this paradox which encapsulates modern theorists' encounter with the uncertainties of understanding.

Second, it has a political significance. The model of moderated government devised in *The Spirit of the Laws* derived from an analytic distillation of every political situation then known of in France and was designed to be the most universally applicable system of governance. It is not only viable in the liberal democratic model used in the USA. Because the system is designed to incorporate difference and diversity, and because its design is built in recognition of the dangers to the polity inherent in a society which includes overt difference, the system can be extended and modified to meet new situations where the differences within modern societies are placing the integrity and identity of the polity and the citizenry at risk. Consider, for example, the many divided societies of the present time which have developed the principles of Montesquieu's system to balance power between conflicting constituent groups. In Northern Ireland, for example, the peace process which began the new century was built upon the (belated) realisation that the differences which threatened to break this society were those which also made it what it was. The differences have to be included and made to work for the continuation of that society, so a delicate mix of a proportional electoral system presentation which ensures that representatives of Loyalists, Unionists, Nationalists and Republicans are on the legislative body, with a carefully constructed allocation of places on the executive given to representatives of those same groupings. Another example is the Malaysian political system. Malaysian society is characterised by a culturally diverse patchwork of (mainly) ethnically defined subgroups. Again, the diverse groups which give it its strong identity also hold the constant potential to rip it apart. Similar situations may be found in the Lebanon, where conflicting religious groups share power through a system of allocating positions of power to representatives of different groupings. A different way in which Montesquieu's idea may be extended is in extra-large polities, such as the USA or the European Union. The danger is that a unitary central government would be out of touch with and beyond the influence of citizens in the outer reaches of the polity. In the USA this problem has been addressed by distribution of governmental responsibilities and power between federal (central) and state (local) government. While each level of government acts as if they are near-sovereign in their own domain, neither is so; not only is the range of their power limited in itself, it is restricted by the powers of the other. Even in the relatively small nation state that is the UK, the Montesquieuian principle of checks and balances is being developed in response to over-mighty central government. In the recently devolved UK, the central governmental powers of Westminster are now limited by powers devolved to the electorally popular Scottish Parliament, the Northern Ireland Assembly and the Mayor of London.

It is no surprise that Montesquieu's recommended system of checks and balances has lasted and is now being developed into ever more formulations, for the principles of the constitutional liberalism were drawn out of his wonder upon Europe's encounter with the varied cultures, economic practices and political systems across the globe. As we enter an age in which politics and economics are increasingly global, liberal politicians and 'captains of commerce' face the problem of how to recognise and include the huge range of diverse cultural and economic systems of life within what they hope will be a commercial, liberal, global society.

Revision notes

1 *Historical*: There is, of course, an intense familiarity to Montesquieu's ideas. In part, this is because his ideas were developed from considerations of the emerging liberal parliamentary government in Britain (although the British system has never had a true separation of powers). However, it is possibly of greater significance that his huge influence on eighteenth-century intellectuals led to a version of his blueprint being adopted by the founding fathers of the USA. The American Revolution occurred in the designing and creating of a new model polity constituted on clearly defined first principles which were those set out in *The Spirit of the Laws*. In making the separation of powers the cornerstone of their constitution, and in prioritising the free flow of goods and ideas in a commercial civil society, the founding fathers shaped the mould of many subsequent modern states designed to deliver security of life and liberty and to enable 'the pursuit of happiness'.

2 *Philosophical*: Montesquieu's argument tracks a line marking out an inherent balancing of tensions in the natural order of things. It begins with an account of the need for checks and balances between desire and need, passion and reason in the human condition to checks and balances between the institutions of the human-serving state. A state which having in-built checks and balances is inherently uncertain (like the human psyche), but which also provides the means to manage the uncertainties of human life. So, using intellect to understand the drives of our inner nature and the conditions of possibility as set by our natural environment, we find that the natural law of human social existence and all the various types of society may be judged as ethical and/or practicable in terms of this natural law. None fit completely, but the implication is that those with the means and will to modify towards the separated powers model will be all right while the rest will slide into despotism.

Bibliography

Aron, R. (1968) *Main Currents in Sociological Thought*, Vol. 1, Harmondsworth: Penguin.

Baum, J.A. (1979) *Montesquieu and Social Theory*, Oxford: Pergamon Press.

Cassirer, E. (1951) *The Philosophy of the Enlightenment*, New Jersey: Princeton University Press.

Cobban, A. (1969) *The Eighteenth Century: Europe in the Age of the Enlightenment*, London: Thames & Hudson.

Durkheim, E. (1960) *Montesquieu and Rousseau: Pioneers of Sociology*, trans. Ralph Manheim, Michigan: Michigan University Press.

Montesquieu, C.-L. (1949) *The Spirit of the Laws*, trans. Nugent, London, New York: Hafner Press.

—— (1973) *The Persian Letters*, trans. Betts, London: Penguin.

Ogg, D. (1965) *Europe of the Ancien Régime 1715–1783*, London: Fontana.

Pangle, T.L. (1973) *Montesquieu's Philosophy of Liberalism*, London: University of Chicago Press.

Sabine, G.H. (1963) *A History of Political Theory* (3rd edn), London: Harrap & Co.

Sparks, C. (1999) *Montesquieu's Vision: Uncertainty and Modernity in Political Philosophy*, Lewiston, Queenstown, Lampeter: Edwin Mellin Press.

Stark, W. (1960) *Montesquieu: Pioneer of the Sociology of Knowledge*, London: Routledge & Kegan Paul.

Further reading

An excellent introduction to Montesquieu is provided by Judith Shkar's contribution to the Oxford University Press Past Masters Series: *Montesquieu* (1987) Oxford: Oxford University Press. The classic bibliographic study is R. Shackleton (1963) *Montesquieu: A Critical Biography*, Oxford: Oxford University Press. Useful contextual studies are provided by C. Franklin (1969) *The Faith Of Reason*, London: Octagon Books, and N. Keohane (1980) *Philosophy and the State in France: The Renaissance to the Enlightenment*, New Jersey: Princeton University Press.

Jean Jacques Rousseau

Man is born free and he is everywhere in chains.

(*The Social Contract*)

Political theorists and actors have been chewing over the writings of Jean Jacques Rousseau since he burst on to the scene in 1750 with his prize-winning essay, *Discourse on the Sciences and the Arts*. Whether viewed from the perspective of the political theorist or from that of the historian of ideas, Rousseau's work is a rich dish placed before a hungry table and, like all great dishes, its magic lies not in its simple constituent parts, but in the mix of texture and flavours which constitutes the whole. What has consistently struck commentators on Rousseau's work is its sweet and sour concoction of apparently opposing trains of thought. It is often noted that his work is marked by an overt individualism, and, in seeming contradiction with this, an apparent advocation of the supremacy of the state. In addition, the work is noted for the apparent contradiction between its romantic attachment to the idea of a non-political and rustic familial life and its arguments for a totally politicised city state. As is immediately apparent, Rousseau's work is going to confound anyone seeking an easy interpretation, and indeed commentators have interpreted his work in a host of ways, some painting him as a romantic individualist, others as a totalitarian collectivist, while others have tried to align the opposing tendencies in his thought. These different interpretations of his ideas have often been integrated with assessment of his impact on the world of political action, particularly his influence on the events of the French Revolution.

Rousseau's central political idea was that inequality – so integral to the socio-political order of the *ancien régime* – was unnatural and produced the immiseration of humankind. This argument has had an impact on the French revolutionaries who not only saw him as an intellectual forefather, but as a rebel, and gave him a unique status: the revolution's iconic figurehead.

The reason why this involvement intrigues so many commentators is that the French Revolution is viewed as a historical watershed. Along with its counterpart, the American Revolution, it was the first attempt to construct anew a democratic, secular, sovereign nation state. All the features of these two great events – the method of revolution, the construction of a centralised elected legislature, the tying of nation-hood to statehood – have become commonplace in modern political activity, and are now the norm (with the exception of revolution, even though revolutionary ideology and practice has had a long and influential life in modern politics). The French Revolution stands apart from its American counterpart, however, in that it dissolved into bloody factional conflict for control of the state – a scenario known, with chilling simplicity, as 'the terror'.

The fact that many of those involved in the terror were self-declared followers of Rousseau has meant that his status as a political theorist has suffered ever afterwards from association with revolutionary terror and dictatorship. Thus a central concern for many commentators is the degree to which Rousseau's ideas promoted the establishment of the modern nation state, and/or contributed to the emergence of a modern politics in which control of the state is the overwhelming goal and terror the means to achieve it. Pursuit of such issues drags the commentator towards examination of the relationship of Rousseau's theory to the historical situation of his time. (It should be noted that Rousseau was not directly involved with the French

Revolution. He died in 1778, some ten years before it erupted, and lived in a world dominated by the affairs of the *ancien régime*.) The commentators ask 'How might Rousseau's work have been involved in the radical changes to the political environment which followed his death, and how might this new environment, with its allegedly Rousseauian theoretical core, have set the terms for the later common model of modern nation state?' These are the intriguing and important questions about Rousseau and we shall consider them in the final section of this chapter, but before doing so it is necessary to sort out the basics. We need to establish what was the socio-political context in which Rousseau worked. We also need to familiarise ourselves with the basic ideas and central arguments set out in Rousseau's original texts. We shall approach these two tasks, first, by way of an exploration of the social struggles, and the philosophical and political issues which dominated Rousseau's time and profoundly influenced his whole way of thinking. Having completed this contextualisation, we shall then examine in more detail the arguments which Rousseau subsequently developed in the text which made his reputation as a political theorists: *The Social Contract*.

Rousseau and the *ancien régime*

By the beginning of the eighteenth century the demise of the Catholic Church's authority, and consequently of its power, had stimulated questioning of the legitimacy (moral authority) of the established power-holders within the *ancien régime*. This catalysed disputes between pretenders to power, with the Church, the monarchy, the aristocracy and the increasingly influential bourgeoisie each questioning the source of others' authority to rule, while attempting to present theoretical grounds for differing perceptions of legitimate power.

This scenario involved the political theorists of the time who tended to recognise their role as architects of ideologies, mapping out blueprints for ethical and practically functional orders of power (Mann 1993: 175–179). Many, including Rousseau, offered their ideas to powerful political players. Thus while they were, as theorists, concerned primarily to clarify and explain the fundamentals of political life in general, their arguments were run through with the concerns of the times. It is significant that while the focus and method of the individual theorists varied, all attempted, with flashes of insight that only gifted participants and firsthand observers could achieve, to clarify the source, structure and scope of a legitimate sovereign power. Prior to the seventeenth century, the term 'sovereign' was little used and only loosely understood. However, as ever-more secular territorial states increasingly became the dynamic centres of political power, the implications and importance of the idea of sovereignty became more profound. In the hands of political theorists of the seventeenth century, the idea of sovereignty moved from a rough conception of 'kingship', often meaning only limited powers within a theocratic continental system of power, towards the current conception, which rests on the definition of an ultimate decision-making power governing a collection of people living in common within an identified territory – an idea which was focused on and honed into various monarchical, republican and liberal parliamentarian forms, to be used as an ideological weapon for and against the various bodies struggling to establish new terms of political power. Thus, by the early eighteenth century, the issue of sovereignty was of central importance for both political activists and theorists. Viewed in this context, it is hard not to see that Rousseau's political theory, like his immediate forebears and contemporaries, is shot through with a concern to establish the principles of sovereign power (Wokler 1995: 139–150). His arguments are aimed at establishing the universal principles of sovereignty, and, in this respect the insights they reveal and the uncertainties which beset them are of import to political thinkers and actors in general. His work is loaded with implications for his immediate political environment, and its historical significance derives largely from the conjunction of his arguments with the popular concerns and political needs which dominated the political events of eighteenth-century France.

As the eighteenth century moved into its second half, the power struggle between the monarchy and the aristocrats which dominated the politics of the *ancien régime* became increasingly infiltrated by the activities and concerns of a slowly developing bourgeoisie, a class centred on commercially propertied entrepreneurs. At the time, the growing presence of this emerging class was unclear in France. While in England a distinct group of Anglican freeholders had already established full citizenship rights for themselves, the emergence of a new property-owning gentry in France was obscured by the tendency of the aristocracy to expand and incorporate newly wealthy people into it. Thus, while the English aristocracy remained distinct and struggled to combat its new rivals, the much larger and socially diverse French aristocracy incorporated strata of noble gentry.

 Rewind

Go to Chapter 5 for details of Montesquieu's social and political theory.

It was perhaps for this reason that the twin pillars of the Enlightenment French thinking, Montesquieu and Voltaire, sought to prescribe remedies to the constitutional and socio-cultural tensions of the *ancien régime*, in terms of balancing or mixing the aristocratic and monarchic strata into variations of constitutional monarchy. Montesquieu's and Voltaire's political vision may also have been affected by their own status as members of the aristocratic classes. In contrast, Rousseau saw things with the eyes of an outsider. He was not French, but, as he proudly announced himself in his writings, a 'citizen of Geneva'. Furthermore, he was from the artisan classes; he was a watchmaker's son who struggled and failed to cope with the subordinate life of an apprentice in several different trades. He had to earn his living as a footman to a female aristocrat, and only in his late thirties did he begin to earn income and fame through his writing. After winning the prestigious Academy of Dijon prize for his essay 'Discourse on the Sciences and the Arts' in 1750, he became a celebrated figure within the world of the *philosophes*, but he and they were always very aware that he was not of their class, and did not even share their common status as French citizens.

Rousseau was a stranger in a strange land. He was always on the outside and he knew it. This separateness provided him with the critical perspective which, so sought after by the rest of us, was to him an almost unbearable burden. He ended his days hounded from country to country by malevolent powermongers, religious leaders whose dogma he offended, and conservative politicians seeking to appease them. Beset by degenerative illness, driven by resentment and hostility into a world of isolation, he fell into a state of paranoiac semi-madness (Cranston 1997).

KEY PEOPLE

The *philosophes*

The term applies to those theorists who formed the intellectual elite of eighteenth-century France. Most *philosophes* were generalists; they discussed ethics, mathematics, art and politics with confidence, but they were not a 'school' in that they did not all adopt the same arguments or methodologies, and their discourse was as marked by disagreement as agreement. What they did share was a belief that science and rationalism spread through education would liberate humankind from the errors and unhappiness created by religious superstition. They worked towards the creation of 'a society governed by rational, universal principles, administered by merit' (Mann 1993: 167). Politically, this common belief set the *philosophes* against the Catholic Church which used its great influence over the monarchy to dominate all aspects of life.

Apart from Voltaire and Montesquieu, the two most influential *philosophes* were Diderot and D'Alembert. In addition to their individual work, these two combined as editors of the *Encyclopédie* regarded by many as the 'manifesto of the Enlightenment'.

Rousseau did initially mix with the *philosophes*, but fell out with them, one by one, following personal disputes. In his final years the *philosophes* regarded him as a pariah.

Rousseau's life's experience fed his desire for inclusion as an equal participant in a civil society. In such a light it is possible to understand why Rousseau not only mounted a critique of the absolutist tendencies of the *ancien régime*, but also rejected Montesquieu's and Voltaire's arguments for a system of limited inclusion into a parliamentary system for the propertied classes, arguing instead for the inclusion of members of all social classes into political life as citizens. It was for this reason, along with 'the power of his exhortation and the excitement of his prose' (Hampson 1983: 55), that Rousseau's argument would also hold such great appeal both to the intellectuals of the emerging bourgeoisie, and to the peasantry, whose resentment and energy were deployed by the bourgeoisie in effecting the revolution.

Rousseau against civilisation

In the seventeenth and early eighteenth centuries, European culture was inspired and shocked by contemporary explorers' encounters with different and apparently more natural human societies in the 'new world'. A flood of travel writings by adventurers in the 1600s, and fantasy adventures such as *Robinson Crusoe* and *Gulliver's Travels* in the early 1700s, excited the European imaginations with stories of worlds apparently beyond recognisable civilisation. In many cases, these worlds were said to be peopled by humans still living in a state of nature. The Europeans' sense that they too had been/might be like the aboriginals of the new world catalysed a series of reflections on the virtues and limits of the civilising process.

Rousseau's response was a series of passionately intense works, some fiction, others political theory, which, taken together, express grieving for the loss of natural simplicity, and bewail the over-presence of artificial civilising customs and institutions. In *Emile*, Rousseau writes, 'from the beginning to the end civilised man is a slave. At birth he is sewn up in swaddling bands, and at death nailed down in a coffin' (Boyd 1966: 15). In contrast, he writes in *Origins of Inequality*,

> There is, I feel, an age at which an individual man would want to stop. You will seek the age at which you would want your species to have stopped. Dissatisfied with your present state for reasons that portend even greater bounds for dissatisfaction for your unhappy posterity, perhaps you would like to go backwards in time.
>
> (Rousseau 1992: 18)

These comments, along with many similar ones found throughout his writing, are driven by a desire for a quasi-mythical simple and natural life that he believes has been lost. They amount to a call to think negatively about the civilising process which had brought Europeans from the ancient into the modern world. A theoretical issue which derives from this, and which has much bearing on the political significance of Rousseau's work, is the degree to which this stance is deployed as a device to highlight what is lacking and what is detrimentally present in his world, and the degree to which it is an emotive appeal to retrieve a quasi-mythical lost utopia.

This is a big issue, since it feeds into the question of whether Rousseau's following arguments on the best political order are built on an emotive appeal to alternatives which could not exist and that could lead to misguided pursuits of unobtainable polities, or whether they provide a reasoned basis for analysing the needs of humans to which any order of social power should be addressed. With this question in mind, we shall explore Rousseau's presentation of a pre-civilised 'golden age' (Cullen 1993: 52) and examine the ways in which it informs his notion of a desirable and achievable political order of life.

From the state of nature to the virtuous republic

The cultural fascination with the primitive state coincided (not accidentally) with the unhinging of theological edicts and scientific procedure which accompanied the decline in Catholic dominance over European thought and practice. Together, these events set political theorists a new task – to establish if there was a God-given and/or naturally prescribed order of human life, and if so the relationship of their own 'artificial' civilisation to it. They responded by trying to set universal grounds for the moral and practical conduct of human lives by establishing how humans would live in a state of nature. The logic was that you cannot know what's good for people if you don't know their fundamental needs. To understand this you need to know how humans function as a natural species type, and how they fit into the general context of their natural world.

By Rousseau's time, this approach was well established. He employed the method at the outset of his political theorising (in *Discourse on the Origins of Inequality*, 1755), but with one distinction; he was acutely aware that it was extremely difficult not to read into the interpretation of natural man's behaviour contemporary modes of understanding and activity which are products of what we might call modern Western socialisation, and what eighteenth-century theorists would call the products of civilisation. He asks: 'How will man be successful in seeing himself as nature formed him?' (Rousseau 1992: 17). His attempt to answer this question involved the construction of a 'hypothetical history' of what, he argued, must have been the human condition before the development of civilisation (Rousseau 1992: 17).

His argument goes as follows: in the state of nature humans lived in the immediacy of their natural environment and their immediate physical needs and pleasures. Rousseau present this creature, 'satisfying his hunger under an oak tree, quenching his thirst at the first stream, finding his bed at the foot of the same tree that supplied his meal; and thus all his needs are met' (Rousseau 1992: 19). Self-absorbed and solitary, the natural human did not need or possess language. Lacking language, their potential to reason, to build abstract images of potential futures from present experience, to plan and to build, is undeveloped, as are the social constructs which such activities produce. Thus, even though they possessed the latent potential to reason and to construct an artificial order of life (a civilised society), they lived, contentedly and independently, as animals. Like other animals with the exception of the basic natural sentiment of pity (see below), they lived with regard only to their own self (Rousseau 1992: 24). They are, Rousseau says, motivated by a basic sense of 'self-love'. This is not vanity; it is a simple condition of constant reaction to basic experience of immediate desires which expresses a concern with immediate well-being.

The idea of self-love remains vital to Rousseau's thinking, since, he reckons, though we have become something far more sophisticated than this simple natural creature, we too experience life as moments of our own individuality and are driven towards self-satisfaction through volition – the active expression of our individual will. To be true to ourselves – that is, to be human – we must remain in connection with our essential natural being. To do this, we must remain alert to our individual needs and wants.

The one expression of care for others which Rousseau allows for natural human beings is pity – an emotion which creates empathy with others (Rousseau 1992: 36–37). Pity plays an important role in Rousseau's argument on the development of humans from natural solitude to social life. As a basic and fundamental human emotion, pity performs the vital function of bridging the island of self to others present and, combined with what we would call psycho-sexual desires, it expresses the fact of basic relations with others who exist for the individual as an extension of their biological being – their mate, their mother and other family members. In doing this, pity establishes the links between individuals, which stimulate humans' latent capacity to think and act beyond animal immediacy.

The family: pre-political society

Although families spring directly from natural emotions, they are not simply of nature. They are early forms of social life, in which humans exhibit the qualities which Rousseau's contemporaries and we, his later readers, would ascribe to human beings.

Familial life, requiring communication, facilitates speech, and, with this, the capacity to reason abstractly which enables individual people to understand the dimensions of their relationship to others. It takes humans into a realm where they have the capacity for moral decision-making, and places them in situations where moral decisions would have to be taken. The moral being who, produced by family life, has a conscience which acts as a guiding go-between for its reasoning self and its natural desires. Rousseau argues that conscience is vital to each and every individual's well-being because it stimulates reasoned action, with the utmost respect for our natural desires, and in so doing drives our will towards right action.

Overall, then, the family is a social form of life which incorporates natural human experience, while giving it a social context – a sphere of other people with their own feelings, desires and volition – against which each member negotiates their own position and thus becomes self-consciously distinct. In this way family living creates liberty, a space prescribed and preserved by rules, in which free action becomes understood and valued.

Historically speaking, simple family living provides the juncture between 'the "first times" and the present' (Cullen 1993: 54). It is the moment in which the unreflective solitariness of the natural condition is transformed into the self-awareness of individuality, which is the necessary condition for a fully human existence.

Rousseau's picture suggests not only that the simple family must have existed, but also that it must have done so prior to the complex societies familiar to us. He speculates that it was the change in the economic organisation of collective life, from family-centred hunting and gathering to agrarian modes of production requiring the integration of families into larger social groups on a regular basis, which brought to an end the golden age of pre-political existence.

In the gradual shift towards larger society, the simple emotional bonds of the family are subsumed into complex relations produced by the conversion of the shared environment into property. He writes, 'the first person who, having enclosed a plot of land took it into his head to say *this is mine* and found people simple enough to believe him, was the true founder of civil society' (Rousseau 1992: 44). As this quote indicates, relations in such a society are competitive; individuals and factions protect their property against others; property gives relative status (that is, each evaluation of themselves as a property owner by measurement against others in the society) and so socio-economic classes arise. In such a development, simple, natural, self-love is transformed into *amour propre* – a love of the self over and against others. Vanity and greed break humans' basic link with their natural sensibilities, pity is overwhelmed by self-interest, and we enter a war of each against all, from which we need to construct a state for protection. States brought into being through this process were a product of malformed beings – cut off from their natural sensibility (due largely to the unnatural creation of property), and, as a product of malformed beings, the states' logic and structure expressed their corrupted thinking. Such states, argued Rousseau, existed everywhere. They worked as vehicles of warring self-interested parties seeking self-aggrandisement and power over others. Whether despotic emperors, absolutist monarchs, or even elected Parliaments, they all used their powers to enable factions to gather up and possess material goods in excess of their need at the expense of others. In short, the states of the civilised world manufactured and maintained inequality, an inequality which reduces the propertyless to material deprivation – whereas in nature they had abundance – and which seduces the rich and powerful to such a degree that they all but lose entirely their natural sensibility, and become corrupted, broken versions of their natural selves. Thus civilisation is not an expression of human progress, but of humans' alienation from their natural self – a condition which breeds psychological unhappiness and material immiseration: 'Man is born free and he is everywhere in chains' (Rousseau 1986: 49).

The body politic

So the question he puts to his contemporaries, and to all those following in the civilised world, is: 'How do we liberate our human selves?' Civilisation fundamentally separates humans from their natural selves; for human happiness in an age where natural life is lost, the first task – a task of anyone attempting to liberate humans from the double enslavement of moral and intellectual impoverishment and social inequality – is the facilitation of the basic human qualities once nurtured by the family. In an age where the family is overwhelmed by more powerful social institutions, the task is to engineer a social order of life in which the basic human qualities, that were once maintained by the family, are artificially produced. Rousseau is suggesting the need for a radical constitutional politics – the building of a new social order in which the humanising of social members operates as the benchmark for all social and political arrangements.

Such a task could be carried out only by someone who is not already dehumanised and immiserated by civilisation. The task must be performed by a founding father. Rousseau describes this person as 'the legislator' – an outsider with 'a superior intelligence' who can understand 'all the passions of men without feeling any of them; who (has) no affinity with our nature, yet (knows) it through and through' (Rousseau 1986: 162). He is a person of great wisdom, who being an outsider would have no personal stake in the social and political order he would create and could be trusted to act impartially according to the needs of all. To ensure no corrupting self-interest creeps into the design, the legislator must leave once they have designed the new constitution, and so remain uninvolved in the social and economic relations maintained by the political order they design. In an ideal scenario, the legislator would be given the task of constructing laws that will build social institutions and processes which promote the development of simple self-love and care for others, and that will exclude any social organisation which promotes the advancement of *amour propre*. In short, the legislator would constitute the ideal state.

The general characteristics of Rousseau's ideal state

Rousseau's analysis of humans in a state of nature and of pre-political familial life provides a guide to the type of socio-political order the legislator would have to introduce to the civilised world. The main features of such a state are as follows.

The simple family is the model for the social order

In Rousseau's presentation, the size, and the inclusiveness and exclusiveness, of the simple family were important factors in its capacity to provide well-being for its members. Direct close living produced familiarity and nurtured a social order which was informal, and egalitarian, which required participation in economic protective and cultural activity and so kept the community together. The only way to reintroduce familial communality into the civilised world would be the construction of small-scale political communities – in which the prevailing conditions established the requirement and the means for full-scale participation in ethical and practical communal life and in the collective discourse on the conditions of communality. Thus the ideal political order presented in *The Social Contract* is 'a very small state where it is easy for the people to gather together, and where each citizen can easily know all the others' (Rousseau 1986: 180).

The ideal state would be a direct democracy

For the people to have their humanising liberty while collecting under the rule of a government, the government must express the will of the people. To do so it must actually be as close as is possible to the same thing as the people. Representation, while sometimes necessitated by limits of time or by the large numbers of citizens even within a small state, cannot express the will of citizens. Being represented means not speaking or acting for oneself. It means not making decisions but having them made for you. It means being excluded from the act of volition. Where representation is absolutely necessary, delegates who do no more than voice the will of those who elected them can perform a limited governmental function, but free thinking and independent representatives of the kind elected to Western Parliaments are the mark of an elite ruling over and possibly against the will of the people. Thus he says, 'the English people believes itself to be free. It is greatly mistaken; it is free only during election of the members of parliament. Once they are elected, the populace is enslaved; it is nothing' (Rousseau 1986: 198).

The ideal state would be Spartan

In Rousseau's time it was commonplace to look to the ancient Greeks and the Roman Republic for guidance on good political order. In following this trend, Rousseau produced a model of such a community in (a highly romanticised) image of ancient Sparta. The Spartan city state was fiercely egalitarian. It did not allow private wealth, it allowed little distinction in social status, and so, Rousseau argued, there was little chance for the corrupting development of *amour propre*. The collectivity, acting as the state, enforced a requirement for each individual's totally committed involvement in the economic, political and military engagements of the community. The Spartan state was the collectivity, reinforcing its common purpose through its laws, which were its customs imposed. Individuals who deviated were punished with fierce severity. Rousseau argued that the Spartan requirement for each individual to give total commitment to the community produced strongly ethical and supremely practical people. For the ancient Greeks, the combination of ethical and practical excellence in a social member was conceptualised in the notion of the virtuous citizen. For Rousseau, the life of a virtuous citizen was the best option available to humans deprived of the environment of the rustic family. Thus the legislator had to replace natural isolation with artificial collectivity: to make it so that 'each citizen can do nothing except through the cooperation of others' (Cranston 1986: 85).

The ideal state would be a nation state

The one major modification of the Spartan system in Rousseau's ideal model was the replacement of the city state with the idea of the public body as a nation. Rousseau's work is often marked out by contemporary historians as the fountain-head of modern nationalism, but in truth, the concept of the national identity had already been made popular by Montesquieu in his discussions of '*l'esprit général*' (the general character) specific to each nation. Many, including Rousseau, took up and developed this idea, presenting it as a fact. For Rousseau, the specific character of a nation, with its enclosed inclusive order (membership being perceived as dependent on genetic stock and historical 'roots' in the national terrain), with economic independence and self-protective capacity, provided an alternative quasi-natural order to the pre-political family. The ideal model he then set himself to construct would be one in which the dimensions of the Spartan city state were developed, in the constitution of the larger entity of a nation, in the form of a national body politic.

KEY CONCEPT

Nation and nationalism

The term 'nation' is commonly used to denote a body of people who possess common physical traits; emotional behaviour, language and culture derived from the communities' history of existence in the unique environmental circumstances of their place in the world. Historically the ideal of the nation was a key element in the construction of European nation states, which in turn set the model for the modern state as we know it. The nation is also a key concept in nationalist thinking. The commonly

continued

held belief in the natural and enduring identities of nations has remained unchallenged, extending into a common belief that each nation had a natural right to have its own state. Only very recently in the wave of intractable conflicts in such places as Israel/Palestine, Ireland and the Basque country has it fallen from its position as unquestionable truth.

Knowing which political order is right for a society is not, in itself, enough to provide legitimacy for imposing such an order. The act of imposition brings questions about the power relationship of the legislator and those who will live under the legislated constitution. It throws open the question of where the legislator comes from. Which brings, in turn, the question 'from where do they get the authority to legislate?' Who asked or authorised them to legislate?

Rousseau answers these questions in traditional terms, presenting the legitimate source of the legislator's authority as a founding social contract. The initial social contract expresses the will of the people to build a polity which nurtures the qualities of human beings. The root of a human being is the act of willing. For any political order to be legitimate it must meet the ethical requirement that its power derives from the freely given consent of each of them; they must choose it, and they must want it.

The initiating social contract would involve an agreement to set up a legislator because pre-contractual society is one in which alienation from natural selves creates a greedy and amoral people. Such people are unable to move beyond their corrupted private interest in self-aggrandisation, to create a commonly serviceable order. It is the shared need of each and all for the security of a stable social order and the capacity of each and all for reason which must have compelled them to see that they need an objective and incorruptible person to design the constitution of the new social order. This person will be the legislator. The legislator is a founding father, 'but he is neither magistracy nor sovereignty' (Rousseau 1986: 163). In the newly constituted order it is the people collectively who are sovereign, since the institutions which govern are the people organised into the political constitution. The constitution as designed by the legislator is a rationally conceived machine for the organisation of the people into a working order of power. It empowers the people and thus they remain sovereign only for as long as they maintain it.

The social contract is power founded on consent

The discussion of the legislator implies, for Rousseau, that legitimate government can only be rooted in the consent of those governed, and not, as is so often the case, the use or threatened use of force to give the state the power to govern. Rousseau points out that any social order imposed by force lacks an ethical basis, since the rulers lack authority. That is, they have not been authorised, an act which expresses the will of those who are to participate in the order; logically this must include those ruled. This requirement negates the claim of social orders ruled by force to be built on a genuine social contract. In practical terms this also ensures that they will be weaker for it, because force cannot ensure the participants' willing involvement, and the moment that those who impose the contract become weak, those who were forced to agree, and those who agreed willingly but perceived it to be a fraudulent contract in their favour, will break the relationship. A social order built from such a contract will be riddled with intra-factional tension, with people pulling in different directions, exploitation of false common goods for factional ends by the powerful class at the expense of the oppressed, and subversion of the law by the oppressed in pursuit of denied ends. Properly speaking, Rousseau points out, though forced arrangements may be described as contracts, they are not really contracts at all. A genuine, binding contract may be made only by willing participants; fraud is the denial of will by sleight of hand, while giving in to force 'is an act of necessity, not of will' (Rousseau 1986: 143). It is only in the act of consent that individuals create an external sovereign – an ultimate decision-making body with power over them all.

As Rousseau points out, consent involves surrendering individual power to the state, but expresses individual will. This argument has strong implications for Rousseau's understanding of political sovereignty. If sovereignty is rooted in human will, and human will cannot be severed from individual willing, the life of the sovereign body – its identity and activity – must be a direct expression of each and every individual's will. Thus, the contract which sets up the public sovereign body cannot do so by taking from individuals their decision-making power (as is suggested to varying degrees in liberal theory); rather, it must establish a common condition, which is an expression of each and every individual's will. As Rousseau puts it: 'The difficulty . . . can be stated in the following terms: "find a form of association which defends and protects with all common forces the person and goods of each associate, and by means of which each one, while uniting with all, nevertheless obeys only himself and remains as free as before?"' (Rousseau 1986: 148).

In attempting to clarify the substance of legitimate sovereign government, Rousseau has hit upon a fundamental problem in political thinking: 'How do individuals combine so that in decisive moments they become unified into the collective "we"?' The answers to this question depend on what exactly constitutes the 'uniting' of people. In current re-creations of a 'classical liberal' presentation, the creation of common wealth is often presented as little more than the regulating of a code of conduct for the pursuit of individual interests, in regard to points of overlapping or integrating activity (the trading of goods, for example). At the other extreme, the concept of unity can imply a merging of parts into an indistinguishable whole, the way eggs are merged into the single whole of an omelette. For theorists trying to dig a path through the dangerous complexities attending the shifting political orders of seventeenth- and eighteenth-century Europe, the difficulty of mapping a practical path through the tensions set by the desire for a unified sovereign body and the newly minted perceptions of individual liberty, the task was urgent (though with the wisdom of hindsight we might also add insurmountable). Rousseau's contribution to attempts to solve this problem was his notion of the general will.

The people's sovereignty is expressed in the general will

Rousseau argues that, in making the social contract, 'Each one of us puts into the community his person and all his powers under the supreme direction of the general will; and as a body, we incorporate every member as an indivisible part of the whole' (Cranston 1986: 61). This totality will function without internal conflict, 'as every individual gives himself absolutely, the conditions are the same for all, and precisely because they are the same for all, it is in no one's interest to make the conditions onerous for others' (Cranston 1986: 60). No individual would mind being integrated because, 'since each man gives himself to all, he gives himself to no one; and since there is no associate over whom he does not gain the same rights as others gain over him, each man recovers the equivalent of everything he loses, and in the bargain he acquires more power to preserve what he has' (Cranston 1986: 61). In other words, as we are all equally subject to the condition of life set out by the common will, each and every one of us will be equally hurt by any foolhardy or malicious policies which the public body would make. We therefore all have an equal interest in ensuring that every policy is to the benefit of each of us. Furthermore, tendencies towards conflict will be minimal, since we give ourselves to a single, whole, public body and therefore do not place ourselves into the service of any sectional groupings, be they political factions or socio-economic classes.

In total, by merging ourselves into the establishment of a unified sovereign body (the state) maintained by its own (general) will, we are freed from imposed subservience to others' self-interest, in addition to which we gain the totality of all the powers of our fellow members (citizens), in ensuring that the conditions we do want are enforced. Underpinning this presentation is a notion of the imposing logic of reason. Reason is equally present and substantively the same in each person. Reason will dictate to all that the terms of the contract must be as Rousseau sets out, if they are to be legitimate and to work. Reason will compel individuals similarly in considering individual laws. Laws, to be laws, must be universal – they must set out general conditions which apply to each and every citizen. An example of this kind of law would be 'no citizen can be discriminated against on the grounds of their religious belief'. This type of law is distinct from despotic edicts, because it cannot be aimed solely at specific events or particular people. The ultimate purpose of this design is that 'Every authentic act of the general binds or favours all the citizens equally, so that the sovereign recognizes only the whole body of the nation and makes no distinction between any of the members that compose it' (Cranston 1986: 76). Here Rousseau is setting out a distinction between rule by edict – that is, statements of will imposed by powerful elites on all social members – and the rule of law in which the rationale of the law compels all who encounter it to admit each law's rightness by the force of its rationality. Because humans are rational, they will see the coherence of the laws, and they will note that only such universal laws could serve each individual's liberties while also holding together the community which facilitates their individuality. For this reason, individual citizens will want the laws they have to obey, and there will be no clash between individual will, the general will, and the law which shapes and governs the community. The general will is thus more than a common agreement. It is a total unity of opinion and desire derived from rational analysis of what is objectively best for all.

Despite the implication that the general will must be an expression of total unanimity. Rousseau does not rule out majority votes as a means of getting the general will. On some occasions, individuals, while seeking the common good and applying their best reasoning, will come to different conclusions concerning specific policies or pieces of legislation, for, after all, differences of opinion are not the same as differences of interest. For this reason, Rousseau argues, the best system for arriving at specific expressions of the general will is the use of plebiscites. In such situations the majority vote will express the genuine general will. Even in a republic of ethical and rational citizens, some individuals will either reason wrongly or fail to perceive the influence of their private desires on their reasoning and vote against the majority opinion. In such cases, he writes, 'when . . . the opinion contrary to mine prevails, this proves only that I have made a mistake, and that what I believed to be the general will was not so' (Cranston 1986: 153). Clearly, the ethical and rational citizen in this situation will feel obligated to defer to the majority opinion and will continue to participate as a member of the community under the terms of the newly established law. In such ways, the general will makes and keeps all of its members complex, reasoning, passionate, virtuous citizens, where once they had been simple self-serving animals.

This is not an assertion of the simple majority principle that the greater the proportion of citizens expressing an opinion, the more the opinion genuinely expresses a common will. The majority principle only expresses the general will in a republic in which the citizens are educated to perceive the ethical need for all decisions to provide for the good of each and everyone. What is hinted at in this idea is that there is a special relationship between reason, debate and true knowledge. Individual reasoning can be faulty, individual experience limited, and individual judgement shaped by prejudice, yet when all are tested in debate and informed by the great range of experience available to the collectivity as a whole, most individuals will perceive the influence of their own prejudices and personal desires in distorting their reasoning, will understand the best means of achieving what is good for the citizenry and, knowing in principle that this is the best for them as individuals also, vote for it.

An important point to note here is that though the expression of the general will can be achieved through the same mechanisms as the will of all, they are totally different. The moralising and unifying qualities of the general will provide it with its legitimacy and distinguish it in essence from consensual arrangements that express a mere aggregate of individual or sectional interests and opinions. The distinction is important. Any collective vote expresses a general agreement over a political issue, but few express total unanimity on what is the best for the common good. Often the consensus produced by democratic processes is a compromise balancing out sectional interests. A consensus on educational reform, for example, would typically be reached only after hard-fought lobbying of the government by representatives of teachers, administrators, parents and students. Each group would have its own concerns and goals and these would often clash with the goals of others, and the outcome, if it was to lead to a working arrangement, would be a 'deal' in which each party gave up some ground and in return achieved some of its goals. At its worst such scenarios can degenerate into a 'fudge', in which deep conflict interests are obscured and/or left undealt with, only to arise at a later date, rupturing the supposed unity of the political community.

For Rousseau, then, the will of all actively works against the unity of a political community for three clear reasons:

1　Though such scenarios are produced by fully democratic processes, and end with apparent unanimity, they obscure the anti-communal self-serving of sectional groups, and are fundamentally distinct from expressions of the general will.
2　As the uncorrupted needs of each and every human can only be expressed in the unanimity of purpose that desires the good of each and all, such sectional trade-offs cannot express genuine human desires and needs. They therefore lack the legitimacy of the general will which works as an expression of such desires and needs.
3　Such scenarios undermine the democratic order through which they operate.

In making these points, Rousseau clearly challenges liberal notions that the value of a democratic process is its functional policing of individual and sectional competition towards commonly acceptable arrangements. During his time these liberal notions were spreading from England to French political culture. In our time they dominate world politics, and Rousseau's challenge, rather than losing its power, is, if anything, more important. Its importance becomes clear when the notion of the general will is considered in relation to the ideal of a national political community. Rousseau believed that only a political community with a defined enclosed membership debating freely and acting in concert – that is, reproducing the effects of simple family life – can provide a context for each and every member to be their true selves. The location of each member's genuine human identity and the identity of the political community are locked together in an organic whole only at the moment when the general will is expressed (Cullen 1993: 118). This understanding provides the foundation of generations of opposition to the dominant liberal ideal of pluralist democracy by communists, socialists, nationalists, theocrats and conservative communitarians.

Issue areas discussed by commentators

In setting out an idealised political order which is small, homogeneous, participatory, and in which the state dominates individuals' lives, Rousseau's argument runs into a number of difficulties which commentators have been quick to seize on. The difficulties may be arranged into four related categories: (1) The applicability of Rousseau's simple model to complex modern societies, (2) issues of participation, (3) issues of democratic rule and the liberty of citizens, (4) the issue of whether *The Social Contract* is a utopian tract or a prescription for action. We shall examine these below.

The issue of the applicability of Rousseau's simple model to complex modern societies

As Rousseau portrays them, both the simple family members and the Spartans directly derived a sense of communality from the sameness of their common experience. To differing degrees, the two social organisations required their members to have a common set of skills for collective survival, and both provided strong and uniform normative cultures, which ensured that group members gave a common evaluation to their common experience. The problem in using such communities as models for modern polities is that they are so unlike larger and much more complex national societies.

The early twentieth-century sociologists Emile Durkheim and Max Weber pointed out that, in complex modern societies, common experience of situations is lacking. Not all people will be at or near important events or involved in important processes. They point out that the uniform possession of skills is also missing, as many social and economic activities have become the specialised terrain of exclusive groups, such as lawyers, doctors and philosophers. With such diversity of experience, skills and knowledge, there is little common ground in which to embed a strong common normative culture. The critical edge of their analysis comes from their common insight that these conditions were not only present during Rousseau's time, but showed a trend away from the simple to the complex. Implicit in this sociological analysis is the suggestion that even at the time that Rousseau was writing, his ideal model was more a piece of nostalgic daydreaming than a realistic plan for a new order.

To leap to such a conclusion, however, would be simplistic. Given the historical context in which Rousseau worked, he would not have been unaware of the increasing complexity of European society, and his private correspondence shows a keen awareness of the religious, economic and social developments within French society. In this light, it is easy to be persuaded by Cobban's claim that 'he had in mind *Parlements* in France . . . and petty privileged groups' (Cobban 1934) who dominated French politics when he excluded sectional interest groups from the ideal polity. It would seem that he was not unaware of the *realpolitik* of his time.

In this light, it might be argued that Rousseau was making an insightful political point to his contemporaries who were locked in constitutional dispute over the relative powers of the Church, the monarch and the aristocratically controlled regional *Parlements*. The point was that a sovereign state can be undermined by competing powerful agencies, and cannot tolerate sectional interest groups, which always challenge or exploit state power to the detriment of the community. Because of this, he argued, those building political constitutions should, where possible, avoid tendencies towards large-scale complex social and political orders and strive where possible for the small and simple. This was not only a reasonable and practical goal for his contemporaries, but might be considered as a theme to be revisited today in a world in which nation states are losing political power to larger bodies such as the European Union, economic power to globalising economic processes and associated institutions, and distinct communal identities to a homogeneous 'Western' culture.

> **DISCUSSION POINT**
>
> Rousseau may be criticised for asserting that pluralist use of democratic systems always undermines the unity which holds political communities together (Cullen 1993: 119). However, he may have a point in saying that tight-knit participatory communities provide the location of full human identity, and you might consider whether the intense commitment to plurality which characterises modern Western societies threatens to destroy the political identity of each and every citizen.

Issues of participation

In Rousseau's presentation, the communality of the simple family and the Spartan city state was sustained by the necessity for full-time participation by their members, and this principle, 'the principle that citizens make their own laws and must not let deputies do so for them' (Plamenatz 1992: 162), is set out as a key feature of his ideal republic. Among liberal commentators, this principle, to borrow Plamenatz's phrase, has 'been condemned as among the more absurd and unrealistic that he put forward' (Plamenatz 1992: 162).

It is only absurd if it is taken too literally. Careful consideration of the whole of Rousseau's work shows him to be quite willing to compromise this principle. He is generally complimentary about representative governments of his time (including that of England). This suggests that in *The Social Contract* he ignores the complexity of real political situations in order to set out the principle which creates genuinely democratic sovereignty in clear terms. His argument in *The Social Contract* is not intended to give real practical advice, and there is little to be gained from concentrating on the lack of practical realism in the language he uses in setting it out. What is worth thinking about is the general principle which it promotes, namely the relationship between the fullest possible participation by as many of the citizenry as possible in political affairs, and the establishment of a government that will be responsive to the needs of social members, and, that will be able, through its dealings with them, to obtain the general authorisation it needs to act decisively – in short, the general democratic conditions for the establishment of a legitimate and practically functioning state. There is nothing absurd about this.

His challenge to supporters of representative government sets the question of whether a system which replaces participation with representation is truly democratic. It is a question which surely needs to be considered when evaluating the modern systems of government under which we live. If modern Western political systems are not democratic – they do not express the will of the people – what are the moral grounds for their superiority over other modes of government such as benevolent dictatorships, or super-efficient bureaucracies?

The general point made by many commentators in response to Rousseau's challenge is that modern pluralist societies have developed many participatory mechanisms such as pressure groups, trade unions and political parties. These provide a constant and sophisticated network of discussion, influence, policy-making and dissent, enabling everyone to have some input if they wish to participate. With such a full range of access available to the active citizen there are grounds for doubting the need for full participation in the single activity of legislating.

A more defensive argument is that in a large national entity, the sheer numbers of people involved make full participation virtually impossible. If any attempt was made to include all the citizens all the time, decisions would be ridiculously hard to arrive at, discussions and voting would be constant, the legislative process chaotic. Furthermore, we would never get any time to do all the other important and enjoyable things in our lives and that would make us miserable.

These arguments do show that there are problems involved in applying a simple model of democracy to complex modern societies, but this does not mean that Rousseau's argument can be dismissed as absurd.

DISCUSSION POINT

Is Rousseau's challenge powerful enough to force us to review our system? Is it absurd to suggest that most members of a mass society could participate in the ongoing debates on policy and legislative matters? Two methods that could be used to this end are: (1) devolving decision-making to localised government, (2) using new technologies for mass participation in internet forums and electronic voting.

Issues of democratic rule and the liberty of citizens

Rousseau's challenge to the liberal democratic process is valuable not only for its insights into the issues of participation, but also for its critique of liberalism's commitment to finding workable compromises between sectional opinion. From these insights, one can make a case for adopting Rousseau's position of having nothing to do with liberal democracy. However, we can also see that it is possible that the rejection of all aspects of liberal democracy may have led Rousseau into constructing an alternative democratic model which, rather than individual liberty, produced its opposite. We shall now explore the cases for and against this possibility.

For

Rousseau's greatest insight in his dismissal of liberalism is that the democratic process is not enough in itself to guarantee that a common will is expressed. In liberal societies which tolerate individual and sectional self-interest the outcome of any collective vote will obscure the fact that many participants will use it to pursue the best deal for them as individuals or as members of a sectional group at least as much as they will use it to pursue the common good. Classic examples of this are issues of taxation and state provision of welfare. While these issues affect everyone and are therefore issues in common, most people vote on them with an eye to their personal needs, or their sectional interests, as employees of the state, or users of welfare, or likely candidates for higher taxation. Despite much rhetoric about the common good and an electoral process which appears to express 'the will of the people', it is the 'will of all' which prevails.

From the position of Rousseau's democratic ideal, everyday life in stable civil society can look unappetising. In situations where there is little communality, Rousseau's challenge to liberal democracy is even more striking. At the end of the twentieth century democratic processes were being used to broker agreements which aimed to end wars between sectional groups in the disputed territories of Ireland/UK, Israel/Palestine and the remnants of Yugoslavia. Can these agreements which are trade-offs between hostile factions create a common good? Armed with Rousseau's insight into the difference between the full and complete unanimity of the general will and the superficial agreement of the will of all, it is easy to see how such agreements can create a superficial peace, a fake expression of unanimity, providing cover for conspiratorial factions to plan the next wave of sectarian warfare.

Powerful though this insight is, it begs one question: Does it have to be all or nothing: reason and unanimity or irrational self-interest-driven greed? Just because peace agreements almost always harbour sectional conspiracies, it does not mean that such agreements preclude the establishment of genuine communality. It may be argued that, on the contrary, by forcing people to deal with each other and by giving them the chance to get to know each other in the non-hostile situation of a shared everyday life, these fudged agreements can nurture the peace enjoyed by inclusive equalitarian and democratic communities.

Against

Consideration of the current work towards various peace agreements suggests that perhaps Rousseau placed too great a hope in reason and virtue, while failing to see the necessity of pragmatic compromise in establishing and maintaining any community. In pursuing this critical line some commentators have challenged his claim that the combination of natural reason and an education in moral sensibility will produce a democratic community of free individuals. Hayek (1992) has pointed out that it is unlikely that there will be agreement between all individuals in all their discussions of all the things which fall into the domain of legislation. In many situations where people are ethically motivated, the issues at stake are complex and right answers hard to come by (current issues concerning education typify this). Reason can, in fact, take many paths to many different conclusions and ethical commitment to communality does not provide citizens with a basis for deciding which, if any, opinion is closest to objective truth. Indeed, far from revealing the superior rationality of the majority argument, the ethical commitment to the community can lead people to act against their rational sense of what is for the good (examples of this abound in hyper-nationalist attempts to ethnically cleanse political communities; perfectly sensible and rational people become irrationally bent on saving their national community from corrupting aliens). For this reason, Hayek argues, even in the ideal state of ethical rational citizens, the majority principle cannot provide a general will as conceived by Rousseau. Furthermore, when this idea has been used in practice, it has allowed majorities to use the argument of ethical obligation to the general will to impose their opinions on minorities. In many situations, it would be nigh on impossible to distinguish between an inclusive-minded communitarianism (a general will) and coercive majoritarianism (the will of all). Indeed, it could be argued that they are the same thing seen from different standpoints. From such a perspective the conceptual distinction between the general will and the will of all is viewed as an academic irrelevance, since what prevails in actuality is the tyranny of the majority.

Here the problem becomes one of potential coercion, for in Rousseau's insistence that all citizens abide by the 'general will' there is no opt out for the conscientious objector – the individuals who, having participated in the collective deliberative process, find themselves unable to go along with its conclusions and stay true to their moral selves. Such people, Rousseau argued, used their liberty to undermine the participatory conditions which provided liberty and should therefore be forced to participate. In the infamous Rousseauian phrase they would be 'forced to be free'. This intimidating conclusion indicates, rather than resolves, the problems revolving around the relationship of individual liberty to collective power. These are the most central to Rousseau's political philosophy.

In many commentaries, the concern with this problem extends into further consideration of the entwined issues of the fate of sectional socio-political factions and individual citizens. From Edmund Burke in the 1790s to C.E. Vaughan in the early years of the twentieth century, commentators have argued that, by giving sectional groups no place in the ideal constitution, Rousseau throws such weight on to the relationship of the individual and the state that the individual will inevitably be overpowered. Individual citizens have nowhere to turn if they do not agree with the majority, and as the majority control the state, nowhere to run if they disobey. It is hard to conceive how this could be a condition of liberty, while it is possible to see how individuals in such a situation could become entrapped by despotic state terrorism. The individual's situation becomes even less a condition of liberty, when the attempt to establish a general will is inevitably undermined by the failure of reason and ethics to produce conclusive right answers to political problems. It takes only one situation in which rational disagreement overwhelms the ethical sense of obligation to the community for the unity of common purpose to be lost; and what then? If there are irresolvable disputes concerning the best rationalisation of a legislative problem, can any common sense of a general will remain? If not, how can any argument for a law claim or show the authority necessary for any attempts it might make to convert its conclusions into law? In such situations, the inflexible unity of the sovereign body will be likely to fracture into disputing factions, and these factions, having no provision within the constitution, would be lawless and, by necessity, act like mafias. For the remaining citizens, isolated individuals each and all, the choice would be to join or submit to one faction or another. In short, the situation would degenerate into the anarchic society which Rousseau preached against.

DISCUSSION POINTS

(1) Has Rousseau got a point? Is it simply that we have a choice between living in weak and fractious sectional societies dominated by political power games of self-interested factions, or surrendering our private interests to the will of the communal majority? (2) Does communitarian democracy topple into authoritarianism? (3) Is there a third way which might steer between the extremes of Rousseau's model and the liberal democratic model?

The issue of whether The Social Contract is a utopian tract or a prescription for action

This issue is important because our conclusions will aid us to make judgements about the appropriateness of the many interpretations of the text as a manifesto for action, and in this way obtain a sense of the significance of Rousseau's work in the history of political thought and action.

The fact that the French revolutionaries used his ideas in establishing their new republic has had the inevitable consequence that his work is often treated as a prescription for a working political order. Writing against this trend, influential commentators such as Judith Shklar (1969: 2), John Plamenatz (1992: 165) and Maurice Cranston (1986) have argued that Rousseau's work is a purely theoretical exercise, and to criticise it for being unrealistic is to miss its purpose and its virtue as a moral commentary on the possibilities of modern political life. However, the fact that Rousseau prescribed constitutions for actual states (Corsica and Poland) suggests that his mind was never far from the practicalities of real political life. Linking the strands of practicality with those of idealistic detachment, it is possible to be persuaded by Alfred Cobban's claims that *The Social Contract* is a romanticised model of the type of polity which Rousseau believed could be developed from the existing republic of Geneva, and which was being offered as a recommendation to the fractious political actors of France. Similarly, one might take Rousseau's representation of the legislator as a clear sign that he was not prescribing for an actual polity. The legislator is an almost God-like figure endowed with total objectivity. Any flaws in his judgement would create flaws in the very structure of the polity. Thus the completely legitimate polity must have a perfect design which could be designed only by someone with superhuman wisdom. This design places extra-human responsibility and overbearing power in one person's hands (note that there is no mechanism for ensuring that the legislator gives up power when he has finished founding the new order). In the real world no one is that wise, and because of that, no one is trustworthy enough to be given unchecked constitutional power. For this reason it may be argued that Rousseau surely could not have meant his design to be a prescription for actual people to establish a new order. Yet J.L. Talmon has argued that it is exactly this element of Rousseau's theory which made it attractive to tyrants who psychologically tend towards unrealistic self-aggrandisement and the belittling of people with differing perspectives.

The French Revolution 1788–1789

A poor economy and peasant food riots combined with an aristocratic and bourgeois challenge to undermine the power of the monarchy. Under pressure, Louis XVI agreed to a new constitutional government including representatives of the bourgeoisie. The National Assembly was set up.

1789–1791. The Assembly set about reform, replacing vestiges of feudalism with a republican nation state. Its two major constitutional innovations were the 1789 Declaration of Rights, setting out basic civil rights for citizens, and the 1791 Constitution, separating Church from state, and replacing royal dictate with the rule of law. Its most impressive display of power was the suspension of the dissenting King.

1793–1795. Factional conflict overran the new government. The Jacobins, a radical liberal faction dominated by Robespierre, captured power from the Girondins in an armed coup. Radical constitutional changes were forced through including universal male suffrage. The Christian Church was replaced by a new civil religion. Shortly after, the reign of terror began. All opposition was forcibly put down by widespread use of imprisonment and execution. The reign of terror and the period of revolutionary change ended with the overthrow of Robespierre in 1795.

In *The Origins of Totalitarian Democracy* (1952), Talmon marks out a direct line between Rousseau's model – a prescription for totalitarian power – and the activities of Robespierre in the French Revolution (following the logic all the way to Hitler's Third Reich and the Stalinist USSR). Talmon and others who present the totalitarian thesis are in turn charged with distortion of history and misrepresentation of ideas (Wokler 1995: 272).

When you weigh up these arguments you may well find it hard to come to any strong conclusion. You will not be helped by the fact that in all his writings, Rousseau did prevaricate on the issue of the relationship of his presentations to factuality. What is clear is that the ideologues and the leaders of the French Revolution and their contemporary critics read Rousseau's work as prescriptive, and his influence was everywhere during the revolution. After the fall of the Bastille, a bust of Rousseau was carved from its stone and engraved with the revolutionaries' slogan, *Liberté, Egalité, Fraternité.* A national assembly was established, which proclaimed itself the embodiment of the general will. Norman Hampson points out that 'faithful to what were believed to be Rousseau's ideas, *The Declaration of the Rights of Man* proclaimed that "the law is the expression of the *volonté générale*"' (general will) (Hampson 1983: 153). In this way his ideas became involved in the world of action; used first as ideological dogma in the execution of the revolution and, throughout the nineteenth century, as a means of criticising the failings of the revolution. Despite the overt connections between theorists and revolution, historians have found that, while the tenor of a Rousseauian stance strongly flavoured revolutionary polemic and attitudes, the connections between Rousseau's ideas and revolutionary actions were somewhat forced. Beyond the cultish adulation given to Rousseau, and the abundance of vague references to his ideas on equality and liberty, and the general will, there was little in the way of careful map-reading of the theoretical structure of the ideal republic as set out in *The Social Contract* (this was, in fact, barely read before the revolution) (McDonald 1965: 44–47; Cobban 1934: 29). Joan McDonald has highlighted how the structures and policies of the revolutionary state (which altered frequently as power swung between factions) were very different in detail from those set out in *The Social Contract*. The most glaring difference was that, contrary to the arguments against representation in *The Social Contract*, 'the revolutionaries asserted precisely the opposite principle, that sovereign rights could not be exercised except by representatives' (McDonald 1965: 95). However, the Declaration of the Rights of Man – a definitive moment in the establishment of revolutionary government – proclaimed that 'the law is the expression of the *volonté générale*'. Ominously, Robespierre, a driving force in the Jacobin capture of the state, saw the general will 'in terms of the State as a collective moral and political body, with absolute power over the individual'. At this point an interlocking of conceptual problems with theoretical models, and with actual tendencies in attempts to deploy such models in practice, becomes observable. The failure to establish a constitutional regulation of political factions, and the contempt with which those in power dismantled and terrorised the other factions, uncannily echoes the tendency towards Mafia-like gangsterism which is, we have seen, an inherent possibility in Rousseau's ideal model. Disputes were fought out by Girondists, Montagnards and the Jacobin club. The governmental body split into factions, as the Paris *Parlement* and the National Assembly disputed who exactly voiced the general will. By 1794, bloodshed was rife. The monarchists, the Girondists and many radicals were executed. The populace as a whole was divided into a range of subgroups involved in conflict and, at times, civil war, and a small group of half a dozen men, believing all the other citizens of France to be either misled or traitorous, used power and terror and the words of Rousseau to impose their version of the general will.

While we have to take great care regarding the vexed issue of the precise relationship of Rousseau's ideas to the activities of the revolutionaries, one cannot help but note the great irony that the attempts of leading revolutionaries to deploy Rousseauian principles in political practice led to the very end which Rousseau had intended such principles to stop: factional civil war and the dissolution of the revolution into 'the terror'.

Given the fact that Rousseau's name was so attached to the actions of the revolutionaries, it is not surprising that his ideas were subjected to intense criticism in the backlash which followed the revolution's demise. In an early post-revolutionary reaction, Mournier described *The Social Contract* as 'the worst book ever written on government' (Boucher 1994: 119). Joseph DeMaistre influentially developed Burke's argument that Rousseau had conceitedly challenged the practical wisdom of French society embedded in custom and traditions. Bonal, in a very personalised attack, accused Rousseau of sacrificing a society for an idealised nation of man (Boucher 1994: 123). In every case, a direct link between Rousseau's arguments and the terrors of revolution were taken as fact. This line of criticism continued into the twentieth century when he became identified by commentators such as Talmon (Talmon 1952: 38–50) as a crucial figure in the development of totalitarian ideology.

Clearly, Rousseau's presentation has become theory with practical consequences, whether or not the author intended it. It is therefore very significant in the history of political action. Yet evaluation of its precise significance is difficult, for its exact relationship to the activities of later practitioners and theorists of politics is unclear. If it is prescriptive, its appropriation by the revolutionaries is not unjustified and the outcome of the revolution – the crashing failure of romantic utopianism to govern the real world – is directly linked to Rousseau's shortcomings as a theorist. If, however, his work is a utopian tract, then the revolutionaries' failures to achieve Rousseau's goals must be largely down to their naïvety in misunderstanding the gulf between what was achievable in their time and circumstances, and the ideal model offered by theorists. In truth, it is impossible to know exactly what Rousseau's intentions were, though two general points may be drawn after consideration of the political use made of his name and works. First, if it is recognised that idealisation of the certain elements of political life is what we do in order to provide a map of intent, and to articulate the common emotional desires for security, belonging and self-expression, the possibility of establishing a pure political order in which such contradicting desires can be unproblematically achieved will be seen to be what it is – an illusion. In such a light, ideal models may be used to provide insights into our desires and the difficulties in achieving them without obscuring the fact of political existence, which is that, insofar as any community is political, it is fractious and dangerously uncertain. Second, the use of Rousseau's name and ideas as ideological weapons in the conflicts between constitutional liberals and revolutionaries exemplifies how all theory is open to misuse by political practitioners, who tend to reduce issues of meaning and value to practical prescription and to reduce statements made in the spirit of inquiry to rhetoric designed to achieve results.

Revision notes

1   Rousseau saw small communities in which the mutual recognition of the natural equality of each member shaped the communal discourse of collective and individual goals as the seat of humans' ethical being.
2   For Rousseau, eighteenth-century civilisation was the end result of centuries of corruption of ethical social organisations by larger powerful organisations, each expressing in institutional form the vices of vanity and the lust for power.
3   An ethical political life could be achieved only by the formation of small republics expressing their sovereignty through fully participatory democracy.
4   Equality of political status and full commitment to the common cause are essential requirements of citizenship.

Bibliography

Boucher, D. (1994) *The Social Contract from Hobbes to Rawls*, London: Routledge.

Boyd, W. (ed.) (1966) *Emile For Today: The Emile of Jean Jacques Rousseau*, London: Heinemann.

Cobban, A. (1934) *Rousseau and the Modern State*, London: Allen & Unwin.

Cranston, M. (1983) *Jean Jacques Rousseau: The Early Life and Work of Jean Jacques Rousseau 1712–1754*, London: Allen Lane.

—— (1986) *Philosophers and Pamphleteers: Political Theorists in the Enlightenment*, Oxford: Oxford University Press.

—— (1991) *The Noble Savage: Jean Jacques Rousseau, 1754–1764*, Chicago: University of Chicago Press.

—— (1997) *The Solitary Self: Jean Jacques Rousseau in Exile and Adversity*, Chicago: University of Chicago Press.

Cullen, D. (1993) *Freedom In Rousseau's Political Philosophy*, Illinois: Northern Illinois Press.

Durkheim, E. (1960) *Montesquieu and Rousseau: Forerunners of Sociology*, Indianapolis, Cambridge: Hackett.

Hampson, N. (1983) *Will and Circumstance: Montesquieu, Rousseau and the French Revolution*, London: Duckworth.

Hayek, F. (1992) *The Fatal Conceit*, London: Routledge & Kegan Paul.

Kelly, P. (1994) *The Social Contract From Hobbes to Rawls*, London and New York: Routledge.

McDonald, J.(1965) *Rousseau and the French Revolution 1762–1791*, London: Athlone Press.

Mann, M. (1993) *The Sources of Social Power*, Vol. 2, Cambridge: Cambridge University Press.

Plamenatz, J. (1992) *Man and Society*, Vol. 2, London and New York: Longman.

Rousseau J.J. (1986) *The Social Contract*, trans. M. Cranston, Harmondsworth: Penguin.

—— (1992) *Discourse on the Origins of Inequality*, trans. D.A. Cress, Michigan, Toronto: University of Michigan Press.

Shklar, J. (1969) *Men and Citizens: A Study of Rousseau's Social Theory*, Cambridge: Cambridge University Press.

Talmon, J.L. (1952) *The Origins of Totalitarian Democracy*, London: Sphere Books.

Wokler, R. (ed.) (1995) *Rousseau and Liberty*, Manchester: Manchester University Press.

Further reading

For further details of Rousseau's life read Maurice Cranston's three-part biography (see bibliography). Shklar's *Men and Citizens: A Study of Rousseau's Social Theory* (1969) is a slim and accessible volume which provides a rich and insightful introduction to Rousseau's theory. Plamenatz's *Man and Society* Vol. 2 (1992), contains a long chapter on Rousseau. In it Plamenatz presents an analysis of Rousseau's apparent contradictions, in which popular misconceptions are neatly dealt with and genuine inconsistencies in Rousseau's argument exposed. Cobban's *Rousseau and the Modern State* (1934), uses the author's wide knowledge of the political world of eighteenth-century France to frame a useful construction of the modern, liberal ideas which he believes lie at the core of Rousseau's argument. N. Hampson's *Will and Circumstance: Montesquieu, Rousseau and the French Revolution* (1983) is a classic contextualisation of Rousseau's work which is much referred to by other academics working on Rousseau. McDonald's *Rousseau and the French Revolution 1762–1791* (1965) provides a detailed analysis of all aspects of

Rousseau's influence on the thoughts and activities of the revolutionaries and their opponents. Talmon's *The Origins of Totalitarian Democracy* (1952) gives us a damning, but perhaps dated, presentation of the links between Rousseau's work and violent, dictatorial, totalitarian politics.

Edmund Burke

Good order is the foundation of all things.

(Reflections on the Revolution in France)

Introduction

Edmund Burke was an Irishman born into a Dublin middle-class family. He was educated at Ireland's most prestigious university, Trinity College. Like so many contemporary politicians he went on to study law in London. However, it was not in the practice of law that Burke made his name but as a Whig politician. He first became a Member of Parliament for Wendover in 1766, but it was while serving as MP for Bristol that he became well known. Burke was celebrated for his fluid command of the English language; he is said to have been one of the greatest orators that Parliament had ever known. His writing is equally inviting. Like his Irish literary contemporaries Burke had a way with words, persuasive, passionate and seductive. He wrote a number of books mainly, but not exclusively, concerned with politics: *A Vindication of Natural Society* (1756), *A Philosophical Enquiry into the Sublime and the Beautiful* (1757). His most famous book was, without doubt, *Reflections on the Revolutions in France* (1790). Like so many successful authors he also has a sequel, *More Reflections on the Revolution in France* (1791/1796) which is a collection of his publications from later in his life.

Burke is a political thinker in the tradition of Machiavelli and not a political philosopher, like Hobbes. That is, he does not have a fully explained philosophical system in which to situate his ideas about politics. Rather, he is an experienced politician who has written down his understanding of what politics is, based upon experience. As he writes, 'I beg leave to throw out my thoughts, and express my feelings, just as they arise in my mind, with very little attention to formal method' (Burke 1986: 62).

A great deal of what Burke writes concerns particular political events that were happening at the time he was writing. The language he uses is not philosophical but rhetorical. His interest was to affect the political circumstances that were happening at the time. In a similar way we saw how Hobbes was provoked into writing *Leviathan* by the chaos of the English revolution and, like Hobbes, all the writing must be seen in its historical context. Yet Burke ends up constructing a classic text of political theory that has had an influence well beyond its own time.

Rewind

Go to Chapter 3 to read Hobbes' analysis.

Although a Whig politician, Burke's reflections have been taken as a key text in the tradition of 'one-nation' conservatism. One-nation conservatism was first clearly articulated by Disraeli who argued that the Conservative Party was the natural and rightful guardian of the British nation. Only the Conservatives understood that society is a balance between the different social classes, each having their particular role to contribute to the nation but none with any greater rights than the other. Economic inequality was a natural feature of a civilised society where birth, tradition and ability would always differ. However, this did not mean that we are separate individuals; in fact, we were all part of the same British 'family' and, just like any family, we should take responsibility for each other. The rich and powerful had a duty to maintain a just and decent society. In their turn the 'ordinary' classes had to respect the traditional constitutional rules. This was (by and large) a version of conservatism that persisted in Britain until Margaret Thatcher and the New Right challenged these ideas in the 1970s and 1980s. Strangely enough, then, Burke's ideas, which are often said to be the basis of modern conservatism, have been challenged most forcefully by the neo-liberal conservatism we associate with Margaret Thatcher. Yet it ought to be said that the belief in 'one (British) nation', the idea that there is some kind of unifying set of basic values and beliefs that underpins our society has not only been the preserve of the Conservative Party. There are distinctive Burkian elements in New Labour who argue that even in a plural and multi-ethnic society there are some values that we must all share. Essentially, Burke's ideas have been taken, in a British context, to reaffirm the notion of an ordered and unified state, often against real circumstances that point to the contrary. Politicians have been able to do this because at the heart of Burke's argument against the French Revolution is a theory of rights that has been useful to governments (regardless of ideology) who attempt to impose a certain social and moral order. In many fundamental ways Burke's work articulates some of the key political traditions of British government. Not least of all Burke is also considered important for laying down the belief of the Westminster model of politics that an MP is independent and does not have to listen to his constituents when making a decision.

KEY CONCEPT 1

British Conservative Party ideology

The ideology of the Conservative Party is usually broken down into two main schools. The 'one-nation' Conservatives are the traditional Conservatives. The New Right are the modernisers who appeared in the party from the 1970s and are most famously represented by Margaret Thatcher. One fundamental difference between the two is that the first believe economic policy should involve a paternalistic element where the state intervenes so that the better-off help those less fortunate. The New Right believe in leaving affairs of the economy to the free market without government intervention to redress inequalities. Burke does not fit fully into either branch of Conservative thinking, although he has more in common with the traditional Conservative Party. But it is important to remember that he was a Whig politician and many of his ideas fit into the liberal politics of his day.

Reflections on the Revolution in France

Key arguments

Reflections on the Revolution in France is a text without chapters. In fact, it is set out as a letter. Like many good letters these ideas seem to be constructed as much during the actual writing as previously thought through. The book has little structure; it is precisely what the title says it is; a series of reflections, a collection of thoughts that criss-cross each other at various intervals. That said, the text is not without some order even though it has no clearly defined chapters. It is a very easy and accessible read. As stated above, Burke was a great stylist. It was this that gave the book such a wide appeal when it was published. The book itself does not contain any deeply philosophical or original arguments, but it does build a bridge between a number of classical and – for Burke – contemporary ideas. In so doing he comes up with a strong argument which objects to revolution. If we find that this argument may be said to hold, then it may be said to hold as much now, in our own time, as then. As well as developing a kind of classical challenge to the idea of revolution, Burke also develops a distinctive take on arguments about 'rights'. We have seen with the social contract theorists – Hobbes, Locke and Rousseau – that each ties his argument to a certain understanding of 'natural rights'. Today we still discuss 'rights' and what they are as an integral part of our politics. Some even argue that the arguments about rights have gone too far. Almost every individual or group of individuals when making a political argument refer to their 'rights', some inviolable entitlement that they claim is theirs. So today we are familiar with claims of rights which include claims ranging from human rights to animal rights. Burke was right in the middle of the eighteenth-century debates that laid the foundations for our own understandings of these contemporary debates.

Abstract rights and the idea of revolution

In *Reflections* Burke begins by articulating his concern that the revolution in France had to be distinguished from the 'glorious revolution' of 1688 in England. He also wanted to make a case that events in France should not affect domestic politics in England. This is made clear in the title-page of the book which states that *Reflections* is also concerned with 'the proceedings in certain societies in London relative to that event'. Burke seemed to be worried that the affairs of England and France would be connected, 'drawing us into an imitation of the conduct of the National Assembly' (Burke 1986: 91).

Burke did not want to see the massive changes that the French Revolution promised. The French revolution is in many ways a 'model' of a modern revolution, a time where everything changes almost overnight by way of a bloody overthrow of the state. And the French Revolution was an extraordinary violent affair. In terms of political ideas the old understandings between rulers and ruled broke down, in particular the idea that rulers had in any sense an automatic right to rule.

The French Revolution took a lurch into the future, into the unknown. Lying behind the French Revolution was the principle that it was possible for anyone to manage the affairs of state even if they did not have any experience of such affairs. Put like this, such an opinion might seem ludicrous. Surely the management of the affairs of the state, like the management of any business or even household, needs some kind of practical experience? However, this idea and those of the French Revolution were based upon a philosophical school of thought that was highly respected at the time; it was called rationalism. Burke believed that the French revolutionaries had taken up this school of thought and turned it from a philosophical set of ideas (embedded in purely theoretical debates) into a set of ideas that could be used in social terms. The basic idea of the rationalism that lay behind the French Revolution was the belief that on the basis of rational principles it is possible to manage states of affairs better than they have been managed before. In other words, just as Enlightenment thinkers had broken new boundaries of science, maths and philosophy by developing new methods, theories and forms of knowledge, so too could this be possible for government. Just as Descartes had 'discovered' the self as the centre of the human world and Galileo the sun as the centre of the universe, so the rationalists of the French Revolution believed they could find the fundamental principles of good government and turn them into a guide to rule under the terms of 'rights' or 'the rights of man'.

KEY CONCEPT 2

Rationalist philosophy

Rationalist philosophers maintained that only through the use of reason could we understand what is real and true. This view was developed from the seventeenth and eighteenth centuries. The problem with rationalism was that it tended towards purely quantitative schools of thought, leaving no room for qualitative methods, including intuition, experience and human emotions.

Burke was living in the age of the Enlightenment, where science, maths and philosophical reason were believed to be able to resolve all human problems. It was no surprise that eventually this was going to be applied to political problems. If the right foundational principles could be found, with correct reasoning, using correct method, then no political tension was beyond resolution. Rationalism takes it that the principles which drive our knowledge can be understood, a priori, outside of or prior to experience. While this may seem flawed when put so bluntly, it does not appear so when set in the context of the knowledge base at the time, because the knowledge base was centred on rationalism generally.

These ideas were a significant part of the ideology of those who sought revolution in France. In England, too, many supported the aims of the French revolutionaries, believing that revolution was justified on the grounds that in France the rule of law had been lost and the natural liberty of men ought to be restored. Thomas Paine most famously defended the revolution against Burke's view in his book, *The Rights of Man*. Here he proposed that there was an essential and inviolable set of rights to which good government ought to adhere. These rights could be set out clearly and constitutionally. Where they did not exist despotic government ruled and should be overthrown. Burke was against the French Revolution because he was against this view of politics. He was a political sceptic. He was sceptical of the view that you could abstract from experience a number of rights and then apply them generally to all situations. Burke maintained that politics was about particular circumstances and not about generalised principles or grand ideologies. In essence, the debate between Paine and Burke is the basis for continuing debates. On the one hand, there are those who favour a politics based on a clear set of principles that drive policy decisions. On the other hand, there are those who believe in the kind of *realpolitik* of Machiavelli, namely that politics is largely a day-to-day business where long-term planning is not possible because situations change and circumstances arise without warning. As Burke puts it, 'Circumstances give in reality to every political principle its distinguishing colour and discriminating effect. The circumstances are what render every civil and political scheme beneficial or noxious to mankind' (Burke 1986: 60).

 Fast forward

Go to Chapter 9 for Marx's arguments about the 'inevitable' events of history.

Burke takes the notion of 'the rights of man' as abstract rights, rights not rooted in the real circumstances of practical life but in the misguided whim of whoever is proclaiming them. Politics is tied to social existence and, as we know in our own time, life changes without warning. We only have to think of the events of 9/11. Who would have considered such an event, how could an event be planned for and how could a response be justified on any notion of 'abstract' rights? In other words, the decision to make a response to the suicide planes that exploded into the Twin Towers in New York could not be guided by any previously established principles. The circumstances at the time are all the politicians had to reflect upon in order to make their decision and, for Burke, a sense of general political experience, in order to act.

Underlying Burke's antagonism to the French Revolution is thus a disposition articulated as an argument against rationalist-like politics. However, although he is challenging a whole school of philosophical ideas that underpinned the revolution, his principal argument against is quite straightforward. Quite simply, Burke does not believe that we, as merely human mortal beings, are able to predict or foresee the future. Nor are we, for that matter, able to try and control the events to come through our actions now. However radical and revolutionary our acts, we cannot determine future outcomes. In this way Burke is against the kind of prediction of the future that both Hegel and Marx got themselves into. He also follows Machiavelli in his scepticism regarding our ability to control events as they unfold. More than that, Burke states his argument as one of fact. The manner in which societies work, as such, is on the basis of continuity. It is not possible to have a society if it develops upon the grounds of periodic ruptures. This is not to say societies do not change, but change comes from within, determined by the slow internal changes that alter our societies rather than being imposed from external factors. Internal changes may be demographic, or they may concern the gradual changes and reform of the law, as different generations interpret the meaning of the law to reflect their own comprehension of their mode of living. Further, change may come about as new understandings of concepts such as 'democracy' or 'liberalism' develop over time. Thus society is not stagnant for Burke but change occurs upon the slow shift of what already exists.

KEY PEOPLE 2

Michael Oakeshott

Oakeshott, like Burke, has often been labelled a conservative thinker and, in his case, the modern Burke. However, like Burke, to call him a conservative is to 'box' him rather narrowly and reduce the content of his thought. Since his death in 1991 Oakeshott's work has been reinterpreted as authors have pointed to its classical liberal aspects (see Franco 1992). It would be true to say that the same interpretation needs to be undertaken for Burke whose so-called conservatism may also be found not to fit into any ideological box too easily.

It may be argued that under certain circumstances revolution is justifiable. If a society is iniquitous or simply misruled, surely revolution is necessary, if not morally justified? But at this point Burke's basic argument comes out. Revolution may be morally justified, it may seem like a good idea, but ultimately it is a dangerous short cut to change as we do not know what the future will bring. Revolution may end up by bringing about a form of government and social being that is far worse than what exists already. Revolutionaries may have certain intended outcomes, they may have a grand plan, but they actually have no way at all of knowing what the consequences of their actions will be. Furthermore, what tends to happen when events do not unfold the way the actors intended is that more and more desperate measures are taken to try and influence the outcome. Violence, unlawful bloodshed, death, is only a small step away from the most worthy intentions of the revolutionary. Rationalists, of course, believe that they can socially engineer events, acting as a kind of political or philosophical mechanic. As long as the right buttons are pressed and the right mechanisms are put in place the outcome can be predicted. Burke contends that politics is not like engineering a well-oiled machine. Unlike machines people are not amenable to manipulation and perfecting. To learn to manage states of affairs one needs to develop practical reason. Politics is a matter of praxis not theory. This view may be highlighted another way by drawing on the twentieth-century ideas of Michael Oakeshott (see his *Rationalism in Politics and Other Essays* (1962)) who some consider to be the modern Burke (although this is an oversimplification of Oakeshott's philosophical politics). Oakeshott argues that in every activity, including political activity, there is a degree of technical knowledge required but also practical knowledge. Take cooks, for example, who can have a recipe book in front of them and follow every detail perfectly. Yet the cake they bake at the end of the process may still not be very good. If they have not made the cake before, if they have not tried various minor alterations, learned by trial and error until it becomes instinctual, they will not make a good cake. As Oakeshott states, it is not the thoughts in their heads but the tastes in their mouths that matter.

Burke makes this same argument much earlier on in the modern period but without the philosophical understanding of knowledge that underpins Oakeshott's work. Yet he reasons through much the same kind of argument. Politics cannot be based on rationalist knowledge alone. The art of government cannot be taught. It is something that has to be learned. If one agrees with Burke and his understanding of politics, it leads to some quite fundamental conclusions regarding the possibilities of political and social change and revolution. For those who see many injustices in their current state of politics this may appear rather unsatisfactory. To this Burke can only say, 'That's life'! Better to get on with what is local to you, what you understand practically, than to try and alter the whole of the existing state of affairs. The past will always be with us, there cannot and should not be any complete rupture from it. If what has been taken to be right in the past becomes implausible then we will inevitably look for new ways of thinking. But there can never be completely new ways of thinking. The past will always hang around with us, we must take the past with us, and consequently whatever you try to think in the future you may transform the past, but there cannot be a true revolution.

Burke and rational liberty

In *Reflections* Burke outlines the three main rights associated with the principles of the French Revolution. He then goes on to attack them as 'fictitious rights'. They are, first, the view that men ought to have the right to choose their own governors, second, that men have the right to cashier them for misconduct, and third, that men have the right to frame a government for themselves (Burke 1986: 99).

First, Burke argues that the King does not owe his crown to the choice of the people. For example, under the English constitution there was no written law which stated that the King was the choice of the people. Rather, what could be found was that the *Declaration of Right*, which followed the glorious revolution, was designed to settle the succession of the crown. The rights and liberties of subjects are bound to the right to succession given in the constitution. It is this hereditary succession that gives 'peace, quiet, and security of the realm' (Burke: 1986: 101).

In other words, Burke is arguing implicitly that because there is an acceptance of the fundamental importance of the continuity of the monarchy other freedoms are guaranteed. There is no need for each generation to redesign the government; in fact, to do so would endanger those freedoms which people enjoy. This view, then, brings out Burke's own view about rights. They are tied to history and tradition, not to abstract principles. It may be said that this position is the beginning of Burke's notion of 'rational liberty' that is developed throughout his famous text and which ought to be understood as a challenge to the idea of abstract rights. What Burke calls 'abstract rights' we might term in a more contemporary fashion 'ideology'. So, Burke's theory of rights sets out an early modern argument against a form of politics that was to become dominant in the twentieth century, and led politics ideologically along the lines of various 'isms': socialism, communism, fascism, liberalism.

Burke continues that the English revolution replaced the idea that succession was by common law with the idea that it was by statute law. This was not the same as France where one traditional system of government was being replaced by a totally new system. Furthermore, power was being placed in the hands of a new political class. For him this was dangerous. Burke argued that it was the people with property who were best suited to govern. The essence of property was inequality between people. Those who had property in large amounts understood the need to conserve it and to pass it on as a hereditary possession. This experience gave them the knowledge needed for government and the preservation of the state. Power ought to be kept away from those who did not have property. He maintained that people should be allowed to move social position and own property but this change was best as a slow change. Similarly he argued that all states change and, without the means to alter, a state will not be maintained. For him, the English revolution was a process of a state changing and conserving its political traditions, whereas the revolution in France was advocated as a total change where all political traditions were rotten and ought to be discarded. Burke maintained that if you threw away the hereditary crown you threw away *hereditary rights*. In France these rights were looked upon as wrongs but in England, 'They look on in the frame of their commonwealth, such as it stands, to be of inestimable value; and they conceive the undisturbed succession of the crown to be a pledge of their stability and perpetuity of all the other members of our constitution' (Burke 1986: 111).

Rewind

Go to Chapter 4 for discussion of the glorious revolution.

Burke does not argue that the King is king because of a divine right given by God (the argument of the medieval monarchs). He believes this view is as 'dogmatised' as the ideas of the French Revolution. But he believes that the King has a right to rule based on history, the constitution and the will of the people. Only this form of government secures peace.

Burke's second argument concerns whether men have the right of 'cashiering' (that is, finally judging) their governors for misconduct. He argues that no government could stand for a moment if it had to be open to the opinion of the people in this way. The abdication of King James (which led up to the glorious revolution) was not due to the charge of misconduct but because the constitution was in danger. The new constitution under King William made sure that succession of the Crown was tied to the idea of frequent parliamentary meetings and a limited monarchy in order to preserve the traditional government of England, not overturn it. This new constitution as well as giving politicians constitutional liberty made sure that 'the vices of administration' that had led to the abdication could not happen again. According to Burke, this whole situation was much more grave than the idea of cashiering rulers for misconduct which was why it was called a revolution. It still meant that the King of Great Britain was the ruler and the people were under his rule. The constitution stated that the people were to obey the law invested in the king but that he is not responsible to the people. As the House of Commons and House of Lords are the embodiment of his law they too are not accountable to the people for their conduct. It is this constitutional settlement that the architects of the French Revolution ignore. Burke warns that the cashiering of kings rarely continues without the use of force. If a war were to start in France this would not be a war like the war of the revolution of 1688 in England. This was because it was not based upon saving the constitution. It is these kinds of warnings that Burke became famous for, as soon after he wrote the Jacobean terror began in France where hundreds of members of the French aristocracy were killed including, of course, the monarchy.

The third and final part of Burke's argument regarding rational liberty concerns another aspect of rights. He argues that the right to form a government for ourselves is not a 'real' right. For him a 'real right' can only be one given to us as an inheritance from our ancestors: 'All the reformations we have hitherto made, have proceeded upon the principle of reference to antiquity' (Burke 1986: 117).

The oldest reformation was the Magna Carta and every political change ever since has had its basis in this document. All peoples' most sacred rights are given to them from this inheritance. Burke quotes the 'Petition of Right' written by Charles I and part of the British constitution which says that subjects have inherited their freedom not as abstract principles or 'as the rights of men' but because they are the rights of Englishmen. It is this 'practical wisdom' that Burke believes gives 'real rights'. He argues that the same understanding of the rights of Englishmen may be found in all English law. It is not something that can be put into strict principles but is given as part of the history of England to all people. This has nothing to do with the right to form a government.

'People will not look forward to posterity, who never look backwards to their ancestors' (Burke 1986: 119)

It is clear that Burke is arguing not only against the principles of the French Revolution but all claims of 'abstract rights' that were not embedded in a nation state's history and culture. For him 'real rights' were only those that could not be fully articulated in a written document precisely because they were so all-pervasive. 'Real rights' were simply *there*, part of the ways of doing things. They may be gleaned in constitutional law and political traditions, but they could never be categorised, systematised or otherwise captured in their entirety. This notion of rational liberty is most famously articulated in Burke's statement about a true social contract which was, for him, 'A partnership not only between those who are living, but between those who are living, those who are dead, and those who are to be born' (Burke 1986: 194–195).

For Burke, 'the rights of man' is not just nonsense (that is non-sense, making no sense at all as a rational argument), it is dangerous nonsense! It is dangerous because it does not recognise that the basis of all rights is law, and that to challenge this relationship is to challenge the legitimacy of law, opening the door to subversion and anarchy. The modern notion of rights, for Burke, is then a most dangerous doctrine.

DISCUSSION POINT

The language of rights is so embedded in our moral, legal and political vocabulary that we may be excused for thinking of them as natural. Yet, as we have seen, the idea that individuals are entitled to certain rights was a process of slow historical development. We have moved from the idea that rights are natural and God-given, to an idea of rights as morally and legally supportable. The United Nations Declaration of Human Rights 1948 is perhaps the most famous of all our modern rights. How far do you think that rights are an effective means of upholding principles of justice in the world? Would the world be radically different without human rights?

Burke is arguing that rights exist not prior to society, but they exist in society. In Hobbes and in Locke one finds a doctrine of natural rights, expressed differently but there in both cases. Similarly in Rousseau and Hegel and Marx there are ideas that there is something distinct from society, some sense of justice that transcends society (like the general will), even though most of what we are structured on is consequent to society. Burke argues that civil society, if it was made for the advantages of man, then what comes out of that becomes the right of men within it. Men have a right to live by that rule of civil society, they have a right to justice, as between their fellows, whether their fellows are in politics or in an ordinary occupation. They have a right to the fruits of their industry, and the means of making that industry fruitful. They have a right to the acquisitions of their parents for the nourishment and improvement of their offspring, and so on. He goes on to say: 'Whatever each man can separately do, without trespassing on others, he has a right to do, for himself. And he has a right to a fair portion of all which all society, with all its combinations of skill and force can do, in his favour' (Burke: 1986: 71–72).

In his sense, then, the 'real' rights of man are actually quite substantial. They are not just ephemeral ideas, but mean something more than merely the abstract 'rights of man' for Burke. He goes on to say that all men have equal rights but (unlike Marx) not to equal things. For example, if someone has put 5 shillings into a partnership he has as good a right to it as the person who has put in £500, but he does not have an equal right to an equal dividend in the product of the joint stock. Thus you have equal rights to have what you own, but not equal rights to share in that richer society. A clearer way for us to understand this today might be to say that the millionaire has just as much right to his Rolls Royce as the person sleeping in a cardboard box has to his cardboard box! They both have an equal right, an equal right to whatever they have. How is this to be known? Burke says it is something to be settled by convention. Ultimately there are no external rules by which you can decide such matters. It is in society in which the rights of men exist; they do not exist outside of society. There is no natural right. Burke is as firmly against the tradition of natural right. That said, he does not think that rights are entirely matters of convention either. That would open up the way for any kind of claims of rights. There are restraints on claims of rights but not ones that may be understood through abstract principles.

DISCUSSION POINT

Without perhaps fully knowing it, Burke sets out an argument against ideological politics. For him politics is not about which party has the best plans for the future, who can write the best manifesto for the next five years. Rather politics is about statecraft, experience and practical wisdom in day-to-day circumstances, the outcome of which cannot be known. Do you think that there is anything beneficial to gain from his understanding of what politics is all about? Or does it belong to a bygone era?

Analysis and critique

It could be argued that many of the arguments that Burke puts forward in his *Reflections* have been vindicated by history. The French Revolution did turn to violence while the British constitution remained relatively untouched (although with a gradual and increasing limitation on the direct power of the monarchy). Domestic peace was, by and large, maintained in Britain while the rest of Europe shook with the sound of revolution over the following sixty years or so. The French political tradition returned after the revolution in the strong presidential system that was established. It was a more modern democratic system of rule but it nevertheless mirrored in many ways the institutional practices and hierarchical organisation that had also existed under the monarchy.

Yet it is not so important to rate the correctness of Burke arguments on the historical outcomes of the events he was writing about. It is just as easy to dismiss Burke's arguments on historical grounds as to maintain that they are justified. Burke was writing at a time when the historical study of society was rather new. Since his time our understanding of history has changed quite considerably. Many different historical methods compete for a truthful understanding of the events of the past. Burke's use of history as evidence for giving rights appears rather naïve when set against more contemporary forms of analysis. For example, a common criticism of

Burke's use of history is that he seems to believe that there is only one true history of the nation. Yet this is patently untrue. In Chapter 2 we looked at the 'alternative' history of Britain and the role of radical politics which is not always considered a part of the development of modern Britain. As we have seen, in the thought of the Levellers, the Diggers and other English radical groups, there is another component to British political history that indicates that it has been far from peaceful and one-dimensional. The classic work on these radical movements by Christopher Hill is a testament to this view (Hill 1991).

   If we cannot look to history to make our judgements on Burke's text where can we look? We have to judge the coherence of his arguments based on what he has written, thinking through the arguments of the text. Burke's *Reflections* is an important text of political thought, not because it is a deeply philosophical text, nor even because of any great originality, but it is important as a kind of bridging text. What it does do is to bridge a number of ideas and draw together a number of different facets of the kinds of debate that had been going on in his time. It also presents a classic objection to revolution; objections that if you agree that they ring true, that they are coherent, have enormous implications for how we might think and do politics.

   Burke is also important because he bridges two traditions in political theory. A key ontological question that any serious author of political thought has to answer is: What is the source of individuality? Some authors in the modern tradition have argued that individuals are the source of society, others that individuals are the outcome of society. In the first model the individual is seen as largely prior to society, and in the second model the individual is seen as largely a consequence of society. Although this is a rather basic way of dividing the history of political thought it is a useful distinction between authors. Any categorisation that enables us to fit the jigsaw pieces of modern thinking together is helpful, as long as we remember that there are many ways of creating such divisions, and many different categories. As far as the thinkers with whom we are concerned with here, Hobbes, Locke and Mill take the individual to be largely prior to society, whereas Rousseau, Hegel and Marx under-stand the individual to be its consequence. Of course, each of these authors has his own ways of reasoning through his views on human nature, and these are specific and distinct in each case. One of the interesting things about Burke is that he straddles these two traditions in some important respects. He sees individuals as part of society, but he does not take them to be completely socially structured in every way. He does see individuals as social beings, which means that any revolutionary shake-up of society will affect individuals deeply. But at the same time Burke also holds to a Christian doctrine of individual souls. Thus Burke's ontology is in the middle of two important schools of thought within political theory.

 Rewind

Go to Chapter 5 for further discussion of the Enlightenment.

In many ways Burke's general weakness is undermined by being too much of a 'piggy in the middle' – time-wise, that is. He writes after the Enlightenment and during the development of modern history. But he is at the table while many ideas are still being cooked. He is caught between traditional outlooks and modern methods. He therefore knows that it is important to discuss society as such, but he does not have the conceptual language to do so, writing before sociological method had fully started to emerge (even if we accept modern sociology was a process started by Montesquieu). He uses history as the factual evidence to back up his claims and his arguments concerning rights, but his history is rather 'potted' and not really thought through in terms of its methodology. He makes what could be termed interesting philosophical remarks regarding human nature, but he has no philosophical system in which to situate them. And his politics was already becoming the politics of a bygone age as Europe (and, indeed, North America) started to change before his eyes. An aspect of Burke's work that has often been criticised is his 'conservatism'. There was one point in our political history in Britain (perhaps from the mid-1960s until the early 1980s) when in some quarters (including many university politics departments) to simply label someone 'conservative' was ample criticism for their ideas to be dismissed without further investigation. Thankfully, that time has passed and such ideological 'boxing' of important authors is less common. Thus to state that Burke is a conservative thinker (which many, but not all parts of his work undoubtedly are) is not a conclusion but rather a starting point for further investigation. What is important is the content of his conservatism and if it has anything to say to us, whether or not it stands up as an argument is the key. Burke was certainly conservative in many of his arguments. We have seen how he values tradition, how he understands society as fundamentally developing along slowly evolving grounds rather than through giant leaps of reorganisation. Most importantly we have tried to understand the reasons for these views. It is often said that behind them is a belief in natural order. For Burke, God organised the world in terms of an organic society. This meant that every person had a specific role to play in life. If you were King it was because this was your God-given role. If you were a farm labourer this too was God-given. Today we might impose our own sociological perspective upon Burke's notion of society and say that he believed that the natural order of society was based upon a very well-structured class system. However, it is important to try and contextualise Burke in the understandings of his own time. It is not easy to think ourselves away from our contemporary discourse and plant ourselves in a world of experience prior to our own. Although there are similarities between our world and Burke's, the vocabulary of science, history and politics was quite different. Furthermore, although Burke seems to justify a hierarchical society, what he means by 'society' is not the sociological definition we take for granted today. Modern society would have been a new thing for Burke, only just developing in a way in which we would conceptually recognise. For Burke, society was 'civil society', a much more political entity that had more notional correspondence to Plato's 'polis' or political community than today's diverse and complex 'society'. So, when Burke writes of society being naturally hierarchical, he is not concerned with its justness or otherwise. This is an argument that does not really fully develop until Marx comes along, although Rousseau and the English radicals begin – in a small way – to take us there. Rather he is merely following a very classical argument that also comes from Plato and Aristotle and early Greek society that very few people are capable of ruling.

KEY CONCEPT 3

Political community

A concept that goes back to the Greek notion of the 'polis' and to Rousseau's 'general will' where all citizens had a direct say in running the affairs of their state. A political community is different to the modern notion of society. It is not concerned with the economic dimensions of society (wealth, inequalities), or with its demographic make-up. A political community is one where there is political equality, not equality of status or wealth.

As we have seen, Burke has a very specific sense of rights. For him rights are embedded in the culture in which one is born. To say that individuals are fundamentally unequal does not, under the terms of his argument, mean that people do not enjoy their rights. Under the terms of Burke's rational liberty, rights cannot be handed down, nor are they the preserve of a few. Society is organic, tied together by everyone, regardless of wealth or status having a role. It follows that rights must be similarly organic. In this way, while to our contemporary mind Burke may be conservative in his view that society is fixed in a natural inequality, under the terms of his own reasoning (and in the context of his time) Burke is actually rather liberal in his theory of rights. Rights belong to all, they do not come from the 'top down'. They cannot be written down, and therefore are not easily taken away. Rights are not granted by government but belong to all by virtue of, literally, a birthright. In the light of this view Burke's conservatism is rather less than straightforward. It needs to be unpacked in order to understand what is meant by it. And when we do unpack it we see that to label him 'conservative' and to leave it at that is a perversion and reduction of his meaning.

KEY CONCEPT 4

Fear of the masses

Modern commentators of all political persuasions have been afraid of the masses. Even before the universal franchise there was a fear of the 'tyranny of the majority'; that is, that if ever the uneducated classes were given political power they would misuse it and end up destroying a civilised culture which they knew nothing about. Burke was by no means alone when indicating his concerns about popular government. It is fair to say that liberals (Mill) and socialists (Marx) were equally worried about the masses. In the political ideas following Burke we often find arguments for democracy moderated by concerns about ensuring that the best rulers rule.

It was not unusual for writers of the early modern period to consider the 'masses' rather dangerous. Indeed it was something of the norm. The 'masses' were not the same as the citizens of today. The majority of people were uneducated, not only unable to read and write but also politically uneducated. Even in Marx's writings, as we shall see, there was a deep distrust of the 'masses'. Burke followed many of his contemporaries in saying that if the uneducated groups in society were given political power they would misuse it and very soon events would turn violent. Even an extremely liberal thinker of his day, J.S. Mill, who believed in a form of women's rights (which was extremely rare and radical) was concerned about the masses having political power. Again, this may appear to us today as a conservative position and we certainly would not tolerate such views as part of a modern liberal democratic system, but the criticism to be made of Burke here is that it was a rather unoriginal comment for his day. The argument he proposed to justify this view was also rather unoriginal and takes something from Lockean ideas. Property ought to be a measure of political experience according to Burke. Families who had managed their own affairs successfully for a number of years and had prospered were the best people to manage society. The management of property gave the wealthy classes an insight into how to manage the nation's affairs. This seems a fair enough observation. Again, in our own times we all participate in society. As individuals we manage a wide range of our own affairs. Most of us do have property, family, responsibility at work and so on. We are educated and literate, we live in a world where political communication and debate is everywhere. It would follow thinking logically along the same lines as Burke that our world, made up of individuals like us, is suited to democracy. But the social world that Burke was living in was very different. Most individuals did not have the experience of the management outside trying to help themselves and their families to survive. However unfortunate a situation this was and however much we may argue for change, the facts were for Burke that it was only the upper classes who had this kind of practical knowledge. It may be correct to say, then, that in this respect Burke's conservatism stems from his realism (and perhaps lack of political imagination) rather than from an ideological point of view.

A final point of analysis is worth considering. This is Burke's notion of liberty. As we have seen with the social contract theorists – Hobbes, Locke and Rousseau – as well as with the French Revolution itself, the notion of liberty was a central feature. By opposing the revolution and in differing from the social contract theorists by not writing extensively on freedom, Burke has sometimes been deemed to be a rather authoritarian thinker. It is true to say that he was against the political cause of the masses, as described above, but that is not to say he does not have a view about liberty. Burke's notion of liberty was not tied to the idea of equality. For him, to be free one must be part of a nation. Although his views on equality set him radically apart from Marx he identified liberty with being part of a community in the same way that communism does. Both are communitarian theories. But there the comparison ends. For Burke, without a sense of the history and traditions of a nation an individual is a lost soul. If we wanted to use a modern concept we might say that Burke is thinking sociologically here again without knowing it. He seems to be touching upon the ground set out later by Durkheim and his contemporaries that if an individual does not feel a sense of belonging they can become dysfunctional. This was Burke's argument; following Hobbes and his concern with order he maintained that the social glue which stopped people being continually in a 'war of all against all' was a sense of national identity. Again here we see in Burke his 'bridginess'. That is, he is beginning to touch a foot into the nineteenth-century territory of nationalism and national identity, as well as sociological argument, but he does not carry it through. This is perhaps both the genius of his work and its ultimate weakness. Burke brings together a number of arguments that had been going on throughout the modern period. He brings them to bear on the events of the day, particularly the revolution in France. In so doing he broaches many modern themes that were to form a great deal of the debates right up until the present, yet he cannot follow them through because of his time and place. Such limitations on his ability to conceptually structure all that was happening around him is by no means his own personal failing. It is to do with time and place. But it does leave his work ultimately unsatisfactory in many ways and we have to move on in the modern period to see what others have said more substantively about some of the issues that Burke can do no more than intimate towards.

Revision notes

1   Burke is often seen as a conservative thinker. However, it may be better to regard this as a starting place rather than a conclusion and to examine the exact content of his conservatism.

2   Burke is a bridge between traditional thinking about political practice and more modern ideas. This gives him both a singular place in the conversation of modern political theory and also a rather weak position regarding the methods he uses to justify his arguments.

3   A key part of Burke's work that is often underrated is his theory of rights. This may be taken as a central focus point. It leads into the examination of other areas of his work such as his notion of liberty.

4   What Burke has to say about revolution needs to be thought through for its contemporary relevance. If what he says may be said to hold for his own time, then it may be said to hold for our own times.

Bibliography

Burke, E. (1982) *A Vindication of Natural Society*, ed. Frank Pagano, Indianapolis: Liberty Classics.
—— (1986) *A Philosophical Enquiry into the Origin of Our Ideas of the Sublime and Beautiful*, London: Penguin.
—— (1992) *Further Reflections on the Revolution in France*, Indianapolis: Liberty Press.
Dreyer, F.A. (1979) *Burke's Politics: A Study in Whig Orthodoxy*, Waterloo, ON: Wilfrid Laurier University Press.
Franco, P. (1992) *The Philosophical Politics of Michael Oakeshott*, New Haven, CT: Yale University Press.
Freeman, M. (1980) *Edmund Burke and the Critique of Political Radicalism*, Oxford: Blackwell.

Hill, C. (1991) *The World Turned Upside Down*, London: Penguin.
Macpherson, C.B. (1980) *Burke*, Oxford: Oxford University Press.
Oakeshott, M. (1962) *Rationalism and Politics and Other Essays*, London: Methuen.

Further reading

A useful supplement to Burke's *Reflections on the Revolution in France* is D.E. Ritchie, (ed.) (1992) *Further Reflections on the Revolution in France*, London: Liberty Press. Burke's work is often read alongside that of Paine who can be taken as his theoretical jousting partner (T. Paine (1969) *Rights of Man*, Harmondsworth: Penguin). However, although on many politics courses you may find Burke and Paine situated together, it can often mean that you do not have time to study either in depth. For good secondary commentary see J.G.A. Pocock's lengthy introduction to Burke's *Reflections* (1987), Indianapolis: Hackett Publishing Company. And, for a general introduction to debates about rights, see P. Jones (1994) *Rights*, Basingstoke: Macmillan.

Part III

ALL THAT IS SOLID MELTS INTO AIR: THE INDUSTRIAL REVOLUTION

John Stuart Mill

What more or better can be said of any condition of human affairs than that
it brings human beings themselves nearer to the best thing they can be?
(On Liberty)

The life of John Stuart Mill (1806–1873) spanned the historical period in which the processes and consequences of industrialisation came to dominate the social and political structure of European society, and his life experience provided him with the knowledge and education necessary to get to grips with understanding the dynamics of this 'brave new world'. In his autobiography Mill sets out the story of his personal and intellectual development. This clearly shows how the major events and issues of his time shaped his intellectual development and how in turn his understanding of these things developed into an argument for the primacy of individual liberty and its vital necessity to each human's happiness and social progress.

Rewind

Go to Chapter 5 to see the similarities between Mill's and Montesquieu's work. Both theorists are very eclectic. They both mix scientific rationalism with classical theory and both are criticised for a subsequent lack of coherence in their work.

Mill's writings covered many fields and included influential works on scientific methodology (*System of Logic* 1843), economics (*Principles of Political Economy* 1848), philosophy (*Utilitarianism* 1861), political constitution (*Representative Government* 1861), gender politics (*Subjection of Women* 1868) and his great contribution to political philosophy, the essay *On Liberty* (1859). As this list indicates, Mill was an eclectic thinker, willingly mixing elements of social scientific theory and method with elements of utilitarian ethics, classical Socratic dialectics and classical liberal individualism. A negative result of this eclecticism is that Mill's work is noted for problems of coherence. Many readers have spied a particularly telling uncertainty about the relationship of the scientific pursuit of truth to public debate, and, even more problematically for a modern political theorist, about the value of democracy. Confusion on such basic issues in modern social and political life has led to doubts among some commentators about the importance of Mill's writings to our understanding of politics in the modern world. Against these doubts, however, we shall see the vitality that Mill's arguments obtain from his willingness to experimentally mix social scientific and classical modes of thinking. Furthermore, such criticisms often miss the point that part of the reason why Mill's work is important is historical. In modern times, traditional modes of enquiry, and with them much of the basis of classical liberal theory, came under challenge from the newly emerging social sciences. Mill rose to the challenge of accommodating the new modes of analysis, while reminding his contemporaries of the enduring relevance to human affairs of classical philosophical conceptions of 'the good life'. Beyond this there is the enduring status of *On Liberty*. This essay, widely regarded as the expression of his core philosophy of social and political life, is a lively, moving and, as many commentators believe, convincing restatement of the necessity of the key features of the classical liberal constitution. What is of particular interest is the way in which Mill takes a standard liberal theme – the primacy of individual liberty, expressed in the dynamics of a unfettered civil society protected at its boundaries by a minimally intrusive state – and integrates into it a theory of social progress, involving a notion of political life as educational and an argument that education is a necessity for social progress.

Mill's personal pursuit of happiness

John Stuart Mill was the eldest of nine children born to Harriet and James Mill. James Mill, a noted political thinker in his own right and a man known for the strength of his personality, cast a long shadow over the life of John Mill. A self-improving Scot, James worked hard to establish a reputation as an academic and a diplomat, rising swiftly to the second most senior rank in the East India Company and building up friendships with cutting-edge intellectuals such as economist David Ricardo and philosopher Jeremy Bentham, the leading establishment thinker of his day. Bentham in particular became a strong influence over the Mills' intellectual life.

KEY PEOPLE 1

Jeremy Bentham (1748–1832)

Jeremy Bentham originated the philosophy of utilitarianism. This philosophy sought to establish the idea that all human endeavours could be evaluated in terms of their utility; that is, their usefulness in producing a general condition of human happiness. He defined happiness as a condition derived from maximising pleasure and mini-mising pain, and argued that varying intensities of happiness were measurable on a scale which calculated the levels of pain and pleasure in any given situation (this was know as the Felicific Calculus).

His novel approach led him to challenge prevailing political conceptions of 'the good life', to challenge legal conceptions of rights and duties and to campaign for radical reforms in social policy and criminal law, to increase education and inculcate principles of civility. He also campaigned for the extension of the franchise, believing that an educated and politically involved population would perceive the sources of happiness and direct their government to work towards them. Although he wrote copiously on many subjects, his philosophy is best captured in his *Introduction to the Principles of Morals and Legislation* (1789).

Bentham's philosophy of utilitarianism influenced the intellectual and practical thinking of James Mill who in turn became renowned as a leading utilitarian in public circles. In private, he filtered his utilitarian philosophy through a strict regime of practical and moral living that had a profound impact on his son.

In his *Autobiography*, John Stuart Mill presented an intense, but heavily muted, loving relationship between himself and his father. A classically Victorian suppression of emotions squeezed the father's expression of love into a strict and rather authoritarian paternalism, centring on a hyper-rigorous programme of educational development for his son. James Mill initiated lessons in Greek when John Stuart was but 3 years old. Latin was introduced at the age of 8; logic, economics and philosophy followed, and during this time he became fully inculcated with the principles of utilitarian philosophy.

The father's influence was double-edged, not only shaping the son's intellect but also shaping his emotional constitution. Psychologically, John Stuart Mill was almost overpowered by his father's presence. Indeed, he struggled so much to fulfil his father's expectations that he attempted to replicate features of his life. He followed James Mill into the civil service of India and, moving through the ranks of bureaucrats like his father before him, he came in the end to occupy exactly the same position. Similarly, as a young man, he copied his father's public advocation of Benthamite philosophy by setting up The Utilitarian Society.

Not surprisingly, the stress of his struggle led John Stuart Mill into clinical depression and eventually into a full-scale nervous breakdown. Reflecting in his *Autobiography* on this dark time, John Stuart Mill reveals inner struggle and mental confusion. He mourns repeatedly the absence of affection and of play from his youth: 'I never was a boy, never played at cricket' and then, swiping at his father's regime, 'it is better to let nature have her own way' (Thomas 1992: 250). On the other hand, he refused to blame his father's rigid programme. It 'was not such as to prevent me from having a happy childhood' (Riley 1998:9). His recognition of his father's strangled expression of love as discipline is expressed with a resentful undertone: 'I believe my father to have had much more feeling than he habitually showed' (Riley 1998: 11). Despite his reluctance to blame his father, he believed that it was an inability to feel emotion that dragged him into depression – and he did see this as a problem rooted firmly in his upbringing, notably in his father's intense dislike of displays of affection, writing that James 'expressed the greatest contempt' (Riley 1998: 9) 'for passionate emotions of all sorts' ((Riley 1998: 10).

Significantly, it was an outburst of weeping (over a play about a failed father–son relationship) that triggered Mill's release from depression and from the overbearing presence of his deceased father. It was a release that gave him the freedom to reflect upon and reinterpret the stuff of his education, and it is at this point that John Stuart Mill's unique philosophical mix of utilitarianism and humanist liberalism makes its entry into the public sphere.

With this in mind, it may be seen why Mill's political and social arguments have at their base the struggle to understand and articulate the constitution of human happiness. It is both a personal and a philosophical struggle. Its personal quality, deriving from his bleak childhood, ran into his adult life. In 1830 he met a loving, affectionate and intellectually gifted woman who shared the name of his dull and loveless mother – Harriet. Unfortunately, given the strictness of Victorian family values, Harriet was married, to a John Taylor. Mill and Harriet Taylor had to conduct a semi-clandestine relationship that could be normalised by marriage only after Taylor's death (and a period of mourning) in 1851. Even then, the happiness they were to have was brief; Harriet died from TB just seven years later.

The philosophical struggle took the form of Mill's quest to break free from the utilitarianism of his father and of Bentham. The philosophy of utilitarianism is built upon the maxim of 'the greatest happiness of the greatest number'. Happiness, as defined by Bentham, was a condition consisting of a state of pleasure, defined in part as sensory enjoyment of experience and in part as the absence of pain. Benthamites believed that although different people had different pleasures, they all amounted to variations of the same substantive condition. All states of happiness are substantively the same and can therefore be weighed against each other in calculating which combinations of individual happiness amount to the greatest total of happiness for the whole of society. Mill knew from personal experience that happiness was much more complex than this. His lack of happiness derived from a lack of feeling altogether; this in turn derived from a lack of contact with his emotional self and a consequent sense of misshapen development. To his own mind, his upbringing had not made him into a fully balanced person but rather into an unemotional 'calculating machine'.

We have seen that Mill's own environment had a part to play in his early unhappiness. Living in the great metropolis of London in the nineteenth century, the heaving centre of the Industrial Revolution, Mill could not but see also that the environment of his contemporaries played a significant role in shaping the possibilities of their achieving any degree of fulfilment and lasting happiness. Mill was struck by the condition of the great numbers of urban working-class people, particularly by the way in which they were squashed together in great un-individuated masses of poverty, uneducated ignorance and squalor. Reflecting on his condition and on the condition of his less fortunate contemporaries, he came to recognise that the Benthamite version of happiness was psychologically crude and that its use as a measure of appropriateness of governmental activity was simplistic. He saw that vast numbers of people lived a daily existence which was miserable not simply because they lacked pleasure – which was readily available in the crude form of laudanum, gin, sex and gambling – but through lack of access to humanising agencies, which he, like his reforming Victorian contemporaries, Dickens and Arnold, saw as the high arts and the sciences and crucially an education which would enable common people to appreciate them.

With the help of Harriet Taylor, Mill mounted a retrieval of the ancient Greek understanding of happiness as *eudaimonia* – the individual's fulfilment of their positive potential. This condition, he noted, was achieved over a lifetime and was not just a superficial and momentary pleasure.

In his theory of happiness, he builds a strong sense of the individuality of the condition of happiness, involving a clear picture of the uniqueness of each individual's pursuit of their happy condition and of the environmental factors that could aid or impede them. A point of confusion for commentators ever since is that Mill attempts to fuse this Hellenic notion of happiness into utilitarian theory, by deploying Plato's hierarchy of pleasures. In this hierarchy, the immediate sensory gratification of animal pleasure corresponds to our lowest animal needs. It does not stimulate or meet the needs of our intellectual or spiritual being. These levels of consciousness have higher needs which can be gratified only through ever-increasing and ever more entwined emotional and intellectual pleasures which are food to the life of the soul and of the mind. This amendment removed from Mill's theory any need to build his arguments on explicitly utilitarian principles – although he did continue to claim that his arguments were driven and bound by them. More significantly, perhaps, his notion of higher levels of happiness strengthened the marked intellectual elitism that

Mill inherited from Bentham's utilitarianism. Bentham claimed that, as every person held a different sense of pleasure and pain and each and all were involved in relationships in which the distribution and value of pleasures would be disputable, only an independent observer with a rare intellectual ability could perform the necessary task of legislating to create and maintain the greatest happiness for the greatest number. In J.S. Mill's writings, this elitism is retained in the modified notion that only a 'gifted few' can perceive the true consequence of actions and potentialities of situations in order to judge the most happy outcome for all those involved. However, the elitism is also notably offset by Mill's belief that the numbers of those who could be included in the few would greatly increase if common people were given access to education.

Finding his own voice in *On Liberty*, he argued that to find happiness, people needed space to think and act and they needed education to arm them with the great sum of wisdom available to guide their thoughts and actions. Although Mill's unwillingness to completely disown his father's and Bentham's ideas (and his interest in a wide range of scientific and philosophical schools of thought) led him to mix his core ideas into some confused passages of reasoning (as many commentators have noted), these ideas remain consistently at the core of his philosophy of liberal humanism.

The radicalism of Mill's liberal humanism became clear to his contemporaries in the years following Harriet's death. In 1865, Mill committed himself to a more public life in politics and was elected Member of Parliament for Westminster. In this capacity, he revealed his radicalism, to a degree which is often obscured by the elitist streak in his writings. In 1866 (with the support of Richard Pankhurst, father of the famous suffragette family), Mill presented a Private Members Bill for Women's Suffrage to the House of Commons (it failed). He associated with the leaders of the growing Trade Union Movement, which he saw as an educative, improving school for the working classes, and in 1869 he fulfilled an intellectual pledge to Harriet Taylor, by publishing the major feminist work *On the Subjection of Women*.

Context

By the nineteenth century it had become apparent that the collapse of Catholic hegemony left the modern world without a clear-cut overarching foundational moral philosophy. It was also apparent that the competition to fill the void left by the collapse of Catholicism had become dominated by the combined intellectual weight and practical power of scientific rationalism. This new and therefore entirely modern way of thinking and acting could, it seemed, explain the physical universe, the evolutionary processes producing the human species at the apex of global life and even the evolution of human societies from the 'primitive' animality of the Stone Age to the sophistication of industrialised modern society. Furthermore, it alone provided the understanding necessary to radically modify human technologies, so as to further improve people's conditions of life and thereby advance human society towards a perfect end.

The massive confidence of this general belief stemmed from the very real experience of technological development and its attendant increase in productive and destructive power. Increasingly rapid advances in the technological manipulation of the environment, in methods of production and distribution of goods, exploded with the practical application of the ground-breaking invention of the steam engine – factories to mass-produce goods and locomotives and steam-powered ships to transport them dynamised the Industrial Revolution and catalysed the growth of large-scale urban conurbations.

The nineteenth-century world – now incorporating the Americas and the massive European empires running through Asia and Africa – revolved around huge industrialised urban centres, in which clearly defined socio-economic classes comprising thousands, and in some cases millions, of people, existed cheek by jowl.

KEY PEOPLE 2

Harriet Taylor Mill (1807–1858)

In addition to acting as Mill's soulmate and partner in life, Harriet Taylor Mill also played a role in the development of Mill's political thinking. Mill claimed that Harriet directly influenced his thinking and contributed to the content and structure of his major writings. He directly credited her with co-authorship of *Principles of Political Economy* and of *Subjection of Women*. Despite Mill's claims, there remains widespread doubt about her alleged contributions to his work. Contemporaries found her less than impressive in discussion, and biographers can find little, if anything, to show that she directly contributed to any texts other than the *Subjection of Women* and possibly the *Principles of Political Economy*. She published very little herself. She is usually credited with having written an article entitled 'Enfranchisement of Women', published in *The Westminster Review* in 1851 and arguing for the enfranchisement of women, on the grounds that enabling women to participate in politics would not only enable them to articulate and pursue their interests in public affairs, but would alert men to many dimensions of social policy that they tended to overlook, with the net result that both sexes would become better educated, more articulate and therefore more rounded human beings. Intriguingly, we find these arguments in Mill's *Subjection of Women*.

While the exact degree of Harriet's involvement in Mill's output is unknown, it is clear that she functioned as his muse, providing the loving support and intellectual companionship necessary to fire his intellectual creativity.

Those living in such times could not help but be impressed and amazed at the contrast with the largely rural and relatively low-populace societies from which they knew their world had sprung. Nor could they help but be struck by the intensity of the depravation that industrialised urbanisation carried in its wake. Mill's contemporary, Charles Dickens, a frequent commentator on the conditions of the great masses of impoverished Londoners, wrote that 'the amount of crime, starvation and nakedness or misery of every sort in the metropolis surpasses all understanding' (Ackroyd 2000: 652–653).

In industrialised Europe, the cities were characterised by large-scale popula-
tions of severely impoverished and uneducated people. In London – the epicentre of
the new industrialised world and home to John Stuart Mill – the extent and intensity
of wide-scale impoverishment was at its worst. The city's massive population, largely
reduced to hopelessness, was prone to widespread drug abuse, made easy by the
ready availability of a cheap new spirit – gin and opium-based laudanum – and subject
to large-scale epidemics of killer diseases. The full dimensions of the squalor were
made clear near the end of the nineteenth century by Charles Booth's studies of
the working class in London and Seebohm Rowntree's first study of poverty in
York. Booth found 32.5 per cent of London's population to be living in deprivation,
while Rowntree found over 40 per cent of the population of York to be living in
absolute poverty.

Yet, despite the radical displacement of peoples from stable traditional modes
of living in country and town and the *ad hoc*, chaotic and often anarchic urban scapes
that replaced them, the massive changes wrought by the Industrial Revolution were
viewed by the majority of the middle and aristocratic classes, including political
practitioners and intellectuals, as 'advances'. Following tens and thousands of years
of human history, marked by ultra-slow and relatively minimal technical change,
this era of sudden change was truly wondrous to those involved (if also rather
frightening).

In such times, the key ideas of classical English liberal political theory, originally
formulated in the seventeenth century, appeared unconnected to the experiences
of everyday social and political life. Classical liberalism (as it has become known) was
forged from the fires of the English civil war and the desperate need of people to
establish safe and civil societies, and by Mill's time, the professional theorists'
discussions of individuals' contractual relations and the limits of the state appeared
to many to offer little understanding of the problems and issues involved in the
emergence of mass society.

In a time when the intensity of mass urban society dominated people's consciousness, the processes and conditions of the social classes became far clearer to
the observer's eye and they appeared to have a stronger impact than individual
actions and efforts in shaping the life-chances of the citizenry. Subsequently, analysis
of power relations – namely of the function and role of the state, of economic relations
and of the actual, possible and desirable living conditions of the citizenry – was
becoming dominated by the theories of social class and their economic and political
relations. This intensification of urbanised industrialised and overtly class-ridden
social existence catalysed the rapid development of the labour movement across
Europe – a movement consisting of a loose mix of trade unionists, romantic socialists,
radical liberals and revolutionaries. In France, this combustible mix exploded in the
failed revolution of 1848, while in the UK it fired activities of the growing trade unions
and the huge mass meetings of the British Chartists agitating for the extension of the
franchise to the working classes.

Many of these new radicals were informed by ideas derived from the new
disciplines of the social sciences, each of which highlighted the apparently deter-
minant power of impersonal forces in human affairs. Philosophical observers
of human affairs created new kinds of social scientific analyses of politics, seeking to
locate alternative explanations for the purpose of human activities in scientific,

rational exploration of large-scale social structures and processes over long periods of time. Auguste Comte (whose terminology Mill often employed in his social analysis) influentially pioneered the idea in his novel science of sociology that the possibilities for all human life were dominated by the functional processes of social institutions.

 Fast forward

Go to Chapter 9 for more information on Hegel's philosophy,

Similarly, the philosopher Hegel pioneered the idea that human progress was shaped by the driving force of historical processes. Both of these ideas were incorporated (along with a modification of contemporary economic theory) in Karl Marx's presentation of a historical evolution of economic, social and political structures towards a communist utopia. This incorporated Hegelian and sociological elements along with a modification of popular economic theories of the time, in an attempt to prove the dominant role of economics in human affairs. Such ideas prospered at the expense of traditional liberal political philosophy and, as a consequence, new formulations of the human condition, incorporating new definitions of its determinates, demands and possibilities, threatened to overwhelm and replace the traditional definitions, arguments and concerns of liberal political philosophy.

KEY PEOPLE 3

Auguste Comte (1798–1857)

Auguste Comte is known today as the 'father of sociology'. In his own time he was known as the creator of positivism – which was a philosophy of science and a philosophy of history, and the basis of a novel science of social development given the name 'sociology' by Comte. These three elements were tied together through the notion of historical progress, operating as the development of the human race towards full rational scientific society. These ideas were set out in the six-volume *Course of Positive Philosophy*, which was published between 1830 and 1842.

Today, Comte's philosophical ideas appear clumsy and his sociology naïve, but he was very influential in the nineteenth century and remains of historical significance for this reason. J. S. Mill was one of a number of establishment writers and thinkers who declared themselves to be positivists.

The considerable persuasive power of this new approach was, however, limited and indeed undermined by one specific and significant flaw in the scientific rationalist position. While scientific thinking had successfully shown the flaws in religious thinking, it had not replaced it with a new set of guiding principles for living. For all its capacity to explain how things worked and to enable people to do powerful things,

193

science could not provide any *ethical* grounds for judging the moral value of these things because it did not provide a context which would give meaning or value to our lives.

Mill was, among other things, a philosophical advocate of scientific rationalism and had little doubt about its capacity to produce real knowledge, 'Science', he wrote, 'is a collection of truths' (Thomas 1992: 302), but he had a sensitivity to the loss of meaning produced by the overthrow of theocracy. So, while he agreed with Comte and Hegel that historical perspective showed that the age of Christendom had ended, he was also aware that scientific rationalism had not yet provided the gap in meaningfulness and morality left in the wake of Christendom's fall. For this reason he disagreed with Comte's and Hegel's optimistic claim that a new age of scientific rationalism was unfolding with certain inevitability. He countered their claims with the argument that, while the old age had died, the new age, built on scientific rational principles, had still to be established. Summing up the situation as he saw it in *The Spirit of the Age*, he wrote, 'At all other periods there exists a large body of received doctrine covering nearly the whole field of the moral relations of man. This state of things does not now exist in the civilised world' (Cowling 1963: 4). It was a period in which 'the progress of enquiry has brought to light the insufficiency of the ancient doctrines' but the new social scientists have 'not yet sanctioned any new body of doctrine' (Cowling 1963: 4). Thus 'Mankind lose their old convictions without acquiring any new ones of a general or authoritative character' (Riley 1998: 3). In contrast to Comte's and Hegel's assertions that the new age of reason had arrived, Mill was presenting an age of crisis which could end only with the victory of 'triumph of a yet more advanced creed' (Riley 1998: 4).

This difference in attitude to the inevitability of the new age of reason stemmed from a basic disagreement about the relative functions of individual endeavour and social organisations – particularly those governing social organisations comprising the state – to human progress. Mill was very aware that the trends towards statism in European political philosophy were in line with the development of mass society in modern Europe. The major cities and many towns had become huge urban con- urbations and the mechanisation of previously craft-based production had deskilled and standardised working practices. It had also standardised produce from the buildings that shaped the cities, to the modes of transport that moved their occupants around those cities. Viewing all this from his home in West London, the greatest mass conglomeration of them all, Mill reflected that 'At present individuals are lost in the crowd' (Warnock 1962: 195). His aim was to articulate a way of life in which the vitality and uniqueness of individuals could be protected and re-enervated.

In this context, we can begin to understand how and why Mill's political theory is so eclectic. His concern for the emotional and intellectual growth of individual human beings, tied to his belief in the potential for scientific rationalism to improve the conditions of life – to create the environment necessary for individual and collective well-being – led him to attempt to present a new template for a meaningful existence to human life. In producing this template, Mill brought to bear all the concepts and methods of analysis he had come to value after wrestling with utili- tarianism, scientism and Hellenic philosophy during his long years of education. His familiarity with these diverse approaches, and his belief that he had liberated himself from the shackles of a doctrinaire faith in any one of them, gave him the courage to build a bric-à-brac mixture of new ideas of historical progress and ancient ideas of happiness, tied around a reassertion of the necessity of individual liberty. From this mixture he formulated a theory of happiness deriving from fulfilment which is possible only when an individual lives in a condition of liberty.

Happiness, virtue and fulfilment

Ironically, despite their claims to be thinking anew, the continental theorists of the nineteenth century readily used the ancient Greeks' conceptualisations of virtue, fulfilment and happiness in their account of the progress of humankind towards perfection in modern times. These Hellenic ideas also provided the common ground between the ideas of the continental social theorists and those of J.S. Mill, for he too looked to the ancients, though in his case it was for a means to improve upon the weaknesses of his educators' utilitarianism. This common ground enabled Mill to engage with the influential continental theories, to challenge them and to counter their presentations of the need of revolutionary new forms of state with arguments for the continuing necessity of liberalism.

Mill's return of utilitarianism to a notion of happiness as *eudaimonia* brought him on to common ground with the political and philosophical discourse of continental Europe at that time. This idea of happiness had been central to Jean Jacques Rousseau's political social and political theory that was still very influential on European political thought in the early nineteenth century. Rousseau-esque language had echoed through the discourse of the Napoleonic Empire and, at a more meaningful level, his ideas were taken up and advanced by the hugely influential German philosophers Kant and Hegel. In Mill's adult lifetime, Rousseauian ideas of the collective will, the educative role of political involvement and the retrieval of the ancient idea of civic virtue permeated the social theories of Auguste Comte – the self-declared father of sociology – and the Hegelian school of philosophy including Karl Marx, whose influence on the modern world cannot be easily overstated.

 Rewind

Go to Chapter 6 for more information on Rousseau's notions of fulfilment and happiness. **Go to Chapter 9** for more on Hegel and Marx.

These three notions converge around the interface of the individual and the state – the role of the state in improving the condition of the citizen is no less than an obligation to educate and to civilise – that is, to humanise the otherwise animal individual. They derive their conceptual integrity from the ancient notion of virtuous being which, in a disguised form, also underpins Mill's passionate assertion of the primacy of individual liberty and so must be examined.

Mill and the teleological notion of human fulfilment

The Greeks believed that the destiny of each individual being was in part predestined by characteristics built into their being at birth – everything, they believed, has within it the blueprint of its perfect form – a form which, given the perfect environment, will unfurl itself over the life span of that thing. Every seed contains the blueprint for a tree which will emerge from within it and unfurl its full dimensions over time, if given good soil, light and regular watering. Every baby has within it the blueprint for the growth of the perfect adult, given the right environment, the right physical and mental stimulation, with intellectual and moral education. A perfect outcome (near impossible to achieve since it requires perfect environmental conditions) would be the complete fulfilment of all the individual's various potentials by the time of their death.

The *telos* is the unique principle of each individual's existence – the energy which dynamises them and drives them on to keep living and to grow, which guides the course of their development, physically, intellectually and ethically, and the complete fulfilment of which is their final destination. Aristotle sums up this idea with the description of the *telos* as both 'energetic being', which drives us to fulfil our potential, and as 'the final cause' – the principle which initiates and drives all our self-fulfilling activities. In this definition, we see the beginning of a moral argument for striving for excellence and a notion of happiness as a notion of fulfilment (*eudaimonia*) derived from such striving.

The conceptual framework of teleological development of the self con-textualises the moral imperative: 'to thyne own self be true', which means act in accordance with your inner striving to achieve your best potential, or more simply put: 'Be the best you that you can be.' Here we find the specific teleological core of the Olympiads' notion of virtue as human excellence. To be virtuous is to be the most excellent version of oneself that one can manage, given the circumstances of one's life. To be fulfilled is to be engaged in a constant striving towards excellence of being. Happiness is not a moment of sensory gratification, but rather it is the satisfaction and fullness of being in the world derived from the striving for excellence.

This notion of happiness provides a much richer and more complex concep-tualisation of happiness than the notion of happiness as a state of being, resulting from the accumulation of pleasure and avoidance of pain. It allows us to understand the significance of those moments of our lives in which struggle, discomfort and tiring endurance tests leave us feeling good about ourselves. J.S. Mill's scientific rationalism led him to argue in his *System of Logic* that the story of a human being's life was no more than the sum of their experiences, the sum of the conditions in which they lived and upon which they acted. For this reason, he was not in a position to coherently present in his political writings an Aristotelian notion of human nature, yet this is what he did. In utilitarianism he fully accepts the Hellenic understanding of happiness as the state of being derived from self-development and sums it up neatly: 'Better to be a human dissatisfied than a pig satisfied; better to be Socrates dissatisfied than a fool satisfied' (Warnock 1962: 260). Better to want to be more intellectually alive and to be accomplished as a human being than to seek happiness in the immediate gratification of the animal senses.

Elements of this teleological notion of human development and the achievement of happiness were also central in the work of the great European thinkers Rousseau, Hegel and Marx, and they set out in their theories the moral function of the socio-political order. Like Mill, they argued that society is not simply about providing for human needs. Its function is also to improve the moral and intellectual quality of its members. J.S. Mill sums up the common position thus: 'what more or better can be said of any condition of human affairs than that it brings human beings themselves nearer to the best thing they can be?' (Warnock 1962: 186). Mill also shared with Hegel, Marx and Comte a strong belief that the history of human society was a map of human progress. However, it is on the question of the relationship of the individual to social and economic process in the shaping of progress that Mill takes up arms against the continental philosophers.

The idea that human beings were progressing away from ignorance towards total knowledge of the universe, with its workings and meanings, through the development of scientific rationalism, grew out of the French Enlightenment, and by the early nineteenth century this view was commonly held among intellectuals. During Mill's own lifetime, the idea was strengthened further by Darwin's development of the theory of general evolution. The concept of evolution was readily applied to notions of social development, by influential social theorists in particular, as is made clear in the claim made at Karl Marx's funeral that 'just as Darwin discovered the law of evolution in human nature . . . so Marx discovered the law of evolution in human history' (Wheen 1999: 364). In truth, however, Marx's theory was much more indebted to the work of Hegel, and J.S. Mill's own discussions of individual liberty and social progress may be seen to be in part a reaction against Hegel's idea of human progress and the many variants it spawned in nineteenth-century European social and political theory.

Hegel gave greater depth to the French revolutionaries' formulation of 'progress', by tying into the teleological notion of human self-development first propagated by the ancient Greek philosophers. In his famously complex and rather metaphysical philosophy, Hegel extended the teleological perception of human development into an account of the progress of the human race towards excellence, and in doing so transformed a notion of individual development into a theory of social progress. Each stage of human development expresses an advance in human consciousness. This is the case for every individual and also for human collectivities, which are the expression of humans' conscious efforts to understand and govern themselves and their environment. His idea was that each stage of society was a progressive development towards a mature and perfectible social formation. The mature form would be the most beneficial to each and every human being living within its bounds. From this perspective, history is nothing less than the map of the unfurling of the potential of the human race towards its ultimate fulfilment over time.

Following Hegel (and Rousseau), many European theorists argued that there is a developmental connection between environmental conditions and individual development, which lays down a moral obligation on the state: the best possible state would nurture each and every individual to their highest achievable condition of being – a condition of educated rationality – and the individual would then participate willingly in the continuance of the laws and social and political structures, to ensure that every other individual was also raised to the most achievable levels of excellence that they could achieve. The will of the rational individual and the aim of the state would be in common; the laws and process of social life they govern would be designed to facilitate this communality.

To this way of thinking, the modern state should construct and maintain a social order that maximises the opportunity for each and every individual to achieve the virtuous state of excellence. The implications of this trend of thought are threatening to key liberal ideals of minimal state intervention and maximum individual freedom in social affairs. The threat resonates in Rousseau's statement that the individual who does not consent to the demands of the state can be 'forced to be free' and in Hegel's assertion that 'the state is the will of God on earth'.

Mill, while fully accepting the idea that humans were progressing through the application of rational thought and science, saw that human action and understanding is derived from and expresses creative independence and cannot simply be an expression of unfolding natural processes.

Social progress, he argued, required human creativity, and human creativity was a product of individual genius . . . not species-like conformity. Unlike evolving plant and species life forms, Mill argued, humans beings' development is substantially the stuff of learning, through active participation with circumstances – what he referred to as 'experiments with living'. In short, humans made choices and humans messed up with the same active passion as they achieved improvements. The path of progress was both a learning curve and a task which required human creative action.

From this position, it seemed clear to Mill that attempts to engineer human excellence through state control of social life would in fact close down the vital spaces for human creative development, for free space to think, to express ideas to each other (the state would take a censorious control over academic freedoms, free press, the marketplace, religion and art). For this reason, he was particularly keen to counter this statist trend in thinking and he set about refuting it in his essay *On Liberty*. Mill articulates here the modern liberal concern with the condition of mass society in general, and with the trend towards political management of society – a trend seen by liberals to threaten the civil liberties of citizens and to promote impediments to the free flow of the vital highways of civil society: the free press, free trade, free association, so limiting the conditions of individual expression to the point of negating them.

DISCUSSION POINTS

1 Is it possible that a conception of happiness as the achievement of fulfilment can also be a notion of happiness as the consistent attainment of pleasure?
2 Does Mill's connection of individual liberty with the general condition of happiness for society depend on his notion of social progress?

On Liberty

The aim of *On Liberty* is twofold. It is to show that individual liberty is the foundation of individual fulfilment and the fulcrum of progress towards a society of ethically and intellectually well-developed citizens; it is also to show the exact limits that maximisation of individual liberty imposes on government involvement in social relations between citizens. The linchpin between these two related goals is the establishment of a general principle which simultaneously indicates the purpose of state restrictions on individual activity and sets the limits of such restrictions. Mill 'asserts this very simple principle' (Warnock 1962: 135), which has since become known as 'the harm principle', at the outset of his essay. There is, he says,

> one very simple principle as entitled to govern absolutely the dealings of society with the individual in the way of compulsion and control. . . . The only purpose for which power can be rightfully exercised over any member of a civilised community, against his will, is to prevent harm to others. His own good either physical or moral, is not a sufficient warrant. He cannot rightfully be compelled to do or forbear because it will be better for him to do so, because it will make him happier, because to do so in the eyes of others would be wise or even right.
>
> (Warnock 1962: 135)

Individuality

Underpinning the harm principle is the notion that the state does not need to enable people to do things; people have the capacity to do things for themselves. In fact, by attempting to enable people to do things, the state closes down the spaces for creative self-development of its citizens. Only by taking on the challenges of circumstances, by experimenting creatively with possible modes of living, can human beings develop as individuals actualising their potential in a teleological, dynamic self-growth.

The teleological individualism central to Mill's conception of human nature is explicit in the opening pages of *On Liberty*, where Mill states that, 'Human nature is not a machine to be built after a model, and set to do exactly the work prescribed for it, but a tree which requires to grow and develop itself on all sides, according to the tendency of the inward forces which make it a living thing' (Warnock 1962: 188). The point he is making is that, although people are made up of the same specifically human constituent elements – the particular physical traits unique to the species, plus the capacity for intellectual speculation, rational and ethical judgement – each individual is made up of a unique cluster of these common elements. It is the individually distinct possession of common attributes that not only makes it possible to perceive different people as members of a common species type, but also to distinguish and compare different people as individual identities who are distinct within the species type.

The particular cluster of attributes possessed by each individual combines and combusts in ways unique to that person, and in doing so, makes their being a unique condition. It also ensures that each individual life is a unique event, made up of particular experiences, each of which is perceived, evaluated, understood and communicated through commonly possessed human attributes, but in a unique formulation. Mill has a point to make regarding the centrality of individuality to social progress: the uniqueness of each person's activity contributes the element of creative novelty in human affairs. There are two main elements to Mill's argument. First, without the ability to think and act in new ways, human beings are at risk from their changing circumstances. Second, human progress is, in part, due to people's ability to think in new ways about seemingly unchanging situations and, by using new ideas, to change them to their own advantage.

Underpinning these points is a deeper perception about the nature of the human condition, which is shaped by the continuous opposition of novelty and repetition. Much of human experience is framed by repetition – the continuous replaying of processes to a pre-designed format. Much human activity is itself repetitious, due either to the species uniformity of the human animal (our basic physical needs and drives are the same), or to accumulated practical wisdom handed down from generation to generation in the form of custom and practice. The repetitions in human behaviour have their place; they reproduce responses to repetitious situations in which human beings live most of their lives, and, as such, they represent the accumulated wisdom of past generations, framed as practical activity. However, societies that simply reproduce themselves in slavishly customary ways perish when faced with novel circumstances. Societies need the capacity to change, because environments alter over time, changing, in turn, people's circumstances so that they will encounter novel situations. For this reason, people need to be able to think and act in new ways to survive new situations when they occur.

Less dramatically, societies that do not become challenged by radical alterations in their circumstances may become moribund. Ideas become accepted without critical assessment and so lose their capacity to engage and to stimulate human intellect. People become mentally lazy, customs lose their symbolic residue and their origins; and thus their original utility becomes obscure and eventually forgotten. In such scenarios, societies do not endure endlessly, but suffer from slow entropic decay. Stagnant societies are those in which the individuality of humans is subordinated to collectivity and custom. The creative dynamism of individual intellect is such that, given free rein, it would ensure social development, because even if the environment remains the same, individuals often see old situations in new ways and this can provide improved ways of dealing with old situations (Mill's own times were marked by the advances in preventive medicine springing from imaginative approaches to viral illnesses such as smallpox). Clearly, says Mill, the individuality of each person is the source of new ideas which are vital to social development.

The individual and the state

For Mill, the legitimacy of all state action derives from its functional utility in facilitating human happiness. As we have seen, for Mill, freedom is the unfettered self-expression through which the free individual finds *eudaimonia*. Individuality is also vital to social progress and thus to the greater happiness of the community. Thus the society that maximises individual freedom maximises happiness. Mill is clear that this maximisation is the functional utility of the state, but he sets himself the task of showing how the state might enable maximum individual happiness without directing social affairs and thus impeding the free thinking and acting individuals who constitute society. Mill's conclusion is that the role of the state is to maintain the conditions which facilitate the free expression of the maximum number of individuals possible. This involves maintaining the condition of liberty, by setting up and policing the boundaries which simultaneously protect and confine individual citizens' free actions.

At this point, Mill's discussion of individual liberty is pointing to the social dimensions of individual freedom. Mill is aware that, because we do not live in isolation but with others, we cannot simply do as we want when we want, since an individual acting in this way would seriously impede the opportunity for others to do as they want. In social terms, individuals need space in which to express their freedom of thought and action. This social space is what liberals define as liberty: an area facilitating free action, bounded by areas of equivalent size and quality for others. The social areas which Mill identifies as being established and maintained by these boundaries are: free trade (production and exchange of private property) (Warnock 1962: 227), the free press (Warnock 1962: 141), social expressions of spiritual and political beliefs in 'experiments of living' (sects and communes) (Warnock 1962: 133) and cultural (what we might call leisure) activities (Warnock 1962: 138). Here, Mill is presenting the classic liberal map of the core features of a civil society. Such a society, he argues, is a social condition of individual liberty and it can exist only without political intrusion into its principles of activity (freely chosen and self-directed interaction), if it is policed by state agencies who enforce its principles (when they are violated by citizens) as encoded by the state in law and do not attempt to do more.

The state cannot legitimately attempt to make citizens believe in an ideology which supports this system; they cannot legitimately force citizens to actively participate. They cannot even push them legitimately towards more thoughtful or polite behaviour. In every case, state action would impose upon the free choice of individuals and close down the opportunity for self-development, so negating the end it attempts to achieve. In a classic utilitarian move, Mill argues that the illegitimacy of state action in this regard derives not from its intent, which is often for the best, but in its outcome: state intervention will not function to improve people's character.

Here we see the benchmark that separates the liberal, socialist and social democratic perceptions of the role of the state. The social democrat and the socialist believe that it is often or always the case that the state is the only social organisation with the depth and range of power necessary to raise up those in society who are in poverty and who suffer deprivation. It is the duty of the state to intervene to aid and guide these people – and where they are resistant (deprived people lacking knowledge often misunderstand state aid and are often resistant), the state must drag them fully into civil society. (Social democrats are more tentative than socialists about this enforcement of civility, but do not reject it in principle.) Mill is emphatically denying that the state can effectively do this. The state can and should encourage improvement in its citizens and it should facilitate philanthropic activity wherever possible, but it cannot legitimately or practically enforce any kind of activity for this end alone.

This is not to say that the socialistic notions of his contemporaries have no impact on Mill's liberalism. Unlike his liberal forerunners, he is all too aware of the environmental features shaping individuals' life-chances and, like Rousseau and Hegel, he has teleological grounds for seeing the state provide the best environment for individual development. However, as individuals must enact the process of their development themselves, the state activity on their behalf is limited to provision of an environment which maximises the opportunity for individuals to act. Constantly discussed, and central to Mill's arguments on this topic, is the process of education. Exploration of his argument shows exactly how he sees the role and limits of the role of the state in individual development.

Education

In *On Liberty*, Mill notes that self-development necessarily occurs at the interface of social and individual activity, in processes of educative governance, and is therefore a typical candidate for management by the state. Warning against this, Mill argues that education in the hands of the state is often degraded into a tool for social control and all too often is little more than 'a contrivance for moulding people to be exactly like one another' (Warnock 1962: 238). Genuine education is the facilitation of individuality, not the training of individuals into conformity. It is best that education is provided in the free spaces – the location for free thinking and analysis provided by civil society. Mill faces up to the social facts. For the majority of people in mass industrialised society, access to genuine knowledge is scarce; their 'educators' are simply the older members of their families or communities, who themselves have had little access to genuine knowledge or places where developed analysis and considered debate were constants. Thus the state had to provide a safety net to ensure that everyone had some genuine education. On this basis, Mill argued that, where the individual is undeveloped and requires tutoring, social agencies should paternalistically lead them towards self-knowledge. However, as the individual attains ever greater degrees of general understanding and self-knowledge, the social agencies should retreat in equal degree. The principle of self-growth is general to all individuals, although only a few have the capability to achieve the ultimate goal of attaining a state of full autonomy – that is, the capacity for complete self-management which involves being able to perceive what one is capable of and to manage one's life in such a way as to achieve it. The attainment of autonomy – the true end of individual endeavour – logically precludes external government on any grounds other than the free consent of the individual. The goal of obtaining autonomy demands that the goal of all public bodies must be to provide a maximum facilitation of individuality.

The role of the state is to maintain or create free spaces in which education can flourish, but not to directly educate social members. It can do this through the facilitation, and where necessary either the enforcement or supplementation, of private education. It can also further people's learning through the facilitation of privately owned public media and other locations for public debate.

The implication of this argument is that, although there are social members who, to their own misfortune, have been unlucky enough to live in an environment which has stunted their development, and are not capable of engaging in rational thought and critical discourse, this is not something that the state could or should rectify directly by imposing education in standards for citizenship.

The harm principle

Mill argues that the focus of state restrictions on individual actions must be limited to those activities which impose a harmful intrusion into the lives of others, thereby damaging other individuals' free pursuit of a happy existence: he states that 'The only purpose for which power can be rightfully exercised over any member of a civilised community, against his will, is to prevent harm to others' (Thomas 1992: 329). He contrasts such activity with activity in which the individual actor 'merely concerns himself' and sets out a conceptual divide between 'self-regarding' and 'other-regarding' actions. Self-regarding actions are those actions, according to Mill, which deliberately and necessarily refer solely to the condition of the actor and are not injurious to others (though they may affect them). Other-regarding acts are acts which intentionally impact on the conditions of other people and will directly and intentionally affect their condition of being, in positive or negative ways. It is the latter category of acts alone that are subject to state restriction and punishment. Mill's intention in making this conceptual divide is to draw a clear line between an individual's rightful allocation of free space for action and expression of ideas, and the social space in which the individual's actions are limited by reference to the needs of others.

Mill notes that the division between self-regarding and other-regarding may seem false, and the dividing line may seem arbitrary. A drunkard shouting and swearing in the street may not be harmful to anyone but himself; on the other hand, if he is a married man and the sole wage earner in his family, he may be spending much-needed housekeeping money on drink, failing to help a partner with childcare, frightening his children, breaking the furniture and/or using violence against them. All these are, after all, fairly common characteristics of drunkard behaviour and they clearly negate the lives of others who are not free to walk away from the drunkard. Mill says that 'when by conduct of this sort a person is led to violate a distinct and assignable obligation to any other person or persons, the case is taken out of the self-regarding class, and becomes amenable to moral dis-approbation in the proper sense of the word' (Warnock 1962: 212), by which he means censure and punishment. Similarly, when an individual, such as a judge, policeman or political representative, fails to fulfil his assigned public duty due to private 'errors' he is amenable to public censure and punishment. Mill is keen to stress that in both cases the individual may be judged and punished only for the acts which harm others and not for the personal errors which led to them.

Jonathon Riley has pointed out that Mill's aim in setting up this conceptual division of action is not only to lay down clear limits on state intervention, but to explore the boundaries of social conventions and of ethical paternalism. These three types of behavioural policing are often located together in a set of social norms enforced by paternalistic state legislation. They are not, however, the same thing and therefore are not necessarily subject to the same limitations. Developing Comte's sociology, Mill points out that, while common sense opinion can place great pressure on social members to conform and such convention may be based on misinformation and/or lack of intellectual capacity to understand novelty, it is the social site of normative rules of conduct, and is therefore often also the purveyor of a society's ethical norms. These norms, though they may be reproduced unthinkingly, are often the product of genuine knowledge learned through the trials and errors of past generations. For example, sexual and dietary norms which are now the stuff of social convention are the product of previous generations' encounters with life-threatening viruses and parasites. Sometimes an individual's violation of social norms so clearly violates their own condition and threatens that of others that strong social pressure (short of actual force or threat of force) may be appropriate where not only state enforcement of the norm but also state employment of directive pressure to conform to the norm would not be.

Rewind

Go to Chapter 1 for Milton's discussion of choice and education.

At first sight it may appear that J.S. Mill thinks that freedom is the most precious end in itself. This is not the case. Mill values freedom so much because it is the necessary condition for fulfilment and happiness. Of course it may be argued that those individuals who are targets for state intervention and/or social reprimand are those whose behaviour is obviously not bringing them fulfilment or happiness – drug addicts would be a classic example of this. Mill's insistence that self-abusing individuals be left alone to harm themselves is based on the Miltonian notion that freedom of action is a requirement of self-development. Such development at first requires the obtaining of self-knowledge and that is an educative process. Education is learning through critical assessment and choice – to know what is good one must also know what is bad, and to know whether things are good or bad one must experience them. Through freely choosing experiences, one facilitates the learning process and, through this entire scenario, one gathers intellectual knowledge and practical wisdom, which combines to produce a mature, wise and knowledgeable individual. Of course, this practical learning process is fraught with dangers. It involves experimentation with dangerous and destructive activities that can educate or ruin an individual. The risk, Mill argues in an echo of Milton, is the price worth paying for genuine practical wisdom. While the ideal scenario is one in which all individuals take up pursuits that will develop their potential, in truth many take up activities which will stunt that development or even deform their being. Individuals often do not take a straight and obvious route towards personal development; sometimes they develop through trial and error, sometimes they choose not to develop, not to learn more and become more capable but to remain static; sometimes they lurch towards self-negation. Others, watching individuals falling on the best path, may find the sight repellent and/or frightening. Observers may wish to step in and put the individual on the 'right track', as they see it, either because their bad activity offends or distresses them or out of a sense of social duty to others. While they have every right, and even in some cases a duty, to try to persuade the badly acting individual to stop and alter their course of behaviour, they would be wrong to try to force them to change or to use the state's lawmaking and enforcement agencies to force them to change. Genuine improvement can only be the result of educative practical experimentation; it cannot be produced by the enforcement of custom or dogma.

Evaluating the harm principle

In evaluating Mill's harm principle, it is necessary to consider two significant features. The first is contextual: Mill was writing to an audience who were involved in novel and intense stresses on the fabric of social life. The widespread urban deprivation set huge social policy problems for the governing elite, who were also concerned with the political tensions expressed in the seething working-class radicalism of the union movement and periodic outbreaks of Chartism. It is to this governing elite that Mill's sermon on liberty and the limits of state interference is primarily addressed. For, while Mill was a radical and reforming liberal, he was worried that the interventionist streak of the radical reformers and the ardour of the social movement for what we would now call a welfare state would overwhelm the social order of civil liberties which he saw as necessary for individual and social progress. The argument in *On Liberty* is designed in part to forewarn of the dangers of well-intentioned bludgeoning of civil society into a stunted overgoverned conservatism, in which citizens, though well fed, educated and protected, are browbeaten into a dull and unimaginative conformity. The harm principle is a mechanism designed to delineate the precise boundaries of state intervention and of social reformism, in the light of the necessary retention of individual freedom.

Mill's arguments, however, failed to make much headway against the trends in public policy. The major reason for the failure of Mill's arguments to impact on the mindset of the establishment was not simply that it riled the hyper-conservatism of a landed gentry already feeling threatened by the trade unions, Chartists and the revolutionary movement in France's working classes (although it did so), but that it failed to convince the radical wing of the political elite (Pyle 1994: vii–xii, 184–219).

At the time of *On Liberty*, a reforming agenda was taking shape in the discourse of the radical wing of the political elite. This agenda represented a significant extension of state involvement in social affairs. Mill found a listening audience for his argument for restraint among some of his contemporaries, but clearly his argument was not decisive. In the UK, the reforming agenda became a legislative programme: the Forster Education Act (1870) and the Factory Acts took the government into novel areas of social policy, initiating what was to become a shift from liberal to social democratic government, one which has endured to this day.

The failure of Mill's ideas to take hold with legislatures is probably due to the theory's intense focus on individual actions, which ensured that it simply lacked the compass to produce convincing explanations of how such large-scale problems as endemic drunkenness, widespread lawless violence and mass ignorance could be tackled. Mill's arguments that alcohol and drug abuse are not matters for the state, unless actual harm to others can be proven, and his arguments concerning mass education (which we shall consider in more detail below) in which he insists that education is the rightful domain of fathers and not the state, would hardly convince policy-makers facing the problem of cities full of semi-literate alcoholics.

The second feature of the harm principle concerns its internal coherence. The principle is much more complicated than it first looks, and its apparent coherence unravels under analytic pressure. Mill realises that harm cannot be applied solely to physical hurt. Clearly one individual's action can cause another psychological hurt (bullying, for example, comes into this category). It is also possible to hurt someone by damaging their life-chances (an example would be a parent who does not allow a gifted child to go to university). It is also necessary to harm others' life-chances in undertaking some social activities. For example, beating other candidates in a competitive test may harm their chances of progressing in their career and so reduce the quality of their life.

At this point, it becomes hard to impose the exact conceptual limits that Mill requires for the concept of 'harm' to set a line in the sand for social restraint on individual actions. Indeed, he states that social intervention is not a necessary consequence of an individual act causing harm to others. The social context in which the act is committed must also be considered. If the act involved is regarded as normal by the society in which it is undertaken, such as competing in a test or in the economic competition of the marketplace, it requires no restriction. This concession seriously weakens his argument. Instead of operating as a universally applicable benchmark for state intervention, the principle became a relativistic one and open to conservative use for defence of socially accepted harmful 'other-regarding' activities. The problems in attempting to use the principle may be seen clearly in the following case example.

SMOKING IN PUBLIC

Smoking is now a public health issue, and in most Western nations there is debate about when and where smoking might be acceptable. Smoking, like drinking, is a form of drug-taking and comes into the category of self-regarding activity in exactly the same way as does drinking. Smoking, however, does have a more obvious immediate impact on others than drinking and has for some time now been restricted in public, on the grounds that others find it uncomfortable. This light touch, which has largely been acceptable to both smokers and non-smokers, is pretty much in line with the tone of Mill's argument involving common sense to develop customary restraints supported in a minimal way by the lightest of governmental restraint (not smoking in hospitals and suchlike). Until recently, public health authorities in liberal democratic societies have resisted the anti-smoking lobby's attempts to obtain further restrictions on the activity on the grounds that smoking is a self-regarding activity. It may damage the individuals that do it, it was argued, but they are freely choosing the style and quality of life they desire and they do not harm anyone else by doing so. Recently, scientific evidence of the damage that inhalation of cigarette smoke (passive smoking) causes in people sharing space with smokers has altered perceptions of smoking. Scientific research has revealed new information on the activity's potential for harming others – the issue of the harmful effects of passive smoking has altered the tone of the debate and the willingness of government to restrict individual behaviour in this regard. Anti-smokers present smoking as 'other-regarding', and as a consequence it has recently been banned from many public places by liberally minded public authorities. Interestingly, smokers respond by using another element of Mill's argument, claiming that passive smoking is an acceptable low-level risk in public life because it is mixed in with car pollution, electric pylons, dangerous traffic and so on, and it may be avoided through the simple act of moving away from smokers (though they often concede that this may not be possible in enclosed spaces). The ban on smoking is, they cry, 'a tyranny of the majority'.

DISCUSSION POINT

What exactly constitutes harm to an individual? Is it only physical damage to their person? Can it include psychological damage? Can it include damage to a person's life-chances?

The tension between the few and the majority

Although his argument for limited government stresses the importance of individual uniqueness, Mill makes it clear that in his eyes most people have more in common than they possess in distinction. Most people have a rough equivalence of abilities and a common experience of life. Lacking great originality of mind, most people are also inclined to seek the security of customary practice and the safe status of ordinary members of the community. Their understanding, evaluation and reactions to events and situations will be framed by the limited range of common sense. For the great mass of people, Mill argues, such tendencies are reinforced by the under-stimulating conditions in which they live. Here he is thinking of the conditions common to the lives of the European working classes and those living in what he calls 'despotic' pre-civilised societies – conditions involving a mix of constant labour, immediate gratification, ever-present potential for violence and disease, and no access to education and general modes of 'high cultural' activity.

Here we see the basic tension in Mill's thought on this subject. Everyone has the potential for individual fulfilment, but for many, this fulfilment is limited in its degree of originality, since most people's intellectual and artistic capabilities are fairly commonplace and their products indistinct. On the other hand, there are a few who are unusually able in some areas (art, maths, science, acting, poetry, music, politics and so on) and/or blend these abilities in unusual combinations. The ideas and creations of these few are outstanding and by definition challenging to the common understanding and its commonplace products: 'originality is the one thing unoriginal minds cannot feel the use of . . . how should they? If they could see what it could do for them, it would not be originality' (Warnock 1962: 195). So the few people who become original thinkers and creators will strike the majority as eccentric, because their different abilities lead them to challenge common ways of perceiving understanding and evaluating situations and events. Mill sees this situation – a constant in all human societies – as one of potential political danger for the original few. The unoriginal majority will tend to see the few as amusing at best, and dangerous at worst. They will be tempted to ignore their insights and inventions or repress them in the name of common sense or, where it is a matter of decision-making, the general will.

Here we see Mill's individualism setting him in direct conflict with the communitarian thinking of those influenced by Rousseau, Hegel, and later by Marx. The notion of fundamental human equality and the high evaluation of communality that stems from it overvalues what is common to us and crucially undervalues the vital life-enhancing and progressive force which is individual uniqueness. What it also set him against is the modern faith in the virtue of democracy as a legitimate form of government for modern mass society.

Democracy: for and against

It would be false to present J.S. Mill as anti-democratic, but he was notably ambivalent about democratisation. There were, he believed, key elements of democracy which were vital to a society of free individuals, but in mass democracy – the system of electing government by the popular vote of the majority of citizens – Mill saw the seed of a novel and particularly modern tyranny of the crowd over the individual. It is possible to extract from his writing arguments for and against democracy, each of which we shall consider below.

For democracy

Democracy is attractive to Mill inasmuch as it derives from and is necessary for a relationship between individual citizens and a political community that is essentially pluralistic; that is, a social community constituted by radically distinguishable yet contributory individual units.

A pluralistic society is heterogeneous – it contains many different types of people with different experiences and understandings of that experience. Social understanding of a pluralist society is a kaleidoscopic mirror, reflecting back to the whole community all colours of opinion shaped by the multiple viewpoints and differing perspectives of all its members, all of whom are pushing and pulling the general understanding and common opinion towards their view.

The fact that each individual experiences things differently, evaluates them differently and communicates them differently ensures that there will be a plurality of perspectives and interpretations of any object, event or situation which is commonly experienced by a social community.

Democratic public debate ensures that each and every view is given an equal hearing and tested by public opinion. This can be a good thing, if that public opinion is educated enough to understand and respect the basic pluralistic condition which enables its pluralistic existence (although, as we shall see below, it can be a bad thing if public opinion is shaped by ignorance and weak judgemental faculties).

Public debate subjects each opinion to scrutiny and interrogation by others; arguments will be rigorously tested for coherence, and claims to fact will be challenged until persuasive evidence is produced, tested and verified. In this way, pluralistic debate combines individual freedom of expression with social access to truthful opinions, enabling individual researchers to offer successful social policy (this constitutes the link between liberalism and democracy).

The successful navigation of the experienced environment (minimally acceptable outcome) and the mastering of objective conditions as a means towards the improvement of living conditions (human progress – the best possible outcome) is dependent on establishing the truth content of subject opinions about commonly experienced situations. A debate between the various opinion holders will test the quality of each opinion, exposing flaws and incoherence, and testing each and all theories by critical questioning and demands for proof where possible, thus validating truths.

Such an event constitutes an intellectual community in a public debate and it is, in essence, democratic. If it is to happen, it is necessary that, at the outset of each debate, all participants are allowed to participate, that their views are given equal status and are treated with equal rigour in the testing conditions of public argument and analysis; coherence and evidence are the criteria for judging the truth content of opinions.

It follows that each person is also treated as an equal participant in the debate, a requirement which ensures that relative social and economic status and relationships do not impinge on the participants' freedom to hold opinions and the equality of opportunity to express them. Democracy is necessary as a basic condition for plurality, and plurality is vital for the following reasons:

1. It creates a commonly sensed objectivity grounded in objective fact: 'complete liberty of contradicting and disproving our opinion is the very condition which justifies us in assuming its truth for the purposes of action; and on no other terms can a being with human faculties have any rational assurance of being right' (Warnock 1962: 145).

2. It provides the public sphere in which participants develop the analytical and communicative skills needed for greater understanding of their environment and of themselves. It is a necessary learning environment: 'the mental and moral, like the muscular powers, are improved only by being used' (Warnock 1962: 187), and it provides individual participants with a greater knowledge of commonly experienced events than they could garner as lone observers.

DISCUSSION POINT

It is not clear whether pluralist democratic debate is a good in itself for Mill or whether its value is its utility in obtaining truth. If it is the latter, what happens to pluralist debate when truth is found? Does public debate lose its purpose and therefore its necessity?

It is important to note here that Mill's vision of a developmental democracy is based upon the ancient Athenian model of the small-scale fully participatory polis where every person is fully involved in public discussion and judgement.

Representation functions to serve direct participation, processing the selection of the gifted few to participate in the direct democracy. Thus representative democracy is 'the ideal type of the most perfect polity, for which in consequence, any portion of mankind are better adapted in proportion to their degree of general improvement. As they range lower and lower in development, that form of government will be, generally speaking, less suitable to them' (Mill 1975: 199).

In the large-scale societies of Mill's time and ours, such constant and total involvement in politics is not possible for most people, and, as the map of Mill's anti-democratic arguments below shows, Mill's democratic public sphere did not contain a clear intention that all members of society could be (or should be) fully involved members of that society's body politic.

Against democracy

The anti-democratic elements of Mill's argument are built upon his belief in progress through individual invention and his utilitarian understanding that the legitimacy of government is ultimately derived from its utility in the production of the greatest happiness for the greatest number.

Democracy, he notes, appears at first sight to be the perfect political system for a society built on the greatest happiness of the greatest number. However, when this utilitarian ideal is tied to a view of human happiness as *eudaimonia*, and this idea is tied in turn to a progressivist notion of human history as the unfurling of human potential, the suitability of democracy to the achievement of happiness looks less than certain.

Mill, pointing out that the greatest happiness is derived from living the best possible quality of life at any given time, argues that the majority of people cannot choose the options that would produce the best quality of life, without guidance from the gifted and truly independently minded 'few', because they lack the means to understand what the best would involve.

He notes that the arguments for the suitability of democracy as a means to general happiness – that is, self-government by the people – is built on the belief that the people want what is good for them. The apparent strength of this claim derives from the belief that people share the capacity to rationally comprehend and judge what is good for them. Mill's argument suggests that this is true only to a limited degree. A general limited common sense sets a commonly perceived horizon to human possibilities, and this in turn informs the expectations and desires of the citizenry. The limited imagination and capacity for invention common to the majority of people means that they cannot see what could be better than what they already know. The majority will seek to maintain the status quo. The more genuinely novel an idea, the more likely that most people will not understand it and will reject it. While a generally well-educated and sophisticated people may be comfortable with some advances which are developed from well-understood principles and well-known technologies, even these people will tend to reject radical novelty. On balance, common sense, failing to understand how new ideas and modes of doing things might produce new improved conditions of life, will oppose them. If the in-built conservatism of the common people is allowed to dominate the creative individual, the result will be social stagnation. This is 'not precisely stationariness . . . it does not preclude change as long as all change together' (Warnock 1962: 201). In short, 'the people' will tend to be conservative, while social development depends on daring creativity and the constant challenging of traditional modes of living: 'The despotism of custom is everywhere the standing hindrance to human advancement' (Warnock 1962: 200), because 'All good things that exist are the fruits of originality' (Warnock 1962: 195).

Mill's worries about the shortcomings of democracies drove his counter-argument against the Rousseau-inspired movement for mass democracy as an agency of the 'will of the people'. He argued that the domination of 'genius' by mediocrity is intensified in mass democracies, where it can corrupt into a tyrannical oppression of all novel ideas and even of their advocates. The most likely result of mass democracy is not Rousseau's sovereignty – the complete and total agreement of all in a communion which merges the will of each and every individual – but rather an unequal society in which the powerful majority subjugate to their will the weak minorities and isolated individuals.

He pointed out that the process of mass selection and the de-selection of governments operating at the centre of mass democracy created the illusion that the state represented the will of the people so completely that the people and the state were at one . . . that 'the nation did not need protecting against its own will. There was no fear of its tyrannising itself' (Warnock 1962: 128), but 'such phrases as "self-government" and "the power of the people over themselves" do not express the true state of the case' (Warnock 1962: 129) . . . 'self-government . . . is not the government of each by himself, but of each by all the rest' (Warnock 1962: 129). In making the argument to support this claim, Mill focuses on two themes: the tensions between individualism and mass democracy (a direct concern stemming from his own individualist position), and the anti-egalitarian outcome of mass democracy (an incoherence in his opponents' egalitarian-inspired mass democracy argument).

Mill saw that the machinery of the mass democratic process tends to translate the most popular opinions into state policy. The most popular opinions are those held by the largest groups of same-thinking people. Public debates – a healthy interchange of individual opinions – would be concluded with the crude and simplifying process of a popular vote. Inevitably, the simpler ideas, and the more familiar ideas combined with those that appear to offer the most immediately pleasurable outcomes (a classic example being arguments which illogically, but temptingly, promise increased services combined with tax cuts) will be chosen over the more coherent and intelligent contributions to the debate. Thus, mass democratic process produces as its end result the translation of less original and less intellectually coherent ideas into state policy. Mill saw the potential for the electoral dominance of mediocrity to become a cruel tyranny of thoughtless custom-led populism in which free-thinking individuals would be victimised. All too often in democracies, the novel idea is rejected and its creator pilloried by the majority. If the state represents majority opinion and such opinion is sufficiently offended by the novel idea, it may be deemed heretical and ignored, destroyed or (if it is a piece of knowledge) hidden from public view, and the individual who created it may be punished. 'Genius', he wrote, 'can only breathe freely in an *atmosphere* of freedom' (Warnock 1962: 194). Public common sense can be an illegitimate censor, and in democracies, where the common sense is converted into state policy as the people's will, the illegitimacy of public censorship is given greater force.

Combining his concern for the individual with the democrat's concern for equality, Mill concludes that in such scenarios, the outcome is in direct contrast to the Rousseauian ideal of a unified state of participating equals. It is the powerful majority dominating the weak minorities and isolated individuals. The powerful pretend to sovereign power under the false claim to be 'the people' but exclude the minority from the status of membership in 'the people' until they conform. It becomes, says Mill, a 'tyranny of the majority' (Warnock 1962: 129) over the individual.

Overall, Mill argues, the result of mass democracy, unless it is managed very carefully, and unless it has a prior commitment to respect individual liberty and to provide mechanisms to promote the opinions of the gifted few over and against the opinions of the average majority, would be that power is not taken up and used by the whole people in an act of unison, but rather is taken up and used by a majority, often to the detriment of minorities, which is plain bullying, contrary to the egalitarian ideals of democrats, and nearly always to the detriment of individualism and therefore also to the possibilities for social progress.

As the groundswell of a mass movement for a full democracy became apparent in the UK, Mill argued that, if a mass democracy which genuinely gave liberty to the people and facilitated social progress were to emerge, it would have to be a system which gave a leading role to that intellectual elite, for 'no government by a democracy . . . either in its political acts or in the opinions, qualities, and tone of mind which it fosters, ever did or could rise above mediocrity, except in so far as the sovereign many have let themselves be guided . . . by the councils and influence of a more highly gifted and instructed One or Few' (Warnock 1962: 196). He went on to suggest a constitution which was designed to bring a greater number of citizens into the democratic process, but which also revolved around maintaining the power of the elite governing class.

The constitution of an educative democratic liberal polity

Mill's analytic eclecticism and his ambivalence towards mass democracy produced his work *Representative Government*. This is an attempt to get to grips with the issue of how to incorporate the extended franchise into the liberal parliamentary system of government in the UK. His belief that the latter is fundamentally at risk from the former led him to design a very complex model constitution, which included an extension of the franchise to include the great bulk of adult citizens – including women (a radical suggestion at the time) – and protection for social minorities through the mechanism of proportional representation and sectional candidates for Parliament. This would have the double virtue of drawing candidates from various well-defined social subgroups, who could represent group interests in Parliament, and an electoral system that gave such candidates a really strong chance of being elected. These advances towards a full and pluralistic democracy were to be offset by a reinforcement of elite governance, through an artificial weighting of the voting power of the academic elite designed to ensure that the highly educated members of society maintained a firm grip of leadership over the political process. Mill's model was long viewed as an over-complicated muddle by the majority of commentators. In recent times, however, it has been noted that, as the social constitution of modern society became ever more heterogeneous (due to the increase in international trade and travel, the geopolitical cosmopolitanism of European imperialism, and finally the globalisation of economic and cultural life), the complexity of actual constitutions drawn up for many societies more than matches Mill's plan. In cases such as South Africa, Northern Ireland and Bosnia, the complexity of the constitutions is a necessary fact, springing from the conflict of mutually opposed subcultures. In each case, simple majority electoral systems would place power in the hands of groups who have radically negative dispositions towards their nation's minorities. In consequence, complex consociational constitutions – that is, constitutions which include guaranteed representation of sectional groups by their own members in the major organs of the state – have been put in place. Reflecting on these, Mill's model looks more like an insightful prototype of consociationalism, displaying Mill's sensitivity to the constant potential for conflict in mass society. His much stated concern was the tyranny of a majority group over others, but an undercurrent of this thinking is the recognition of a potential for conflict between social subgroups (the socio-economic classes).

Applied to today's complex, heterogeneous and potentially conflict-full societies, Mill's model has much to commend it. The extension of the franchise to women, and by implication to any minorities excluded on grounds of religion or ethnicity, is now recognised as a functional necessity for working democracy.

The notion that social conflict would be reduced if the legislature consisted of a selection of sectional representatives underpins all consociational government, as does the idea that this 'microcosmic' representation will pull people from all social constituencies into the public life of the whole community and spread parliamentary debate to include consideration of the experiences and needs of all the social constituencies. Such constitutions also replicate Mill's greatest concern, which is to drag those constituencies – often made up of the most excluded, deprived and alienated social groupings – into the public debate, and to educate them towards mature critical and knowledgeable engagement with their social condition and political minority to give them an electoral majority. The aim of this proposal was precisely to create a model of elite-led mass democracy.

Critical problems

Over the last century, Mill's work has been subject to criticism from all sides of the political spectrum. Tellingly, while the politics of the critics have varied considerably, a number of critical points have remained constant, featuring repeatedly through the diverse range and tone of the criticisms. These points, by enduring with such consistency, despite the varied concerns and ideologies of the critics, have highlighted the core crucial weaknesses in Mill's argument. These weaknesses may be summarised as follows:

1   *The problem of establishing the precise delineation between self- and other-regarding action.* This conceptual dualism is presented as being conceptually clear in that it establishes exactly what kinds of action are to be judged and in

what way, and as a consequence as a practical and useful aid to legal and governmental decision-making. The problem of precision undermines its coherence and negates its intended purpose. The problem has proved to be enduring. The dualism not only lacked precise terms of definition in Mill's original version, but it has resisted subsequent attempts to establish a decisively convincing precision in the hands of later theorists attempting to strengthen Mill's case.

2   *The difficulty of establishing the dimensions of harm.* The problems of specificity which beset the self/other-regarding dualism are complicated by the fact that Mill does not explicitly define the meaning of 'harm' in his theory. He makes it very clear that he does not include offending others' taste, nor offending their sense of good behaviour, but he is unclear about hurting people's feelings. This is a problem because hurting feelings may be perceived as emotional violence, and violence to a person is, by definition, harmful. This grey area in Mill's arguments leaves him open to accusation of psychological naïvety, failing to see that every situation involving two or more people is psychologically other-regarding, in that the interactions of participants necessarily impact on their states of mind. Mill's restricted notion of harm fails to allow for the frequency of situations in which there is harm to the emotional and intellectual integrity of individuals. Again, this is damaging to Mill's case. The claim for the harm principle is its utility in a guide for practical legal and governing action. There is a lack of precision in the definition of the term 'harm' necessary to qualify it as a useful tool in legal and governmental decision-making.

Despite its shortcomings, the harm principle has proved to be operable as a technical device used by the legal profession for assessing individual situations. A court, using precedents from previous cases, can come to a common agreement on a particular definition of harm applicable to the particular scenario being considered – for example, a particular case of drunken behaviour may be considered in all the minutiae of its details and assessed for its specific potential for harm (which can and often is conceptually modified by the involved lawyers to incorporate the now common notions of psychological harm). For this reason, it has always had some appeal to lawyers and some utility in protecting the victims of a wide range of harmful activities, including non-physical harm that is often involved, for example, in sexual and racial harassment. It has proved particularly useful in protecting individual members of minorities. Through its use in many legal decisions, it has found its way into the principles of common law and, through this, has been used at times to guide and/or modify government programmes. In the United Kingdom, the most notable case is the eventual persuasiveness of H.L.A. Hart's explicit use of Mill's harm principle to argue for the legalisation of homosexuality in the United Kingdom on the grounds that it is a self-regarding practice which is therefore non-harmful to others (Hart 1963).

3   *The incompatibility between the utilitarian concept of happiness and the concept of happiness presented by Mill.* In his own time, many utilitarians criticised Mill for his traditional formulation of the 'good life' (Pyle 1994: xvi–xvii). In recent times, utilitarians such as R.M. Hare, John Rees and Robert

Hoag have struggled to reinterpret Mill's position to try to render a more functional and utility-oriented reading of his argument (Gray and Smith 1991: 212–239). Liberals who are opposed to utilitarianism, such as Isaiah Berlin (Gray and Smith 1991: 131–162), have pointed out that much of Mill's argument can stand as a coherent proposition without any reference to utilitarian principles. From this angle, *On Liberty* is seen as a fruitful mixture of the classical liberal formulation of the necessary relationship between individual liberty, individual happiness and a functioning social order. This argument, however, brushes over the importance which Mill attached to core utilitarian principles, and to their consistent and often confusing impact on the development of his liberalism.

4 *The analytic limitations of an intensely individualist account of political life*. This criticism is one levelled at liberal theory in general by socialists and communitarians, but it has particular impact on Mill for, unlike the classical liberals of the seventeenth century, he was deliberately challenging communitarian notions of the political good life. The weakness of his analysis is that its focus on the dimensions of individual interactions reduces the practicable scale of the theorist's analytic devices to the methods of identifying and understanding the dimensions of small-scale individual interactions. This is especially problematic for Mill, who is seeking to explain the social dimensions of liberty in the context of large-scale historical epochs. *On Liberty* is littered with attempted comparisons between the social conditions impeding or facilitating individual liberty in Hellenic times, in feudal Europe and in China and the conditions of the industrial modern world in which he lived. Despite this attempt to give social depth and historical range to his analysis, he is unable to assess the impact of long-lasting international cultural and/or economic hegemonies on the life-chances of any particular individuals (it is not possible), so his analysis of individual relations remains abstracted from his social historical theory – neither enhancing the other.

Balancing this weakness is the core strength of Mill's position. His assertion of the primacy of individual experience rests on the firm basis of the existential fact that each of us lives the experience of our own unique and individual life. We cannot merge this experience into that of others or share the fundamental features of it. We feel pain alone, we experience hurt in ourselves alone and we die alone. At this level, profoundly meaningful moments of our lives are intensely individual.

Revision notes

1 Mill advanced the utilitarians' idea that the maximisation of happiness is the right goal for all social and public policy, but in doing so developed a notion of happiness as fulfilment which was at odds with the classical utilitarian ideal of happiness as the maximisation of pleasure.

2 Mill's notion of happiness is tied into a conception of individual self-realisation which requires that the state provides a nurturing and educative environment, but that it

also refrains from hindering individuals' self-expression wherever it is non-harmful to others.

3   Mill's benchmark for public policy regarding the relationship of individuals to society is 'the harm principle', but, when examined, the central notion – that some actions are purely self-regarding and are not to be the subject of public policy – is problematic.

4   Mill's concerns about the possible restrictions on individual liberty by popular opinion in mass society led to ambivalence in his attitude to democracy.

Bibliography

Ackroyd, P. (2000) *London: The Biography*, London: Vintage.

Cowling, M. (1963) *Mill and Liberalism*, Cambridge: Cambridge University Press.

Gray, J. and Smith, G.W. (eds) (1991) *J.S. Mill's On Liberty in Focus*, London: Routledge.

Halliday, R.J. (1976) *John Stuart Mill*, London: Allen & Unwin.

Hart, H.L.A. (1963) *Law, Liberty and Morality*, Oxford: Oxford University Press.

Mill, J.S. (1975) *Three Essays: On Liberty, Representative Government, The Subjection of Women*, Norwich: Fletcher and Son.

Pyle, A. (ed.) (1994) *Liberty: Contemporary Responses to John Stuart Mill*, Bristol: Thoemmes Press.

Riley, J. (1998) *Mill On Liberty*, London: Routledge.

Thomas, W. (1992) 'Mill' in Q. Skinner, R. Tuck, W. Thomas, and P. Singer, *Great Political Thinkers*, Oxford: Oxford University Press.

Warnock, M. (ed.) (1962) *Utilitarianism, On Liberty & Essay on Bentham*, Glasgow: William Collins & Son.

Wheen, F. (1999) *Karl Marx*, London: Fourth Estate.

Further reading

Riley's *Mill On Liberty* (1998) is an excellent and detailed examination of Mill's key arguments and the critical debates they have inspired. Gray and Smith's *J.S. Mill's 'On Liberty' in Focus* (1991) contains a number of essays by leading liberal and utilitarian commentators of current and recent times. Their expertise and familiarity with the subject matter takes the reader into very finely detailed critical analyses of Mill's theory in relatively accessible language. Pyle (1994) provides a series of nineteenth-century responses to the publication of *On Liberty*. These are very helpful in understanding how Mill was seen by his contemporaries.

Karl Marx

> There followed on the birth of mechanization and modern industry . . . a violent encroachment like that of an avalanche in its intensity and its extent. All boundaries of morals and nature, of age and sex, of night and day were broken down.
>
> (*Capital*)

Introduction

Unlike our early modern thinkers Marx was living in a highly industrialised, urbanised world, one where there were fast developing the kinds of communication networks and transportation systems that we would recognise today. He was also writing in an age of revolution, a revolution based not only upon the consequences of the changes brought about by the collapse of aristocracy and the Enlightenment of the eighteenth century, but a revolution that was changing the way people lived, thought of themselves and others in relation to the world. The revolution that Marx was witnessing was the coming of the modern world. Modernity was a process of slow social, cultural, political and economic change. Marx recognised that in his own time these processes of modernity had already brought about profound and irreversible changes. This included, of course, a dominant economic system called capitalism. While Marx was ambivalent about most features of modernity he was not about this new economic structure. For him, capitalism was the root of all social and political evils. It tainted all that was good about modernity and condoned all that was bad. Capitalism was a worm, rotting away the wonderful liberating potential of modernity.

The intellectual origins of Marx's thought

Marx has been claimed by sociology, philosophy, politics and the humanities. We find schools of Marxism in many diverse disciplines from linguistics to fine art. This manifold presence is due in part to Marx's very diverse intellectual background. It is true to say that unless we understand where he is coming from, unless we are fully aware of his own intellectual baggage, we cannot possibly begin to understand Marx's own writings. This is not an easy task as Marx was a lifelong student and a great intellectual. He began his mature intellectual life as a 'romantic subjectivist' following the ideas of Kant. However, as a young, liberal thinking journalist he became more attracted to Hegel's writings as they appeared to unite philosophical Idealism with the real world. In common with many young intellectuals of his day Marx became a young Hegelian, supporting the ideas of the great liberal German thinker, particularly his view concerning the central role of the state. However, these ideas were radicalised through his experiences as editor of the *Rheinische Zeitung*, a liberal newspaper of his day. There is a very attractive account of a specific event that transformed Marx's views and led him to critique Hegel's ideas. The story goes that Rheinische Provincial Assembly decided to stop the poor taking fallen wood from small and large landowners. Marx was so outraged by this that he began to form the view that the state was not a neutral player but worked in the specific interests of one particular economic class.

German Idealism

The context of Marx's thought must be understood in terms of the real political world in which he lived and the vibrant intellectual debates of his day. Marx was a great proponent of the view that there was a strong connection between theory and practice. It was his practice to reflect upon his day-to-day experiences in a philosophical manner. We find in the man himself the embodiment of his own view that a main aim of the intellectual was to define a notion of 'praxis', a condition of action that married theoretical reflection with human labour. Unfortunately the personal context of Marx's life as a young journalist, seeing at first hand the poverty of the countryside, is easier to explain with stories like the one above than the theoretical element of his praxis, for Marx was embedded in a school of philosophy that today may seem somewhat obscure. It also has an internal debate that stretched back in its modern form over two hundred years, and in its entirety to the very origins of Western philosophy itself. That school of thought is Idealism or, to be more precise in Marx's case, German Idealism. Failure to grasp the basic principles of Idealism and Marx's place within this school of thought has led to countless misinterpretations of his work, and many wrongly placed criticisms. Thus it is to an explanation of this once dominant philosophical perspective that we must now turn.

Idealism is a branch of philosophical speculation that was developed by the ancient Greeks, most notably Socrates. Put generally, Idealism takes the objects of experience to be appearances that have their real 'true' essence elsewhere. We live in a world of 'ideals', not in the moral sense of idealistic, but in the sense that we can never know reality. Now, although Marx's own work is deeply embedded in this school of philosophy, his genius was to turn it on its head. If we put Idealism's general principles another way we can say that it holds that the material things of our world (tables, chairs, books, all objects) are not 'real'. Reality lies elsewhere. And if reality lies elsewhere, so too must knowledge of that reality. We cannot know that an object is real simply by touching, smelling, seeing or hearing it. Our senses are not to be trusted. This view goes against an empiricist or rationalist view of the world. It also goes against a materialist view. Yet Marx was to develop a materialist philosophical system through being guided by Idealist principles.

KEY PEOPLE 1

Immanuel Kant (1724–1804)

Kant lectured at the University of Königsberg in philosophy and various sciences. He became Professor of Logic and Metaphysics in 1770 and achieved wide renown through his writings and teachings. The more important among these writings were: *Prolegomena to Any Future Metaphysics* (1783), *Foundations of the Metaphysics of Morals* (1785), *Critique of Practical Reason* (1788), and *Critique of Judgment* (1790).

· Although the Idealist point of view goes back to the very origins of philosophy itself, for an examination of its relevance as far as Marx is concerned we may start with Kant. To a young intellectual like Marx the great star of thought in his youth was Kant. In his *Critique of Pure Reason* (Kant 1933), Kant had set out his 'transcendental Idealism'. He argued that the objects of experience, which exist in time and space (the necessary conditions of experience), were 'things-in-themselves'. These objects were unknowable. He maintained that things which we generally regard as purely external to ourselves are actually made of 'forms' or 'moulds' that exist in the individual's mind. That which we know is a combination of these two elements: the subjective and objective. 'Things-in-themselves' (any objects) are known only by coming into contact with the mind (and in this way they are transformed). What Kant argues is that there is no 'objective' reality which we can grasp. The real objective reality comes from 'a priori' (antecedent to experience) judgements. In other words, our experience presupposes a realm of unknowable reality which affects the senses but which we can perceive only in forms ordered by the a priori categories in our minds. Kant leaves us with the view that empirical phenomena are mere appearances. The empirical world was 'ideal' a picture due to the functioning of the brain.

KEY PEOPLE 2

Georg Wilhelm Friedrich Hegel (1770–1831)

Hegel was born in Stuttgart, the son of a government clerk. During the Napoleonic occupation Hegel edited (1807/8) a newspaper, which he left to become rector (1808–1816) of a *Gymnasium* at Nuremberg. He then returned to professorships at Heidelberg (1816–1818) and Berlin (1818–1831), where he became famous. In his lectures at Berlin he set forth the system elaborated in his books. Chief among these were: *Science of Logic* (1812/16), *Encyclopedia of the Philosophical Sciences* (1817), and *Philosophy of Right* (1821).

From these metaphysics Kant went on to develop a theory of Will and morality. He argued for 'practical reason' and a sense of humility in human intellectual endeavours. Because of this, many see him as a great architect of liberal social and political thought. However, his arguments did not go unchallenged. The next key figure we must look to in order to understand Marx is Hegel. It was from Hegel, who built upon the foundations of Kantian metaphysics, that Marx took a guiding (although critical) light. Hegel agreed with Kant that what we can know must be imposed by the mind, but he rejected the 'thing-in-itself' as an unintelligible concept. Although Kant had stated that we could never know the 'things-in-themselves', he maintained that 'things' were still there. This view betrayed an empirical realism in Kant's thought that stood in a state of tension to his Idealism. Kant never fully explained how the categories of the mind and the 'things-in-themselves' came together. It was through this gap that Hegel took German Idealism.

Hegel offered an 'Absolute' notion of mind in contrast to Kant's metaphysics. For Hegel, all existence was a 'form' of one mind. The subject/object distinction existed only as precipitate of an undifferentiated experience prior to them both. This was 'Pure Being' or the 'Absolute'. The 'Absolute' was the ultimate reality, an objective fact in which all things participated and from which all self-consciousness originated. In the *Phenomenology* (1931) Hegel distinguished three levels of social consciousness from which the 'forms' were said to be abstracted: spirit, religion and absolute knowing. These various forms of consciousness were ordered hierarchically. They were both an individual state of mind and the culmination of collective human history. Hegel argued that humankind moved from a spiritual knowledge of the world, through a religious knowledge until true knowledge of reality was found in the 'Absolute', '*Where appearance becomes identified with essence*' (Hegel 1931: 145).

Hegel's 'Absolute Knowing' challenged the empiricist theory of knowledge. The 'Absolute' was not an empirical phenomenon but the *totality* of all previous forms of consciousness. In other words, what was 'real' was the totality of human experience, not the material reality of our everyday world. For Hegel this totality was evolving, developing, progressing; moving humanity forward towards ultimate knowledge of existence. Although in a non-philosophical way of thinking this may sound, at best, like a replacement for God or, at worst, some kind of non-sense, Hegel argues that the Absolute was ultimately the only 'real' and 'rational' aspect of human experience. The 'Absolute' was the universal that gave meaning to all things. It was also a historical object towards which humankind was evolving. This was understood as a process of dialectical change. Hegel's dialectic was to be of fundamental importance to Marx's system of thought. That said, what Hegel meant by dialectics is not always clear. Suffice to say that it was the dynamic aspect of his system of mind. It was the way that the various forms of consciousness were hierarchically interrelated. Although Hegel was trying to come to grips with historical change, it must be emphasised that the dialectic was a philosophical concept. Hegel separated philosophical propositions from any other. In this way he separated theory and practice, a separation that Marx thought unsustainable. Hegel argued that philosophy was the highest of all forms of thought. Only the philosopher could hope to understand the 'Absolute'. This is because philosophy's form of comprehension is a conceptual one that makes it conscious of its own methods. Philosophy is self-aware of its own assumptions in a way that no other form of human consciousness (such as art and religion) could be. Only philosophy could give a self-awareness of the whole of human intellectual life.

KEY CONCEPT

The dialectic

Generally speaking a dialectic is a philosophical way of thinking whereby contradictions become a starting point rather than a dead-end of thought. A dialectic helps us try to explain a world where paradox is the norm. In classical thought Plato, Aristotle and Cicero all had different dialectical methods. In modern thought German philosophy revived the notion, first with Kant, then with Hegel and Marx. Hegel's

continued

dialectic – which Marx adopted – is a three-step process. One begins with a clear concept (the thesis), then moves to its opposite (the antithesis); these two are then thought through and resolved (the synthesis).

Marx's critique of Hegel

As stated above, Marx was deeply influenced by both Kant and Hegel. His role as a journalist on the *Rheinische Zeitung* meant that the starting point for his thought began not with the isolated individual in the state of nature (a fundamentally liberal position from which to start) but with 'man' as a social animal. Although he approved of Kant's Idealist system of thought, Marx saw in Hegel a way of avoiding Kant's radically individualist conclusions. Initially, at least, he also believed that Hegel grounded philosophical Idealism in the 'real' world. He read Hegel as maintaining that reason was the basis of human existence. The development of reason was a historical process, which had a number of stages leading to the ultimate perfectibility of the human spirit. Hegel's dialectics also explained that as humans developed a tension between the present state of affairs (and what it was to become) existed. This changed into something new, which Hegel (according to Marx) saw as the effect of oppositional elements within a given historical period. Marx's reading of Hegel in this way profoundly affected him. He rejected Kant's liberal individualism in favour of Hegel's holistic, unifying theories. Instead of understanding the world as a place of underlying harmony (in the way that Locke and much of the liberal tradition since has done), Marx began to use his interpretation of Hegel to explain the oppositional character of human existence. Human life was about conflict. For Marx the greatest conflict of all was to be the class struggle between proletariats and bourgeoisie. But to get to this analysis Marx has one more philosophical hoop to jump through.

It was through the work of the now little regarded Ludwig Feuerbach that Marx made his final theoretical journey to find his own philosophical voice. It also enabled him to critique his own intellectual hero, Hegel. Feuerbach had presented a humanist-materialist critique of Hegel's thought built on the ideas of Enlightenment thinkers such as Holbach. It was the metaphysical nature of Hegel's work that Feuerbach most derided, with its concern with the ideal 'Absolute' as its subject rather than the reality of everyday life. Feuerbach maintained that 'Thought arises from being, being does not arise from thought'. He accused Hegel of working upside-down, working with imaginary 'wholes' rather than with real people. His attack (for such it was) on Hegel took the shape of an exegesis on religion. He argued that humankind project their wants and needs on to an imaginary figure of God who was given the human attributes which individuals saw themselves as lacking. God became alienated man, meaning that a feature of humanity was placed under an alien entity. The history of theology was a history of reinforcing this alienation. Furthermore, such a society based on these principles benefited, materially, some groups (the established church, the aristocracy) more than others. Just as theology had alienated man in this way, Feuerbach maintained that Hegel's Idealist philosophy had done so too. Hegel believed that there was an 'Absolute spirit' or human consciousness that was separate from man. This was supposed to exist throughout the world, through political institutions, religion, philosophy and so on. Yet this was a misleading premise; the real subject of human history ought not to be the 'unknowable Absolute' but 'man' himself.

KEY PEOPLE 3

Ludwig Feuerbach (1804–1872)

As a member of the young Hegelians, Feuerbach criticised the connection between Hegel's Idealism and religion in his *The Essence of Christianity* (1841). This had a great influence upon Marx's own materialist philosophy. However, he was also criticised by both Marx and Engels for his inconsistent application of materialism.

Marx's theory of the state

Marx took up Feuerbach's basic critique. However, he criticised him for his lack of attention to the political. In Marx's *Critique of Hegel's Philosophy of Right* (Marx 1970) he uses Feuerbach's methods to try and discredit Hegel's philosophy for putting the 'Ideal' before all else. Hegel, Marx argued, was making the subject the predicate and the predicate the subject. In his *Philosophy of Right*, Hegel had argued that the Prussian state was the high point of human reason, and that it had developed the lessons of history into the most advanced form that any society had ever known. The three elements of the Prussian state – legislative, executive and the Crown – together expressed the universal needs, interests and ideas of individuals in civil society. It acted as a type of 'general will' to develop the best policies for all. The state's bureaucracy was particularly important to this process. Collectively they subordinated the particular interests of the different groups in civil society, to a rational system of hierarchy, specialisation and co-ordination. The bureaucracy represented a 'universal class' that acted only in the interests of the whole community.

In all this Marx accused Hegel of mysticism. He argued that Hegel had not paid due regard to the particular historical development of the Prussian state, as if the state were completely severed from the historical and social circumstances that created it. The separation between social and political was a false one, Marx maintained; the state existed to preserve certain interests. This, of course, goes against the liberal notion that the state is the agent of the people, an idea given expression by J.S. Mill, who argued that in order for governments to be democratic they must be representative. Marx's thought on the state illustrates in a deep and fundamental way his divergence from the liberal tradition that started with Hobbes.

 Rewind

Go to Chapter 8 for Mill's arguments on representative government.

Marx argues that, in fact, the state acted in such a way as to alienate the population from the political institutions. The notion of alienation cuts through the liberal conception of the state being the magnate for all interests. Rather the state seeks to perpetuate the property rights of the ruling class which ensures that the majority remain powerless. This goes much further than Mill's idea of the 'tyranny of the majority'. Marx is not concerned to ensure that the political system is just, as was Mill, but maintains that at its core is a fundamental inequality and injustice which can be changed only when the whole political system collapses. By linking property with the representative system of bourgeois society Marx argues that a dualism arises between the political and the social. This creates a further division between man the citizen and man the worker. Instead of being a complete social being, human beings become egotistical, concerned only with their own wants and needs. For Marx, the divisions in society were reflected in the divisions in the political apparatus; those dominant due to their wealth in civil society would also dominate in the political system. In contrast to Hegel's idea that the state was a 'universal class', Marx argued that class differences based upon property relations carried over into the political system and were central in defining it. By illustrating that it was the material basis of society that gave rise to the state, Marx had not only turned Hegel on his head but provided a fundamental critique of the liberal theory of the state.

Marx's general system of thought

The *Critique* does not provide a systematic alternative view of the state but it does indicate Marx's ideas, many of which were to be found in his later writings. Many commentators have seen a difference in Marx's early works and his later writings. The distinction is usually drawn around the view that his early preoccupation was 'humanist' and dealt with themes such as man's alienation, while his later writings were seen as 'structuralist', particularly his great work *Capital* (1861/79). There is a great deal to recommend this view. Indeed it is a criticism of Marx that these two different methodological approaches are never fully reconciled. However, all that being said, Avineri (1970) has argued that there are similarities to be found in both the 'early' and 'late' Marx.

In his critique of Hegel, Marx proposed that the state was based upon property and production relations. In his later works he continues to develop this hypothesis. In fact it becomes the premise for what most commentators call his method of 'historical materialism' (a phrase Marx actually never used). At the centre of this approach is the theory that the basis of human society and the dynamic of human history is the changing nature of the production process. He maintained that 'The economic structure of society is the foundation on which the legal and political superstructure arises and social conditions and intellectual life' (Marx 1859).

The various social systems that have developed throughout history have produced class-based societies made up of a minority of owners, who ruled, and a majority of non-owners, whole were ruled over. Human history was a process of progressive evolution propelled by the engines of economic and technical change. It may be said, then, that for Marx the world was a place of change and conflict. These basic premises come from his Idealist philosophical heritage. They are not assumptions based on political bias, although they certainly fit in with Marx's communist political convictions, but were based upon the sure footing of his metaphysics. As stated above, authors have made the mistake of challenging Marx for his conclusions rather than getting to grips with the wealth of scholarly knowledge behind these conclusions. One thing Marx was not was a dilettante. He was deeply engrossed, serious, and a wildly passionate man. His intellectual capacity was vivid for all who met him and he was rarely if ever beaten in argument. Marx's firm conviction was that he was well on the way to discovering the universal scientific laws underlying all of human history. He developed a coherent, systematic theory that he believed matched up to the political and social realities of the world. That said, Marx himself was not a worldly man, insofar as he took little interest in the day-to-day activities around him in the numerous countries where he lived. Neither while in Belgium nor France nor living in London did he care to learn a great deal about the culture that surrounded him. In particular, the realities of the working class were a mystery to him and if it were not for his lieutenant, confidant and patron, the ever-loyal Friedrich Engels, Marx may have become completely detached from social life. As it was he barely held together a family life despite having a deeply devoted wife in Jenny von Westphalen (who came from Prussian aristocratic stock, a fact Marx was very proud of) so absorbed was he in plotting the downfall of capitalism.

KEY PEOPLE 4

Friedrich Engels

Engels was born in Barmen in 1820, the son of a successful German industrialist. His father sent him to England to manage his cotton factory in Manchester. Engels was shocked by the poverty in the city and began writing an account that was published as *Condition of the Working Classes in England* (1844). It was about this time when he began contributing to a radical journal that was being edited by Marx in Paris. Later that year Engels met Marx and the two men became close friends. Engels shared Marx's views on capitalism and after their first meeting he wrote that there was virtually *'complete agreement in all theoretical fields'*. Marx and Engels decided to work together. It was a good partnership; whereas Marx was at his best when dealing with difficult abstract concepts, Engels had the ability to write for a mass audience. Engels helped to support Marx and his family financially throughout his life.

There were four aspects to Marx's method, to his historical materialism, which provide the basis for his claim that the days of capitalism were limited and revolution inevitable. It is worth noting that although this is a materialist metaphysics, deeply opposed to Hegel's Idealism, the schema upon which Marx builds is very much that of his old mentor. Indeed, although Marx jettisoned Idealism as abstract and esoteric, he carried on many of the assumptions of Hegel's thought, as we shall see below.

First, his study of historical development was intended to illustrate how human life is progressive; how the character of materialist or economic life determined the process of human development. In the epochal changes witnessed by humanity (from primitive societies to ancient societies, from ancient to feudal and then to modern-capitalist societies) it was, Marx argued, the materialist changes that had fundamentally altered the way people lived.

Second, the key materialist determinate was what Marx famously called 'the means of production'. These are the technology and skills used to produce goods and services. It was not 'ideas' (as Hegel had said) that changed the world but changes to the nature of production.

Third, as the means of production changes so too does 'the division of labour'. The way that specialised tasks are divided in society alters as the economic means of production alters. It is this process that produces economic classes.

Fourth, economic classes are unequal in terms of their 'relations to the means of production'. Each individual's relation to the means of production determines their entire social identity.

These are the key points of Marx's historical materialism. He uses a dialectical method following Hegel. In so doing he characterises life as full of change and conflict, not in the sense of day-to-day antagonisms between individuals, but in terms of a historical epochal battle having taken place throughout history between unequal economic groups or classes. Hegel had argued in an Idealist guise that humankind was progressing towards the Absolute and full knowledge of reality. Marx as a materialist agreed that humanity was progressing, but his materialist methodology saw that progress as being towards a classless society, where the historical class conflict (whether between slaves and their owners, serfs and lords or workers and factory owners) would finally end. That condition would be under communism where the means of production would be in the hands of the workers or, to put it correctly in Marx's conceptual framework, under the control of the industrial proletariat. When the ownership of the means of production was communal, then, following the above theory, everything else would fall into place. The division of labour and the relations to production would be egalitarian.

 Rewind

Go to Chapter 6 to see how Rousseau's analysis of the division of labour is remarkably similar to Marx's. Both argued that the desire for private property led to the division of labour, and this in turn gave rise to the existence of separate social classes based on economic differences.

While Marx did not say a great deal about the actual form of government or society under communism there are hints, here and there, in his work, of what he would have intended. These notions are far removed from the actual forms of state communism that developed after the Second World War in Russia, China and elsewhere. One early, perhaps exaggerated view of life under communism may be found in *The German Ideology*. This was an early 'humanist' work of Marx that was never published during his lifetime but was found in an attic and finally went into print in 1932. In it he describes how once the current life-limiting division of labour was overthrown man would live differently.

He is a hunter, a fisherman, a shepherd, or a critic, and must remain so if he does not want to lose his means of livelihood; whereas in communist society, where nobody has one exclusive sphere of activity but each can become accomplished in any branch he wishes, society regulates the general production and thus makes it possible for me to do one thing today and another tomorrow, to hunt in the morning, fish in the afternoon, rear cattle in the evening, criticize, just as I have a mind, without ever becoming hunter, fisherman, shepherd or critic.

(Marx 1965)

Marx's model of capitalism

For Marx, then, all societies are based upon conflict between classes. This arises out of an antagonism created when existing production processes are being challenged by the new emerging ones. This affects the people who are constrained by their class position; they become rebellious because they are not able to use their labour to its full potential. Above all, Marx was concerned with using this general proposition regarding social change to analyse capitalism. As a dialectician Marx, not surprisingly, was ambivalent towards modern bourgeois society. Even in the *Communist Manifesto* he may be found praising the achievements of the industrial middle classes. He was a true modernist in his relish for the new technologies such as the locomotive engine, and he marvelled at the ingenuity of bourgeois engineering, its wonderful steel constructions, the factories pouring out mass-produced goods and the revolution of communications and the printed word. However, for Marx the motivation for all these marvels of the bourgeoisie was wrong and they would destroy it all without a thought, for one thing – profit. The private accumulation of wealth was all that drove the new entrepreneurial class and this was done at the expense of others. Indeed, Marx argued that in many aspects capitalism, although coming progressively out of feudalism, was in many ways more barbaric then any other form of society that humanity had contrived for itself.

As well as drawing upon his historical materialism to challenge capitalism Marx also employed a range of other economic theories. One of these concerned the exploitation of labour. Marx had studied in great detail the classical liberal economic theories of Adam Smith, David Ricardo and James Mill. During the summer of 1844 he had systematically engaged with these great figures of British political economy and written notes that amounted to around 50,000 words of commentary. These were later published as the 'Paris manuscripts' (Marx 1959). This evidence alone points to how great a scholar Marx was and how seriously he took his task. It is from these studies that Marx derived his theory of labour power, a not uncommon point of view among liberal theorists, although in Marx's hands this theory was deployed for revolutionary intent. Put simply, Marx adopted the classical liberal view that the value of an object is a reflection of the amount of labour power put into it. In other words, the reason why a crafted chair made by a carpenter over several weeks is worth more than one made from a couple of old beer crates nailed together is because it took more labour power to make it. The genius of the property-owning classes, the bourgeoisie, was that they had appropriated (literally taken possession of) the workers' labour power, and instead of giving them the full cost of their labour power paid them a wage. The owners of capital wielded an immoral power over the industrial working class, the proletariat. Because they owned the factories they could force the workers to work for much less than the real value of what they produced was actually worth. They were able to do this because industrialisation and urbanisation had created an army of landless labourers. These poor propertyless souls had nothing to sell but themselves, their labour power. They were at the mercy of the property-owning economic class who paid them no more than a subsistence wage.

It may be seen that when Marx (and for that matter Marxists) discusses exploitation and appropriation it is not said in a merely passionate, rhetorical or humanitarian manner. Rather, Marx argued on the basis of accepted theoretical principles that the workers were actually and demonstrably robbed of the fruits of their labour. The concept of 'exploitation' is now, like many of Marx's insights, a common notion in everyday political vocabulary. Pick up a newspaper and you will find references in many different types of political arguments relating to exploitation. Such a discussion may also be set alongside a concomitant concept, that of alienation. Once again Marx takes the basic principle of this concept from Hegel but turns it upside-down (from an Idealist notion to a materialist one). Hegel had argued that the general human condition was one of estrangement from reality (the Whole or Absolute). For him the struggle for humankind was to progress towards ultimate knowledge, and the state was the most appropriate mechanism to do this. Marx used the term 'alienation' to describe the depersonalised and purposeless condition of the proletariat who had become estranged from the social and economic aspects of their lives. For him alienation was the condition of the working class having lost control over their productive powers and, therefore, over their own lives. In fact, we find in Marx reference to the most iniquitous form of alienation under capitalism that was possible: self-alienation. Capitalism created a 'false consciousness', wherein the working class lived as if in a 'fog', not knowing their real class interests. However, Marx argued that capitalism contained within it the seeds of its own destruction. The proletariat would become a force against capital because of its impoverishment, because of capitalist injustices and because of the self-alienation that eventually the workers would come to realise. In a process of material dialectic the proletariat were the powerful antithesis to the thesis of private ownership of property. They played the leading role in the progress of humankind towards a new epoch of existence.

Marx maintained that when the proletariat became a 'class-for-itself', recognising its true social conditions under capitalism and its real class interests, a revolution would follow. A communist society would replace capitalism. Private property and the wage system of labour would be abolished and with it the whole political and social system which exploited and alienated individuals. For the first time in human history people would be liberated, genuinely free to pursue their own individual interests.

DISCUSSION POINT

Marx distinguished between a 'class-in-itself' (the objective unity of the working class) and a 'class-for-itself' (the subjective unity of the working class). Only when the proletariat became a 'class-for-itself', realising their united class interests, would revolution be possible. Marx created a disjuncture between the objective realities of class and people's subjective perceptions of their own position within society. Thus the working class in capitalist society in the main fails to recognise it own oppression and as such lives under 'false consciousness'. This concept may be theorised in a variety of ways – ranging from a conspiratorial view that capitalists use their ownership of the media to brainwash us into a notion that reality itself is inherently deceptive. This kind of ideological control may also be conceived of as something purely involving beliefs and ideas to something material and involving practices as well. The key question is: How do theorists of false consciousness step outside of it in order to judge it as 'false'? How can they have a vantage point different to ordinary people? Can somebody judge the social and economic position of others better than the individual concerned can him or herself? Can we be told 'you have false consciousness'?

Marx, freedom and rights

It has been argued that the supreme human value for Marx was human freedom. The same has been said of most liberal theorists too, yet Marx's ideas are very different from liberals such as Hobbes, Locke and Mill. His work challenged what he saw as the exploitive ruling class of the liberal state and its subsequent alien-ation as it took away people's freedom from themselves as well as from others. Bourgeois liberal society set individuals against each other and took away any sense of community. Unlike Rousseau, Marx did not argue that being a citizen was an essential part of being human. Moreover, what Marx understood by citizenship was rather different to the meaning Rousseau attributed to it. This was because Marx believed that the social and political would 'merge' under a communist society (and the state would not be needed in the way it was in liberal societies to police people). Citizenship, as such, for Marx was possible and had meaning in the context of a society only where individuals were equal and free.

 Rewind

> Interestingly enough, Marx's conclusions often have more in common with the liberal tradition of Hobbes, Locke and Mill than with the Rousseau, who seems to share his belief in equality.

> Not until the real, individual man is identical with the citizen, and has become a species-being in his empirical life, in his individual work, in his individual relationships, not until man has recognized and organized his own capacities, and consequently the social force is no longer divided by the political power, not until then will human emancipation be achieved.
>
> (Marx, in Stenning 1926)

Unusually among political thinkers who are concerned with communal forms of identity and society, the notion of citizenship is categorised by Marx as only secondary to the more fundamental notion of freedom. In his early works Marx was known for having discussed the notion of freedom (for example, in his *Essay On The Jewish Question*). Yet even at the end of his great later and supposedly more structurally orientated work *Capital* (Marx 1887), he reiterates his view set out as a young man that to be free, humankind must have freedom 'within' material existence and freedom 'from' material life. Self-fulfilment was possible only when individuals were able to move between pursuits that necessitated freedom from material constraints (perhaps to produce great art or writing) and to participate fully in material production (through the endeavours of their own labour). The constitutional and legal freedoms of bourgeois society were not 'true' freedoms. The framework of government and law was just an artificial condition of freedom, which benefited one particular economic class.

This brings us to the rather interesting contemporary terrain regarding discussions about rights. For if any political thinker sets out a theory of freedom there ought to be markers, that is, demarcations, which set out what the boundaries of the freedoms are that enable us to enjoy our liberty. In other words, any notion of freedom is hard to disassociate from a theory of rights because in setting out that notion certain rules are laid down as to the types of freedom individuals may or may not enjoy. And we are thrown into the subject of rights. Marx had no explicit theory of rights. However, in early works such as the *The German Ideology* (Marx 1965) we find Marx's critique of liberal justice, which does touch upon the field of rights. Not surprisingly we find that Marx argues that liberal theories of rights are far from just. Rights can be meaningful only in a genuine community; one of the conditions of genuine community is equality, and capitalism denies this: 'Only in community with others has each individual the means of cultivating his gifts in all directions; only in the community, therefore, is personal freedom possible' (Marx 1965).

Capitalism predetermines an individual's life-course by situating them in a particular economic class. This class identity determines their entire social and political being. It sets the boundaries of freedoms and rights that individuals will hold. Communism as a classless society allows non-predetermined action because an individual's identity is not prescribed by being placed in a particular economic class. Under communism individuals are free to create their own identities unbound by social roles. In this way 'rights' are developed, not as a set of rules handed down by one class who controls the institutions of the state but by the interplay of individuals acting out their own desires. It seems that for Marx, 'rights', insofar as they exist for him, are a creative process. They are not something that can be prescribed but emerge out of the value system that would develop when people are emancipated from the tightly bound class identities of capitalism. As such what 'real rights' may look like is impossible to say, since humankind has never been in the fortunate position of being able to have the freedom to create them.

Strangely enough, under communism individual freedom becomes central to Marx's conception of society. It may be true to say that Marx's final aim was not that far removed from the bourgeois liberals he so detested, namely that of maximising individual freedom. Indeed, at times he almost seems to have a romanticised view of human freedom and he comes close at times to articulating the possibility of absolute or unbounded freedom for individuals under communism. Given Marx's obvious awareness of the structural constraints upon individuals living in communities we may only speculate that some of what he says regarding freedom and rights occasionally falls into a rhetorical rather than a philosophical mode. Marx, a great admirer of Shakespeare, had a penchant for peppering his work with flourishes of creative writing and it is perhaps in this area of his thought where he allows himself the greatest licence to do so.

Marx rejects all types of liberal notions of rights. The idea of 'natural rights' was anathema to someone like Marx with such an historical understanding of social change. For him societies were constructed upon the basis of particular means of production, upon the material circumstances of the age. From this foundation came all political and social structures including the relations of production, the class system. There was nothing natural about this: it was secular, constructed, man-made. Marx also rejected the belief in the 'rights of man'. As stated above, however 'just' such a set of rights were supposed to be they were still embedded in the whole individualistic structure of capitalism and ultimately based upon property rights. Finally, Marx even rejected a notion of historical rights in the Burkian sense. Like Burke, Marx appreciated the historical character of society, and they both rallied against 'abstract' liberal rights. Yet while Burke saw existing traditions and culture as inherent to 'real rights' Marx understood these as part of the ideology of exploitation. Whereas Burke ties people's ultimate identity to their national identity, Marx ties it to their class identity. These two differing kinds of politics, the politics of nationhood and the politics of class, were to become the key features of political debate and conflict throughout the twentieth century.

 Rewind

Go to Chapter 7 to see how Marx shares with Burke a similar critique of liberal rights.

The language of rights constructed by various liberal discourses over the centuries had obscured the real issues of emancipation. Only through establishing communal ownership of the means of production would human beings find their liberty and their real moral worth. Economic equality was the pre-condition for moral equality and freedom. Marx's critique of liberal justice is very seductive. His criticism of liberal freedoms and rights is profound in the way that it situates these debates in the context not only of economic inequality but also in terms of the limiting identities which capitalism imposes. For Marx, citizenship (membership of a political community) is only a partial solution to the ills of capitalism. Such a concept was used by the bourgeois to limit the boundaries of individual freedom to that prescribed by law and liberal morality.

Marx's own concept of freedom and rights (as far as he has one) is rather more sketchy, not the most convincing aspect of his work and one of his least developed areas. We might agree with Marx that citizenship is presented too often as a partial political concept, useful for those who are included in society but meaningless for groups (think, for example, of asylum-seekers) who are excluded and feel disenfranchised. However, instead of rejecting the concept itself as too limited it is possible to argue for a different broader definition (and actualisation) of citizenship. This is something argued after Marx's death by a number of thinkers, including, oddly enough, a group known as the English Idealists. While Marx rejects one particular liberal notion of citizenship he does not offer any real direct challenge to these debates given that it is a discussion with a long pedigree, a conversation that stretches back to Athens and the very beginning of political thought. The same may be said about his rejection of rights. Marx's tendency is to set up a rather one-dimensional version of rights (natural rights are this not that, the rights of man are this not that) without really getting into the detail and nuances of what various authors have argued. Furthermore, while he rejects liberal rights as such, he does make claims for the kinds of rights and freedoms that individuals would enjoy under communism. Yet there is a great deal of difficulty in defining communal or group rights. Marx seems to believe that once there is economic equality then all individuals will, plainly and simply, have equal freedom. As contemporary debates on the construction of communal rights illustrate, this is not something that is so easy to translate into practice. The fundamental problem is that all the individual rights and freedoms we enjoy are riddled with a basic tension with the rights of the group. Even in the kind of stateless society that Marx foresees, there would be many occasions where the rights of the individual may come up against the rights of the group. For example, if one worker in a factory exercised her right to paint during the day when she was needed on the factory floor, whose rights, whose freedom, ought to take precedence? The worker may argue that she needs to fulfil her creative sense by finishing her painting even though the group may be unable to work because of her absence. At a more national level (and Marx does not really take a sense of national identity seriously) one individual's right to speak out may endanger the freedoms of the entire country. Issues of this kind would inevitably give rise to the kinds of debates about rights and freedoms that Marx finds so superficial and 'bourgeois'. Yet in any modern society they are debates which would not simply 'wither away', as Marx believed. In the end it may be said that Marx is a supremely apolitical philosopher. This may seem strange. Yet Marx appears to see such fundamental political debates about citizenship, rights and freedom as subsidiary and secondary arguments that arise out of a corrupt capitalist system. When a 'true' state of being arises Marx sees such discussions along with the political realm itself as disappearing. Instead, individuals could devote themselves to their own self-fulfilment. This is an oddly individualistic conclusion to an argument based upon communal freedom and identity. Marx ends up, strange as it may seem, as desiring a more individualised apolitical society than any liberal thinker.

Analysis and critique

This critical discussion of some of the most important concepts of political debate that we use today brings us to some more general points of critique in relation to Marx's work. There has been an enormous amount of analysis of his writings over the decades, from those sympathetic to his ideas through to those who see him as the anti-Christ of politics and all shades in between. To pick out some of the key points of discussion is extremely difficult. Nevertheless, for better or worse, here are the most pertinent ones as we see them. That is, these criticisms are not based upon a purely ideological antagonism to Marx, simply because he was a communist, but upon his work as a philosopher and political thinker whose genius was to take Hegelian Idealism and marry it to his own theory of historical materialism. Below, then, are three grouped areas of discussion. In the first we look at the issues surrounding the different methodologies that Marx employs. The second group concerns Marx's use of history, and the role of structure and agency within that model. Finally, there is a set of discussions around Marx's economic theories and his model of capitalism.

Marx's work has often been divided into an 'early' and 'late' period. On this basis it has been argued that Marx does not reconcile the tension between his early 'humanist' works and the later 'economic determinist' or structuralist writings. It is said that in works such as his *Critique of Hegel's Philosophy of Right* (1843) and *The Eighteenth Brumaire Louis Bonaparte* (1852) Marx is concerned with the concept of alienation, the outcomes of capitalism and its impact upon people's lives. However, in his later works, such as the *Grundrisse* (1857) and his magnum opus, *Capital* (1887), his concern is to scientifically find the laws of history and society. In the same way that early sociologists such as Emile Durkheim sought to find the fundamental laws of society (echoing the way that natural scientists had claimed to have found the fundamental laws of nature and human evolution), we find Marx, as one of the founders of empirical sociology, trying to prove beyond doubt the inequities of capitalism and the inevitability of communism.

This is an interesting way of approaching the two main strands of Marx's thinking; yet one might also note that there are other elements to be found in his work. There is a 'Romanticist' Marx who simply loves the written word and writes lyrically about modernity and mechanisation. There is the 'political' Marx, the communist agitator who sets out some of the most seductive rhetoric in *The Communist Manifesto* (1888). We find a dogmatic Marx in his myopic self-belief that he can discover the laws of history. And we find Marx the philosopher and open thinker stating that he is not a Marxist! Finally, there is Engels, Marx's closest ally, whose interpretation of Marx's work we rely upon quite heavily at times to understand some areas of Marx's work. Although there may be loose methodological ends in Marx's project (and this is grounds for criticism), it is worth bearing in mind that this also makes Marx a rich and deeply enjoyable thinker.

Second, Marx's work has been criticised for being historicist. The most famous commentator to level this accusation was Karl Popper. He argued that Marx (and Hegel too) was of the view that history had a rational character and meaning that could be analysed with the right method and the 'Truth' (with a capital 'T') be told. It should be noted that this point of view relies upon an interpretation of Marx's work as essentially scientific (i.e. the 'later' Marx). The debate as to the character of Marx's alleged historicism also rests upon how one takes Marx's view that communism was inevitable and the 'end of history' or at least the end of history as human beings had so far known it. Commentators have argued that Marx went too far in trying to predict the future, a dangerous enterprise, as we might know from our own daily lives and not just philosophically! Marx could not possibly have been aware of some of the key sociological features of capitalism which contribute to its maintenance, including the rise of an influential middle class, an affluent working class, the welfare state and the rise of non-class-based political issues such as feminism, issues of race and the environment.

Another issue that arises from this discussion concerns structure and agency in Marx's work. On the one hand, Marx maintains that communism is inevitable, that the proletariat will be so pauperised under capitalism that they will rise up and overthrow it to create a communist society. On the other hand, he maintains that the workers need an organised communist party in order to be enlightened about their true 'interests'. The problem here is that Marx has a rather underdeveloped notion of human agency. The world is either structurally programmed to bring about communism, or the proletariat have to be told to revolt. Either way (and both ways have problems in themselves), Marx does not seem to have any faith, let alone developed theory about the agency, the choices and self-reflecting awareness of ordinary people. As we saw in the discussion of rights and freedom above, Marx's conclusions are not always what we would expect. It seems clear in the debate about the proletariat's historical mission that Marx finds it hard to conceive of them having the capacity to bring about revolution themselves. It is either their uncontrollable destiny or they have to be led there. Furthermore, they would subsequently need to face a 'dictatorship of the proletariat' until they are educated enough to understand their own best interests! It may well be true to say that the supreme value for Marx was freedom, but that does not necessarily mean he was a democrat. Again, although Marx was vehemently against liberalism, he shared with liberals such as Hobbes and John Stuart Mill a scepticism about the collective intelligence of the working class.

The last set of discussions concerns Marx's economics and model of capitalism. If we take the base-superstructure model, that the economic base (the means of production) determines all other structures of the state – the political, cultural and legal structures – we find that even Marxists have found this too 'deterministic' to live with. Following Marx's death many communists became Marxists to the extent that soon one could hardly be one without the other (which was not the case while Marx was alive). Yet as Marxist theorists (for example, the leading Italian communist Antonio Gramsci) soon discovered, putting such a notion into praxis (theory to a practical use) was extremely difficult. The base-superstructure model left very little room for political activity, for agency. It also did not allow for tactical action on the part of the communists trying to get the workers to understand and participate in a revolution. If all actions were determined by the owners of the means of production then any acts to counter capitalism must inevitably play into capital's hands. So why do anything? This dilemma was circumvented by 'humanist' Marxists such as Gramsci emphasising the work of the 'early' Marx and the important battles to be fought against capitalist ideology. So it was that Marxists found themselves engaged in arguments about art and culture as well as political economy in a bid to challenge the representation of capitalism in all its guises. However, although Marxism developed in this way, it does not negate the critique that the base-superstructure model was a rather rigid theoretical piece of Marx's system of thought and caused endless debates in Marxist circles, debates which were never really resolved. Marxist structuralists such as Althusser were opposed to Gramsci's way out of this rigidity and proposed to try and maintain the 'scientific' basis of the base-superstructure model by making it more methodologically sophisticated. However, this project itself became bogged down in all kinds of minute theoretical discussions and again was never satisfactorily concluded.

Another common criticism of the base-superstructure model is that it leads to 'reductionist' arguments. All human activities are reduced by way of explanation to the economic base. All human activities are analysed on the basis of their relations to who owns and controls the means of production. So it is that Marx is able to say that all history is the history of class struggle. Such a universal statement is possible only because Marx 'reduces' all history to what he sees as the essence, the foundational point at the root of all social existence. Yet one wonders if the abolition of slavery, the struggle for women's emancipation, the battles for democracy and the franchise throughout the globe can all be put down to class struggle. Max Weber famously wrote *The Protestant Ethic and the Spirit of Capitalism* (1930) as a retort to Marx's claim. He indicates how the rise of the Protestant value system was a motor for capitalism, religious ideas rather than class antagonisms.

There is no doubt that Karl Marx has been one of the most influential thinkers of the modern age. He has given us a unique way of thinking about the world. Concepts such as economic class, alienation, revolution, equality and so on are embedded firmly in our consciousness and help us interpret the way we live. Many still find a resonance in his critique of capitalism, and *The Communist Manifesto* continues to sell thousands of copies every year throughout the world. While recognising his lasting influence it is important to look dispassionately at his work and make clear the tensions in his theory. Like all our theorists, Marx's work must all be set in its context. Marx was writing at a time when capitalism was struggling through the pains of its birth and not, as Marx thought, the anguish of its death. Capitalism has proved to be more flexible and adaptive to the needs of different classes than Marx could ever have predicted. It has developed and continues to change, from a national to a global force. Yet, as we live through these changes we may be sure that there will be the voice of Marx warning us about its iniquities. As he himself said, 'Last words are for fools who haven't said enough'. It is very doubtful that Marx's words will ever fade from our memories.

Revision notes

1. Getting to grips with Marx's philosophical background is important in order to appropriately analyse his writings. In particular it is important to understand the influence of Hegel and the development of his own historical materialist methodology.
2. Marx's main work is *Capital*; it is here that he attempts to prove that capitalism is both corrupt and destined to fail.

3   There are many aspects to Marx's work. There is the 'early' humanist work that dealt with alienation, freedom and revolution. There is the 'later' work that was more scientifically based and more deterministic. There is his rhetorical work and political publications too. In fact, we may find a mix of these different aspects of his work in each of his writings.

4   Modernity was a positive force for Marx, bringing about the possibility of change. However, progress was held back by the mean profit motives of the bourgeoisie.

5   Marx may be criticised for the lack of overall coherence to his philosophical system: his underdeveloped theories of freedom, rights and, indeed, the political sphere. He may also be taken to task for his historicism and his reductionism. This is particularly the case in his arguments regarding class-consciousness and false consciousness.

Bibliography

Althusser, L. (1969) *For Marx*, London: Allen Lane.

Avineri, S. (1970) *The Social and Political Thought of Karl Marx*, Cambridge: Cambridge University Press.

Gramsci, A. (1971) *Selections from the Prison Notebooks of Antonio Gramsci*, London: Lawrence & Wishart.

Hegel, G.W.F. (1931) *The Phenomenology of Mind*, trans. J.B. Baille, London: Oxford University Press.

Hegel, G.W.F. (1967) *Philosophy of Right*, Oxford: Oxford University Press.

Kant, I. (1933) *Critique of Pure Reason*, London: Macmillan.

Marx, K. (1859) *A Contribution to the Critique of Political Economy*, Moscow: Progress Publishers.

—— (1887) *Capital*, London: Samuel Moore and Edward Avelin.

—— (1888) *The Communist Manifesto*, London: Samuel Moore and Edward Avelin.

—— (1959) *The Economic and Philosophic Manuscripts*, Moscow: Foreign Languages Publishing House.

—— (1965) *The German Ideology*, London: Lawrence & Wishart.

—— (1970) *Critique of Hegel's Philosophy of Right*, Cambridge: Cambridge University Press.

Stenning, H.J. (1926) *Selected Essays by Karl Marx*, London: Leonard Parsons.

Weber, M. (1930) *The Protestant Ethic and the Spirit of Capitalism*, New York: Scribner.

Further reading

For a good summary of the many different notions of citizenship, before and after Marx, see P. Barry Clarke (1994) *Citizenship* (London: Pluto Press). For the issues raised in the discussion of communal rights see W. Kymlica (1991) *Liberalism, Community and Culture* (Oxford: Clarendon Press). For a wonderful general biography of Marx see F. Wheen (1999) *Karl Marx* (London: Fourth Estate).

Mikhail Bakunin
and the anarchists

It is in the nature of the state to break the solidarity of the human race and, as it were, to deny humanity.

(*Marxism, Freedom and the State*)

Introduction

Most textbooks on modern political theory or political ideologies tend to end with Marx. Glance through the shelves; pick up book after book, and you will see that specifically 'modern' political thought seems to have ended with the birth of communism. It is almost as if after conservatism and liberalism this was the last of the truly modern ideologies. When the literature moves from 'modern' to 'contemporary' political thought the latter tends towards post-Second World War political thinkers, perhaps starting with some of the ideas associated with either fascism or nationalism. Yet there is one 'ism' of political thought that is firmly rooted in the modern vernacular but seems to be forgotten about except by specialists. That is, of course, anarchism. This is strange, since anarchism was very much alive and well during the time that Marx was writing. Indeed, it was an equal contender for the radical crown of political ideas throughout Europe during this period, so much so that for most of his life Marx spent a great deal of time attacking anarchist theoreticians such as Proudhon and Bakunin (Thomas 1980).

The anarchist discourse stretches back to the ancient Greeks, to Taoism and Buddhism. Yet like most of the ideas, concepts, ideologies, political movements and philosophical systems we have come across, its chief characteristics developed in modern times, from the Enlightenment. Anarchism was a vital political doctrine throughout the modern period. It has already been seen that anarchist ideas were an important part of the radical groups that were around during the period of the English revolution, especially the Diggers and the Ranters. Furthermore, although it is true to say that it faded for a short time towards the mid-twentieth century it was revived in the 1960s through the rise of the New Left who championed 'grassroots' political activity. In an unlikely turn of events many neo-liberals of the 1980s and 1990s turned towards anarchist ideas. These new libertarians argued that the state (in particular the welfare state) needed to be 'rolled back' to allow individuals' greater freedom to exercise their own ambitions and enterprise. Both Margaret Thatcher in Britain and Ronald Reagan in the USA benefited from this Right-leaning anarchist spirited discourse. More recently some of its central ideas have been employed in the 'praxis' of direct action groups such as the anti-capitalist movement, ecology groups and disability rights campaigners. The impact of anarchism on our streets is far from over.

The most potent image that is conjured up when the word 'anarchism' is mentioned is one of a crowd out of control intent on violence and mayhem. The

Rewind

Go to Chapter 2 for more information on the Levellers.

anarchist is demonised as an individual (perhaps dressed up in black) who is a fanatic intent on creating chaos for chaos' sake. Yet these images could not be further from the truth of the very serious, slightly staid, nineteenth-century gentlemen who advocated its basic principles. They saw in anarchism a sense of social order and justice that had hitherto not been attained by the existing structures of the state. The etymology of the word 'anarchy' points to this. It comes from the Greek *anarkhos* meaning the condition of being without a *leader*, and not, as it is most often translated as without a *ruler*. Not having a leader is an entirely different set of circumstances from not having any rule or set of rules. It is possible to argue for a society where decisions can be made communally without a leader but within an established and accepted set of rules. Jettisoning the rule of law is not an essential part of being an anarchist. Being against the state is. Anarchists maintain that the state, which in liberal theory is meant to be the Leviathan against injustice and oppression, was, in fact, preventing people's freedom rather than enabling it. Hobbes, Locke and the whole edifice of the liberal tradition gave truth to the lie of the benevolent state. Rather than saving us from a '*warre of all against all*' the state perpetuated inequality and the chains of servitude. Anarchism is not merely negative; this is yet another false depiction. At the same time as it is anti-state it is pro the notion of individual responsibility. In other words, anarchism has at its core a belief in the direct democratic participation of all in the decisions that affect the society in which they live. Perhaps more than any other modern ideological discourse anarchism has at the very heart and soul of its rationale a belief in the notion of citizenship; that is, that citizens are what polities are all about. Given this reading it may be argued that anarchism is in some senses a return to the original idea of politics set out by Socrates, Plato and Aristotle. For them politics is about being seen by one's equals to take part in the communal issues of the day, and that in so doing the 'higher' moral questions of what makes a 'good' or 'just' society may be discussed and reflected upon.

 Rewind

Go to Chapter 3 for Hobbes' *Leviathan*.

As we saw with the work of Marx, we also find that central to the anarchist ideology is a privileging of the individual. On the one hand, anarchism is a rather anti-Enlightenment doctrine in the sense that it rejects the nation state, one of the founding political ideas upon which modernity was constructed. On the other hand, anarchism is a prime example of the Enlightenment tradition and the preoccupation with individual freedom. In some cases (for example, in the anarcho-syndicalism of George Sorel – see below) individuals are urged to achieve a heroic status by acting only upon their own intuition and will. Of course, anarchists believed that the gap between the individual's desires and the best interests of one's 'class' was not an insurmountable one. In a certain sense this was a rather naïve position to hold. As social and political theory developed from the late nineteenth century, commentators found that dealing with the tension between individual and communal needs was one of the greatest difficulties they faced. The arguments that we have seen philosophers such as Kant and Hegel rehearse regarding the subject/object distinction were later to be thought through in the more practical realm in this way. How can we reconcile individual needs (the subject) with that of society (the object)? This is a question that anarchists approach but not very satisfactorily.

KEY CONCEPT 1

Anarchist or libertarian?

Anarchists reject all forms of the state and argue that people would have greater liberty and more control over their lives without its structures. Libertarians are not necessarily anti-state. They take freedom to be the supreme value and aim to limit the powers of government as far as possible without endangering national security. That said, these two strands share a great deal in common and commentators often use the terms interchangeably.

Anarchism was a movement based upon equality and, like communism, it sought a working-class revolution to overthrow the state. Although the origins of their thought go back in all sorts of directions as indicated above, there are two principal figures in the modern era who are often said to have been the key players in constructing the main body of ideas upon which anarchism rests. Their work has been dealt with in earlier chapters (see Chapters 2 and 6). The first of these is William Godwin in his *An Enquiry Concerning the Principles of Human Justice* (1793) in which text he sets out the libertarian agenda. The other is Rousseau (although his individualism is rejected by anarchists as 'bourgeois'), who pointed to the corrupt practices of the state and government that could be overcome only by some form of direct democracy. Although in general these two theorists are the guiding lights against the power of the nation state, the anarchist tradition is a broad one and we find different forms of anarchism even within the same society. Often commentators have divided anarchism according to the degree of violence that the various movements have or have not professed. So, for example, in Russia, Tolstoy, one of the country's greatest writers, was a pacifist-anarchist, while Bakunin was one of the leading Russian anarchists who advocated the violent overthrow of the state. While the pacifism of Tolstoy is not without interest it is the ideas and actions of Mikhail Bakunin (1814–1876) that have been most influential to mainstream anarchist ideas throughout Europe. So it is to his thought that we shall now turn.

Mikhail Bakunin: infinite freedom

Like Marx, Bakunin was a complex character. He had a genius for rhetoric and theory, a rational thinker in the tradition of the Enlightenment. But like his communist counterpart he had a passionate temperament, believing deeply in the inequities of the present institutional powers and the possibility of a genuine communal-based society.

I mean that freedom of the individual which, far from stopping as if before a boundary in the face of the freedom of others, on the contrary finds in that freedom its own confirmation and extension to infinity; the unlimited freedom of each in the freedom of all, freedom in solidarity, freedom in equality; triumphant freedom, victorious over brute force and the principle of authority which was never anything but the idealised expression of brute force; freedom which, after overthrowing all the heavenly and earthly idols, will establish and organise a new world, that of humanity in solidarity, built on the ruin of all Churches and all States.

(Bakunin, in Dolgoff 1973)

Boundless freedom was the goal, in the face of the authoritarian polities and legal apparatus that held down the will of individuals to be creative and spontaneous. Here lies a further paradox of Bakunin's thought. While a thinker who appreciated much of the systematic analysis of human life that the German Idealists had expounded, he also had an appreciation of the philosophy of 'will' which looked to the non-rational, intuitive and experiential-based aspects of human action. This Kantian tradition which was expounded further by Schopenhauer and Nietzsche in philosophy and, later, by Weber in sociology, took it that spontaneous human action was as legitimate and valid a part of the human condition as the reflective rational behaviour needed to turn acts into processes of constructive labour. It is this aspect of his work, as a philosopher of action, that makes his ideas so interesting in the context of modern political theory as a contrast to the liberal ideas that had so dominated the epoch. It also contrasts to the other great 'ism' that was to dominate the twentieth century, Marxism. For rather than argue for a 'dictatorship of the proletariat' or any other kind of workers' state, Bakunin believed in revolution from below, a genuine workers' revolution that would establish networks of self-government through syndicalist rather than statist means.

KEY CONCEPT 2

Syndicalism

The word 'syndicalism' comes from the French *syndicats*, associations of working men that united members of the same trade or industry for common interests. Politically the term developed to mean a form of revolutionary unionism that advocated direct action against employers in small-scale revolts or strikes. These 'battles' would lead collectively to the eventual overthrow of the capitalist state. Syndicalism is fundamentally a workers' movement that repudiates interference by intellectuals or any professional political actors.

In his own life Bakunin portrayed the dynamism of his political ideas. He was without doubt an extremely charismatic figure, with a huge amount of intellectual and physical energy. Not exactly a man of the people by birth, coming from an established aristocratic family, he nevertheless sought to develop a 'praxis' of collective action for workers to overthrow the bourgeois state. Even though he was well read in philosophy Bakunin was not a systematic thinker himself. His ideas came partly from his written work, in his theory and rhetoric for the cause, and partly through his own active participation in the anarchist movement. Given this manner in which we understand his ideas it may be said – as it has by many other commentators – that he is often inconsistent in what he said and his work remains incomplete and fragmented. He was through his own admission an excitable character, easily bored, likely to change projects and direction at any moment, always looking for some new form of excitement, something to totally absorb himself into.

> There was always a basic defect in my nature: a love for the fantastic, for unusual, unheard-of-adventures, for undertakings that open up a boundless horizon and whose end no one can foresee. I would feel suffocated and nauseated in ordinary peaceful surroundings . . . my need for movement and activity remained unsatisfied. This need, subsequently, combined with democratic exaltation, was almost my only motive force.
>
> (Bakunin, in Howes 1977)

Many biographers have pointed to some unfulfilled psychological need in Bakunin, in particular looking at his intense relationships with his sisters or his penchant for cloak-and-dagger secret societies, to find an explanation for his erratic and anarchic political ideas. However, such profiling, while interesting in understanding the man, is in the end rather fruitless in getting to grips with his political ideas. Despite its disorganised character there is enough textual material to get to grips with his main doctrines.

It may be that a 'theory of anarchism' is a contradiction in terms. Nevertheless, Bakunin offers us something along the lines of a theoretical explanation for his joining of the politics of Proudhon with the economic materialism of Marx. In addition, Bakunin did have, as stated above, a more than passing acquaintance with the philosophy that had influenced his age and the main thinkers of his day. This, of course, included knowing the main tenets of Hegel (as well as Feuerbach, whose arguments about religion he largely accepted). Like Rousseau, Bakunin begins from the idea that man is born free, free even from God, who he argues cannot exist because of the natural freedom of man. If God existed, Bakunin reasons, men would be born as slaves and it would be necessary to get rid of him anyway. Belief in reason is an abdication of man's responsibilities as a reflective and active being. However, although 'no'-thing either supernatural or natural can impinge on man's natural liberty there are such things as natural laws. These laws, which scientists of the age, such as Newton, were discovering, showed the world to have an underlying foundation of rationality and predictability. The world, for this arch-anarchist, was not essentially anarchic. That is not to say that human beings could not conquer nature. In fact, one of the key characteristics of the human condition was to struggle with and overcome nature. The material struggle of life was at the heart of human achievement. It was human will that separated us from all other animals. The fact that man could consciously determine his life, his future, is what was unique about human endeavours. Men could control their passions and rationally construct the kind of society that they desired. Following Hegel, Bakunin maintained that human history was an evolutionary process leading to the perfectibility of the individual and society. Men are born with their innate rational ability, but it is only in the context of the societies they build that it is possible to assess their ultimate moral worth. In common with Rousseau's sociological insight Bakunin argues that individuals are shaped almost entirely by the societies in which they live. Through their social institutions, particularly education, the moral dimension of individuals is embedded. If the social and political traditions of a society are just, so will be the individuals of that society. Men are social beings in the sense that they rely upon others in order to know how to act justly: 'Everything that lives, does so under the categorical condition of decisively interfering in the life of someone else' (Maximoff 1953).

 Rewind

For explanations of Hegel and Feuerbach **see Chapter 9** on Marx.

KEY PEOPLE 1

Pierre Joseph Proudhon (1809–1865)

The first to call himself an anarchist, the son of a peasant and printer by trade, Proudhon became a leading architect of socialist ideas throughout Europe. Famously he argued 'property is theft'; that society ought to provide access to the means of production for all, not the protection of property for the few. He denounced centralisation and any revolution other than that which came from the working class themselves. See his *What is Property? An Inquiry into the Principle of Right and of Government* (1876).

While Bakunin does not always state these ideas as metaphysics, as foundational points of an ontology that is clearly explained, he does set them out as the basis of his practical belief in anarchism. For Bakunin, then, liberty is the basis of man's natural condition. This natural liberty leads us towards a condition of mutual dependence. Dependence articulates itself in the formation of societies. Societies engineer the type of individuals within them and imbue them with morals. The just society seeks to give the individual the kind of freedom that is natural to man. Although Bakunin calls this freedom 'absolute liberty', what he means by this is not complete unbounded licence for individuals to do exactly as they 'will'. Rather his definition of 'absolute liberty' is specific to his thought:

> The only liberty that is truly worthy of the name, the liberty which consists in the full development of all the material, intellectual and moral powers which are to be found as faculties latent in everyone, the liberty which recognises no other restrictions than those which are traced for us by the laws of our own nature; so that properly speaking there are no restrictions, since these laws

are not imposed on us by some outside legislator, beside us or above us; they are immanent in us, inherent, constituting the very basis of our being, material as well as intellectual and moral; instead, therefore, of finding them a limit, we must consider them as the real conditions and effective reason for our liberty.
(Bakunin 1950)

For Bakunin, 'absolute liberty' means that freedom which is natural to man as both an individual and social being. In other words, individuals may follow their will insofar as it does not adversely affect the liberties of the wider society. True liberty can be achieved only when a society is based upon equality both in material and legal-political terms. In a roundabout way, Bakunin shares something in common with Burke. Although they come to vastly different political conclusions they agree that individuals receive their moral identities only by being part of a community of equals. For Burke this equality was not material but it was political (see Chapter 7). The connecting point of these rather different theorists is that they have come face to face with a perennial dilemma of political theory, how to reconcile the will of the individual with that of the community. This is an issue that continues to generate a great deal of debate today. To what degree should individual needs be privileged over social needs or vice versa. Rousseau believed that individuals should be 'forced to be free', that is, to accept the 'general will', and he set out his arguments for this view in *The Social Contract* (see Chapter 6). Burke maintains that through history and tradition the essence of a nation's customs will be maintained. His theory of 'rational liberty' is articulated throughout his *Reflections*. But Bakunin does not really give us an account of how 'absolute liberty' will be articulated or understood. He leaves us with little more than an assertion that once equality is obtained and the state is overthrown, the natural law of freedom will reign.

Theoretically, Bakunin does not develop his notion of 'absolute liberty' at any great length or with any great success. The whole concept is premised upon a belief, a declaration of faith, rather than a philosophical proposition. Bakunin maintains that once all artificially created authority disappears then natural authority will assert itself. Bakunin constructs a binary distinction that associates man-made/artificial authority with falsehood and natural (scientific verified) law with legitimacy. Bakunin argues that all institutions which attempt to set up authority over others are bound to be limited in the way they establish the rule of law. Such institutions will inevitably reflect the inequalities of power whenever one group attempts to govern another. This is the case whether a liberal system or representatives of the workers in the first stages of a Marxist society. For Bakunin the power that comes with the authority to govern corrupts absolutely. In a society of equals where no institutions of state existed, natural law would prove more powerful than man-made authority. Scientific enquiry showed that the laws of nature were fixed and inviolable. In a kind of reversal of Hobbes' *Leviathan*, Bakunin sees the state as the condition of insecurity and unfreedom and a 'state of nature' of self-governing individuals as a place of order and a just society. Yet Bakunin's use of 'natural law' and even 'science' is not clearly explained. Here his philosophical system becomes undone as he has no metaphysics in this respect. That is, Bakunin leaves unexplained what he means by natural law and the verification of science that will somehow magically effect a perfect balance between the 'will' of the individual and the 'needs' society must have from its citizens to keep it going. Furthermore, it seems strange that someone who in certain respects is the inheritor of the Rousseauian tradition should draw upon natural law theory in order to make a point. For Rousseau virtually killed off natural law theory with his insight that human identities are constructed by the social environment and through the social institutions (such as education, the family, and so on) in which they live. On the one hand, Bakunin accepts this point of view which he uses in his arguments regarding morality. On the other hand, he goes back to natural law theory to justify his claims about liberty and authority as if there were no contradiction in marrying these two opposing concepts.

To criticise Bakunin's theory for its lack of philosophical rigour does not necessarily undermine his whole project. Authors have tended to fall into two distinct camps when commenting on Bakunin's theory of liberty, which is at the heart of the explanation of his anarchism. For instance, Marshall argues that Bakunin's theory is 'both realistic and plausible' (Marshall 1992), while Isaiah Berlin denounces it as 'glib Hegelian claptrap' (Berlin 1978). Given what has been said above, if we are looking in terms of his philosophical system it is clear that Bakunin's ideas are conceptually leaky. However, one must not forget the activist character of his doctrine of anarchism. For his political thought had two dimensions. As well as the traditional Hegelian-inspired aspect of his theory that attempted some systematic explanation of the human condition, there was also his theory of social action and will. The side of Bakunin's ideas that is least successful are his arguments that resemble secondhand objective Idealism. He goes on from the flawed concept of human liberty described above to argue that man can perfect himself. That united with science, human beings have the capacity to create a better and more morally acute society. In this way he follows a fairly standard Hegelian reasoning that human beings are moving through history to perfect their natures and come closer to self-awareness. This rationalist, determinist approach may be criticised along the same lines that Marx has been rebuked for in the previous chapter. Yet the social action aspects of his thought carry a great deal more force. Indeed, it may be said that it is the inspiration of these ideas that has kept the anarchist heritage alive and well to the present day.

Bakunin's praxis: social action and revolution

Bakunin may have deployed the notion of scientific legitimacy to try to substantiate his anarchist theory but he was no fetishist of science. For him, in the last instance, science was a mere tool to be harnessed to the power of will: 'Life not science, creates life; the spontaneous action of the people themselves alone can create liberty' (Marshall 1992).

This spontaneous action reaches a moral and political peak when it turns to revolution. Revolution, violent revolution, is the high point of collective will. In stating this, Bakunin's argument points to the anarcho-syndicalism later developed by Sorel (discussed below). He argues that ultimately the only means to overthrow bourgeois society is to destroy it. Again we see in Bakunin's ideas a vision of a rather romantic return to a state of nature. This is envisaged not as a recipe for a chaotic, insecure and brutal life (as in Hobbes) but as the beginnings of a new phase of civilisation, a higher phase. Initially the workers may embark upon a whole range of political and economic struggles. Bakunin was not against the idea of industrial action such as organising strikes and workers' groups to promote the workers' interests. These actions would provide useful training grounds for the great revolutionary struggle. It should also be remembered that Russia at this time was not a fully industrialised nation. In fact, its economy was still largely a rural one with a small industrial proletariat. It was for this reason that Bakunin further maintained that in the Russian context a revolution could work only by uniting the workers with the peasantry. Without this alliance the revolution would be doomed, since the city workers were too remote from the everyday concerns of the farm labourers. This belief in grass-roots participation, direct action and alliances between different sections of the working class was to be carried on in the Marxist tradition in the work of Gramsci.

KEY PEOPLE 2

Antonio Gramsci (1891–1937)

In many respects Gramsci united Marxist and anarchist ideas. As a leader of the Italian Communist Party in the 1920s and 1930s, he wrote in his famous *Prison Notebooks* how the communists needed to look to strategies that included creating alliances with other groups, forming workers' councils and making sure the revolution came from below not above, all ideas one can find in Bakunin's thought.

In 1870 Bakunin attempted to put these ideas into practice, to turn this theory of social action and revolution into 'praxis'. He did this by leading what turned out to be a failed uprising at Lyon in France. It was in July of that year that the Franco-Prussian war broke out. He hoped that the defeat of the French would lead to a popular revolution and the overthrow of the apparatus of the state. He foresaw the setting up of a federation of communes, self-governing workers' associations, to replace the state. In his *Letters to a Frenchman on the Present Crisis*, he makes a passionate cry for destruction, anarchy and civil strife, suggesting that only with a bloody and violent revolt would the new world dawn. He appeals to the will of the French people to turn their rage into terror and wield it against the forces that prevent them from achieving their true liberty. In September 1870 Bakunin put his might where his pen was and went to Lyon following the victory of the Prussians. Initially he received a warm welcome by anarchist supporters and he declared the abolition of the state. But the revolt was quickly put down and Bakunin had to flee.

Although not successful, the Lyon revolt provided the inspiration for a more spectacular revolt the following year. It was the Paris Commune of 1871 that provided a more legitimate confirmation of Bakunin's notion of social revolution. Indeed, he recognised this himself and set these ideas down in his text *The Paris Commune and the Idea of the State* in the same year. The Commune had come about following the French Army's defeat to the Prussians. With the Prussians on the outskirts of Paris the French authorities had to sign an embarrassing armistice in February 1871. The Parisians were disgusted with their government and revolted. On 18 March

1871 they declared the Paris Commune, a workers' insurrection that was symbolised by their red banners. Communists, anarchists and socialists from across Europe supported the Commune, seeing in it a model of the workers' revolutions to come. They usefully forgot its rather patriotic origins and focused on the fact that it was a popular uprising that sprang up spontaneously from the streets and involved ordinary people in a spirit of equality and justice.

KEY EVENT

Karl Marx and Bakunin

Much has been made of the personal conflict between these two great men of socialism. While there is some evidence that they did respect each other (Bakunin did agree with Marx's economic analysis), they also spoke and wrote damning words about each other's positions. Marx saw Bakunin as an anti-intellectual; Bakunin accused Marx of wanting a 'red bureaucracy' and made anti-Semitic remarks about him. This created a schism in socialism, although some, like Gramsci (see above) were wise enough to see their mutual aims.

See Thomas, P. (1980) *Karl Marx and the Anarchists*, London: Routledge & Kegan Paul.

The Paris Commune had strong anarchist characteristics. Bakunin had written that a revolution would have to occur in a major city that would declare itself autonomous, and would show by example how a stateless society would function: 'Revolutionary socialism has just attempted its first striking and practical demonstration in the Paris Commune' (Bakunin, in Dolgoff 1973).

The Commune called for a federalist structure of workers' alliances to be the basis of communes that ought to be established not only in Paris but also throughout France. This, Bakunin argued, was a clear negation of the state and bourgeois forms of government. He urged the communards not to take on any statist forms of organisation and maintained that the revolution could be spread only when the industrial workers formed a free association with agricultural workers.

Although the Paris Commune was short-lived, collapsing on 30 May 1871, many anarchists saw it as a vindication of their ideas. Bakunin in particular declared it as a victory for his ideas over Marx and the communists. However, Marx claimed that the Paris Commune was in fact an example of a 'dictatorship of the proletariat'. That is, it ought to be seen as a model not of a stateless society but as an example of the working class using state power to control the means of production during the period of transition from capitalism to communism. There followed a disagreement between Marx and Bakunin that eventually led to Bakunin's expulsion from the International Working Men's Association (usually simply known as the International), the umbrella organisation for all revolutionary socialist groups.

Summary

From the analysis of Bakunin's work it may be said that while his philosophical justification for anarchism was flawed, his 'praxis' has been a major inspiration for ideas of social action and revolution that carry us through to the twentieth century. As well as having an influence on the main tendencies of anarchism mentioned above in the introduction to this chapter, Bakunin's thought inspired a body of modern academic literature that was wary of attempts at large-scale rational political organisation, whatever the ideology that inspired it. In addition, Bakunin's work provides us with an alternative socialist critique of Marx as well as the liberal tradition since Hobbes. Moving from the general to the specific, Bakunin's ideas were particularly influential in Spain. Here the federalist movement, inspired by the ideals of the French Revolution, were influenced by two of Bakunin's supporters (Giuseppe Fanelli and Elie Reclus). By 1873 the Bakunin anarchists numbered 54,000 in Spain (Schechter 1994). The anarchist tradition remains strong in that country despite their defeat as part of the republican movement by Franco in the 1930s.

DISCUSSION POINT

Bakunin is a paradoxical thinker; a believer in natural law and the social construction of identities; a rational thinker and a passionate activist; against liberalism as well as Marxism. It is then, perhaps, no surprise to find that Bakunin is arguing that only in a stateless society could there be a genuine social order. Bakunin was, in the end, a defender of individual liberty. He maintained that only through collective action could an individual find true freedom. In other words, it was not until individuals were in an economic and social condition of equality with no higher authority over them that their acts would be genuinely free. Only in this form of society would we be able to judge how we ought to act to achieve self-realisation and social progress. The questions to ask here are: Has Bakunin really reconciled anarchy and order? Are there any difficulties in the way he theorises these ideas as compatible? Is he right in his reasoning and conclusions? Can you see any flaws in attempting to achieve order from anarchy?

Anarcho-syndicalism: Georges Sorel (1847–1922)

As mentioned above, one of the main strands of anarchism Bakunin feeds into is anarcho-syndicalism. Anarcho-syndicalism is the branch of anarchism that is associated with the labour movement. At the core of anarcho-syndicalist beliefs is that only the abolition of the wage system and the establishment of self-management industries can liberate the workers. This strand of anarchism is not in any sense a Luddite organisation, although its name seems to imply destruction of some kind. Rather, anarcho-syndicalism may be thought of as very much a modern industrial movement that takes industry and progress as important aspects of constructing a socialist society. To end this chapter and indeed this book, we shall look at the work of Georges Sorel.

Sorel's work has fallen into disfavour. This is because his ideas have been claimed not for socialism but fascism. The young Mussolini was particularly taken by Sorel's notion of 'social myths'. However, it ought to be remembered that Mussolini was a socialist and a leading socialist in Italy when he was inspired by Sorel's ideas. The fact that he continued to draw from some of Sorel's terminology after he developed fascism says more about Mussolini's politics and ideology than about Sorel's intent. Like many thinkers who have become 'discredited', Sorel's ideas can be made to serve the purposes of extremist ideologies only if his writings are taken out of context. Sorel himself was writing as an anarcho-syndicalist and was opposed to all statist organisations, whether of the Left or of the Right. He is by no means the greatest intellect of the modern age but nor is he the poorest. His usefulness here is not only to illustrate further the trajectory of anarchism but also to highlight one of the key themes of this book. That is, to understand the ideas of particular political thinkers and to be able to substantively critique their work we must take them in context. Not only the context of their times, their particular historical setting, but also their philosophical and theoretical context. If we abstract authors from their intellectual and temporal environment then we are in danger of distorting their work and of committing the crime of turning their ideas into the worst kind of dogma.

Sorel is a unique thinker within the broad church of anarchism because his greatest intellectual influence was not Marx or Proudhon but the anti-positivist philosopher Henri Bergson. Bergson was a famous figure during Sorel's lifetime but, like Sorel himself, he has also fallen out of favour. In his case this was not because his ideas were misused for political purposes but because the anti-positivist philosophy he advocated was severely criticised by his contemporaries as too abstract, pseudo-scientific and anti-intellectual. It is not important to relate the whole of Bergson's philosophical system here, although anyone interested in Sorel's work ought to have a grasp of his main ideas. Briefly stated then, Bergson argued against Darwin that evolution was not only a natural scientific occurrence but also a meta-physical one. Throughout the world there was a life-force, an energy or spirit that he termed the 'élan vital'. This vital energy was not teleological, it had no clear end or progressive route. Darwin had argued in the natural sciences much like Hegel had

---

KEY PEOPLE 3

Henri Bergson (1859–1941)

Bergson was born in Paris to Anglo-Polish parents. He became a famous academic and was awarded the Nobel Prize for literature in 1927. He died after he caught pneumonia from having to queue for hours in order to register as a Jew in Nazi-controlled France. His most famous publication is *Creative Evolution* published in 1907.

in philosophy that human evolution was progressing towards a state of perfectibility. Bergson maintained that this was not the case. The élan vital was creative, an unstructured flux of constant change. In other words, the world was not a place that had an underlying order and rational structure to it. This earth-bound existence was chaotic and this chaos made it a wondrous place, a place where individuals could determine their own ends, where no future or destiny was set, where outcomes were open-ended and inconclusive.

Sorel's contribution to anarchism was to turn Bergson's philosophical understanding of the human condition as a dynamic arena without end or purpose into a social theory that celebrated the vitality of life and action for action's sake. Unlike many socialists brought up on a diet of German Idealism and Marx, Sorel's intellectual influence meant that he was much more concerned with the 'art' of the struggle itself. In this way the reasoning behind his brand of anarcho-syndicalism was philosophically opposed to the mainstream ideas of the anarchist movement even though his conclusions were similar. Only the Bakunin-inspired anarchists in Spain appreciated Sorel's input, taking many of his ideas seriously. It is surprising that not more anarchists could see that his contribution was not so much a challenge but a complementary counterbalance to the scientific materialism of Marx.

In his *Reflections on Violence* (1908) Sorel sets out his anti-Enlightenment Bergsonian political thought. He follows Bergson in arguing that the history of humankind was an unending catalogue of social change. Part of this change was due to science and technology and part of it was due to the direct actions of groups and individuals. While a part of life was no doubt amenable to rational calculation and scientific categorisation, another part was unknowable and could be grasped only through intuition. On the basis of these thoughts Sorel sets out his theory of self-expressive action. He argues that the highest form of human action is a synthesis of thought and intuition. In a sense his concept shares with Bakunin's notion of 'absolute liberty' a preoccupation with the free and naturally unbound expression of self. However, it differs from Bakunin's concept in placing intuition as a key component of this self-expression. For Sorel it is intuition that can grasp the flux of reality and manipulate it in a way that is desired by the individual or group. Yet, despite this difference of emphasis, both anarchists are aware of the potential of spontaneous action. Although Bakunin uses a different language, he too wrote about the desirability to use the unplanned impromptu revolts of the masses for the purposes of revolution. In this respect the two thinkers are no different.

According to Sorel, it would only be through spontaneous, non-rational action that a revolution could be constructed. However, although the action that sparked the revolution itself would be impulsive and intuitive it was possible to prepare the groundwork for revolt in a more rational manner. It ought to be emphasised that although what is notable about Sorel's work is his emphasis on spontaneity and intuition, his theory of expressive self-action is a synthesis of these elements and rational calculation. So it is that he argues that the industrial working class need to be organised into syndicates, or workers' associations. These associations would stand as proto-post-revolutionary organisations, ready to take over the running of industry following the revolution. As an anarchist, Sorel was firmly set against the state and any form of parliamentary or bureaucratic government. As well as providing a model of political organisation the syndicates would also discuss and debate issues.

Unlike many other syndicalists, Sorel was concerned not only that these associations would disseminate socialist ideas, but also moral ideas.

Intertwined with Sorel's notion of creative action is a moral theory. Sorel maintained that the ethical value of action was important to rehearse if the workers were to understand fully the need for revolution. Society had become debased under bourgeoisie morality. Liberal government was a sham, a screen for the control of the masses by a self-serving political elite. Sorel was a strong advocate of politics, in the sense that he saw direct participation in political activities as an essential part of our humanity. Individuals lived in a community with others and as such, practical and moral questions were always going to be contested. Yet bourgeois politics was a debasement of this idea, disenfranchising the masses from taking part in political action. It maintained a class system that not only created economic inequalities but also cultural inequalities. Interestingly, Sorel discusses how it was not only economic class but also social status that set people apart under capitalism. These two were combined for him; not only did the owners of the means of production have an iniquitous degree of wealth but they also determined the status of those who were able or not able to engage in political and moral debate. Sorel is insightful here and such ideas were to be developed much further by sociologists such as Max Weber later in the twentieth century.

It was, then, for moral as well as economic reasons that Sorel concluded that the bourgeois state needed to be replaced with what he termed a 'renascence' society. As with both Marx and Bakunin, when it comes to setting out the possible features of a new kind of society a certain romanticism comes through. Sorel takes the anarcho-syndicalist society as being one that would be constructed by heroic citizens. These were individuals who were able to marry their own egoistic goals to social achievements. Such individuals would rise through the revolution, exhibiting their creative dynamism and ability to affect change on the chaos of life. A key feature in being able to become the heroic architect of such change was the use of violence. This is one of the most controversial parts of Sorel's theory and has been much discussed. Many find his advocation of violence abhorrent. Yet this is no more than Bakunin said and is inherent in all anarchic revolutionary discourses. Why then ought Sorel's admission that violence is a necessary part of revolution be taken more seriously and more emotively than the work of other similar writers? It would seem that the reason for this is that Sorel is not only advocating violence as expediency to form a new society but advocating it as a *moral* imperative. In other words, Sorel does not take violence to be an unfortunate necessity, a temporary by-product of revolution. Rather he argues that violence is the high point of creative human action. It is neither cruel nor barbaric but morally necessary. As the heroic class, the working class are morally justified in using violence to overthrow the state. Furthermore, violence has an important social role, since it reinforces the workers as a community and helps to cement their communal identity.

The discerning reader may have detected a certain preachiness in Sorel's work. That is, the syndicates offered a mechanism for teaching the workers what they 'needed' to know in order to inspire them towards revolution. Now this may or may not have been a necessity to educate the masses. But it was certainly a tendency of socialist thought in this period when the intellectual leaders did tend to be somewhat patronising towards those who they took as the leading class. This comes through particularly in Sorel's famous strategy for sparking off a revolutionary moment. He argued that in order to facilitate the circumstances for a revolt the workers needed to be told a 'social myth'; that is, a story that would inspire them to become conscious of their own creative potential to enact change. Sorel suggested that through the syndicates a 'myth' be created that the best way to change the conditions of the working industrial proletariat would be through a 'general strike'. The general strike would be taken as a clear and rational goal of the syndicates. However, this was a mechanism to be used only to agitate the workers and to trigger off their intuitive sense of action. It was hoped that once the momentum of the strike was underway, the 'real' goal of social change and the overthrow of the bourgeois state would spontaneously occur.

It may be unfair to simply look upon the social myth as a rather patronising strategy by an intellectual to conjure up the revolutionary potential of the working class. To our modern eyes it certainly has that sense to it. But it may also be taken as a rather ingenious way of rallying the masses. Certainly the 'social myth' of nationalism and nationhood has been an incredibly strong motivating force in the modern age, as Mussolini recognised. Perhaps it may be said that most political movements have an element of myth about them, be it the myth of equality, nationality, ethnicity or rights. For when ideas or causes or beliefs are translated into the real world of politics they can never be as 'pure' as they are in thought. Myths are perhaps necessary for mass movements and political ideologies in order to effect social change. Take, for example, Bakunin's notion of 'absolute liberty'. As a philosophical concept it has been shown above to be extremely flawed and undertheorised. But if we take it as a 'social myth' it has more legitimacy as a tool for political agitation. The idea that human beings can have unbounded freedom within the context of being both discrete individuals and members of a community is an appealing one. Yet it is an idea that can never be realised, since the tensions between the will of the individual and the 'needs' of society will always clash at some point. However, as an idea, a source of inspiration, a promise of better days it carries a great deal of motivating force. Given this discussion, it may not be going too far to suggest that Sorel's theory of social action, with its concomitant deliberations on violence and myth, enables us to reflect upon (if not 'expose') many of the underlying reasons for the powerful appeal of the ideas at the heart of anarchism.

DISCUSSION POINT

Of all the anarchists, Sorel may be said to be the most theoretically honest and courageous in tackling the issue of violence head-on. While Bakunin and others were certainly ready to put their lives in the firing line for their cause, they did not do the same with their intellect. Violence is, of course, a serious matter; people die or get hurt in the most horrific of circumstances. Yet most revolutionary writers either gloss over the use of violence or write about it as if it can be controlled in a rational way. Unfortunately, even in our own twenty-first-century experience, we know that despite all the latest technologies innocent people die and suffer needlessly in violent conflicts. It is implicit in Sorel's work that such acts of violence are uncontrollable but few others will admit it. However, is he right to seek a moral justification for violence? Can violence really be deemed to be a high point of human expression? Is violence a legitimate and morally justified tool of social change?

Conclusion

In this chapter a number of arguments have been made that are worthwhile reviewing. First, it has been maintained that anarchism itself is a fitting subject for investigation in texts of modern political thought. The anarchist tradition, so often overlooked, provides us with an important perspective on the politics of the modern age. The idea of a stateless society may seem absurd in a world that is moving towards ever larger and more global institutions. Yet it is a welcome reflection upon the dangers of removing power from the direct control of citizens and the ease by which powerful elites can determine the lives of most ordinary people. It makes the general point that democracy means 'rule by the people' and that this is to be taken literally. As stated in the introduction, this insight has been taken up by a range of new social movements which maintain that an activist, participatory style of politics is essential to any truly democratic society.

Second, the anarchist perspective offers a critique of liberal and Marxist political ideas. Indeed, it is a compliment to anarchism that as the twentieth century unfolded, Marxists and liberals alike took inspiration from many anarchist principles. But anarchism remains distinct from these points of view and cannot be subsumed by them. The advocation of small-scale non-hierarchical organisation alongside their anti-statism marks these radical thinkers out as significant in their own right.

Third, it has been argued that the power of their work is not so much in the philosophical rigour of their concepts as in their praxis of social action and the attempt to construct a realisable context for revolution. Like Marx's writings about the characteristics of a communist state, the claims made by Bakunin for a post-capitalist anarchist society are weakly presented, as all predictions about the future must inevitably be. However, read with an eye fixed upon Sorel's concept of myth, anarchism makes sense as a movement based upon rational social action and spontaneous revolutionary intent. It was the combination of these qualities that was discernible in the Paris Commune and the mix of social analysis and intuitive action that has appealed to the Spanish socialist movement.

Finally, there is nothing shameful in declaring that anarchism is exciting. As a set of ideas it may be loosely held together, often contradictory, certainly under-theorised. But the significance of these ideas needs to be felt as much as explained. Anarchism is a sensibility and, for those who feel it, a very forceful one. There is, of course, a risk here that a sensibility is no more than a prejudice. People have 'felt' many things and have justified acts as horrendous as genocide on the basis of vague theories and 'intuitive' feelings. It is important to be aware of this and humbled by a consciousness of the theoretical as well as practical dilemmas of anarchism. In that case we can take away from the study of anarchism a view of it as imbued with a passionate spirit regarding human potential, and this is just as important to politics as any rationally defined set of ideas.

Revision notes

1   Anarchism should be studied in terms of the specific writings and actions of its late nineteenth-century and early twentieth-century supporters. The popular perception of anarchism is misleading to academic discussions.

2   The appeal of anarchism is in its discussion of social action and revolution rather than the sophisticated character of its philosophical system.

3   Anarcho-syndicalism is a strand of anarchism that is associated with the labour movement. It calls for workers' co-operatives to be the basis of post-statist social and political organisation.

4   Although it shares similar features with Marxism and other forms of socialism, anarchism is distinctive by offering an alternative form of micro-organisation and workers' self-rule.

5   The writings of Sorel lead us to reflect upon the nature of violence in politics and the artifical creation of social myths that form part of most mass political movements.

Bibliography

Bakunin, M. (1950) *Marxism, Freedom and the State*, trans. and ed. K.J. Kenafick, London: Freedom Press.

Bergson, H. (1907) *Creative Evolution*, trans. A. Mitchell, London: Greenwood Press.

Berlin, I. (1978) *A Remarkable Decade: Russian Thinkers*, London: Hogarth Press.

Dolgoff, S. (ed.) (1973) *Bakunin on Anarchy*, London: George Allen & Unwin.

Howes, R.C. (ed.) (1977) *The Confessions of Mikhail Bakunin*, trans. Lawrence D. Orton, Ithaca: Cornell University Press.

Lehnin, A. (ed.) (1973) 'The Paris Commune and the Idea of the State', in *Selected Writings*, ed. A. Lehnin, London: Jonathan Cape.

Marshall, P. (1992) *Demanding the Impossible: A History of Anarchism*, London: Fontana Press.

Maximoff, G.P. (ed.) (1953) *The Political Philosophy of Bakunin: Scientific Anarchism*, New York: Free Press.

Proudhon, P.J. (1876) *What is Property? An Inquiry into the Principle of Right and of Government*, trans. B. Tucker, New York: Humboldt Press.

Schechter, D. (1994) *Radical Theories: Paths Beyond Marxism and Social Democracy*, Manchester: Manchester University Press.

Sorel, G. (1908) *Reflections on Violence*, trans. T.E. Hulme and J. Roth, New York: The Free Press.

Thomas, P. (1980) *Karl Marx and the Anarchists*, London: Routledge & Kegan Paul.

Further reading

If you intend to follow up the anarchist legacy you may want to start with the influential contemporary writings of Murray Bookchin; see M. Bookchin (1982) *The Ecology of Freedom: The Emergence and Dissolution of Hierarchy*, California: Cheshire Books; (1987) *The Modern Crisis*, Montreal: Black Rose; (1990) *The Philosophy of Social Ecology: Essays on Dialectical Naturalism*, Montreal: Black Rose. To see where the critique of bureaucracy went in the twentieth century see M. Weber (1968) *Economy and Society*, Berkeley: University of California Press; R. Michels (1959) *Political Parties*, New York: Dover Press.

Index